PHP and MySQL Recipes

A Problem-Solution Approach

Second Edition

Frank M. Kromann

Apress®

PHP and MySQL Recipes: A Problem-Solution Approach, Second Edition

Frank M. Kromann
Trabuco Canyon
California, USA

ISBN-13 (pbk): 978-1-4842-0606-5   ISBN-13 (electronic): 978-1-4842-0605-8
DOI 10.1007/978-1-4842-0605-8

Library of Congress Control Number: 2016943555

Managing Director: Welmoed Spahr
Lead Editor: Steve Anglin
Technical Reviewer: Massimo Nardone
Editorial Board: Steve Anglin, Pramila Balan, Louise Corrigan, Jonathan Gennick, Robert Hutchinson, Celestin Suresh John, Michelle Lowman, James Markham, Susan McDermott, Matthew Moodie, Jeffrey Pepper, Douglas Pundick, Ben Renow-Clarke, Gwenan Spearing
Coordinating Editor: Mark Powers
Copy Editor: Karen Jameson
Compositor: SPi Global
Indexer: SPi Global
Artist: SPi Global

Distributed to the book trade worldwide by Springer Science+Business Media New York, 233 Spring Street, 6th Floor, New York, NY 10013. Phone 1-800-SPRINGER, fax (201) 348-4505, e-mail orders-ny@springer-sbm.com, or visit www.springeronline.com. Apress Media, LLC is a California LLC and the sole member (owner) is Springer Science + Business Media Finance Inc (SSBM Finance Inc). SSBM Finance Inc is a Delaware corporation.

For information on translations, please e-mail rights@apress.com, or visit www.apress.com.

Apress and friends of ED books may be purchased in bulk for academic, corporate, or promotional use. eBook versions and licenses are also available for most titles. For more information, reference our Special Bulk Sales–eBook Licensing web page at www.apress.com/bulk-sales.

Any source code or other supplementary materials referenced by the author in this text is available to readers at www.apress.com/9781484206065. For detailed information about how to locate your book's source code, go to www.apress.com/source-code/. Readers can also access source code at SpringerLink in the Supplementary Material section for each chapter.

Printed on acid-free paper

Contents at a Glance

About the Author xxix

About the Technical Reviewer xxxi

Introduction xxxiii

■Chapter 1: Installation and Configuration 1

■Chapter 2: Classes and Objects 29

■Chapter 3: Performing Math Operations 61

■Chapter 4: Working with Arrays 77

■Chapter 5: Dates and Times... 109

■Chapter 6: Strings.. 125

■Chapter 7: Files and Directories 143

■Chapter 8: Dynamic Imaging 169

■Chapter 9: Regular Expressions 197

■Chapter 10: Variables 209

■Chapter 11: Functions 231

■Chapter 12: Web Fundamentals... 249

■Chapter 13: Creating and Using Forms.. 271

■Chapter 14: XML, RSS, WDDX, and SOAP 293

■Chapter 15: Data Exchange with JSON... 317

■Chapter 16: Using MySQL Databases... 333

Index... 357

Contents

About the Author xxix

About the Technical Reviewer xxxi

Introduction xxxiii

■Chapter 1: Installation and Configuration 1

Recipe 1-1. Installing PHP 1

    Problem 1

    Solution 1

    How it Works 2

Recipe 1-2. Configuring PHP 17

    Problem 17

    Solution 17

    How it Works 18

Recipe 1-3. Compiling PHP 21

    Problem 21

    Solution 21

    How it Works 22

Recipe 1-4. Installing MySQL 26

    Problem 26

    Solution 26

    How it Works 27

Recipe 1-5. Virtual Machines 27

    Problem 27

    Solution 27

    How it Works 28

■Chapter 2: Classes and Objects 29

Recipe 2-1. Writing a Simple Class 29

Problem 29

Solution 29

How it Works 29

Recipe 2-2. Writing a Base Class 30

Problem 30

Solution 30

How it Works 30

Recipe 2-3. Writing an Abstract Class 31

Problem 31

Solution 31

How it Works 31

Recipe 2-4. Writing an Interface 33

Problem 33

Solution 33

How it Works 33

Recipe 2-5. Class Members as Regular Functions 35

Problem 35

Solution 35

How it Works 35

Recipe 2-6. Protecting Data and Methods 36

Problem 36

Solution 36

How it Works 36

Recipe 2-7. Mixed Static and Object Context 37

Problem 37

Solution 37

How it Works 38

Recipe 2-8. Referencing Class Members 38

Problem 38

Solution.. 38

How it Works.. 38

Recipe 2-9. Instantiation of Classes.. 39

Problem 39

Solution.. 39

How it Works.. 40

Recipe 2-10. Printing Objects.. 41

Problem 41

Solution.. 41

How it Works.. 41

Recipe 2-11. Variable Overloading 42

Problem 42

Solution.. 42

How it Works.. 42

Recipe 2-12. Serializing Types and Object 44

Problem 44

Solution.. 44

How it Works.. 45

Recipe 2-13. Copying an Object.. 46

Problem 46

Solution.. 46

How it Works.. 46

Recipe 2-14. Using Objects as Functions.. 47

Problem 47

Solution.. 47

How it Works.. 47

Recipe 2-15. Overloading Methods 48

Problem 48

Solution 48

How it Works 48

Recipe 2-16. Debugging Objects 49

Problem 49

Solution 49

How it Works 50

Recipe 2-17. Using Objects without a Class 51

Problem 51

Solution 51

How it Works 51

Recipe 2-18. Directory Iteration 52

Problem 52

Solution 52

How it Works 52

Recipe 2-19. Writing Reusable Code 53

Problem 53

Solution 53

How it Works 53

Recipe 2-20. Avoiding Name Collisions 57

Problem 57

Solution 57

How it Works 57

Recipe 2-21. Autoloading Classes on First Use 59

Problem 59

Solution 59

How it Works 59

■Chapter 3: Performing Math Operations 61

Recipe 3-1. Changing the Base Values for Numbers 62

Problem 62

Solution 62

How it Works 62

Recipe 3-2. Converting to a Different Base Value 63

Problem 63

Solution 63

How it Works 63

Recipe 3-3. Storing Binary Values in Integers 64

Problem 64

Solution 64

How it Works 64

Recipe 3-4. Setting and Clearing Bits in Binary 65

Problem 65

Solution 65

How it Works 65

Recipe 3-5. Using Hexadecimal Numbers 66

Problem 66

Solution 66

How it Works 66

Recipe 3-6. Increasing Performance with Binary Shift 67

Problem 67

Solution 67

How it Works 67

Recipe 3-7. Rounding Floating Point Numbers 69

Problem 69

Solution 69

How it Works 69

Recipe 3-8. Generating Random Numbers 70
Problem 70
Solution 70
How it Works 70

Recipe 3-9. Expressing Ratios with Logarithmic Functions 71
Problem 71
Solution 71
How it Works 71

Recipe 3-10. Calculating Future Values 71
Problem 71
Solution 71
How it Works 72

Recipe 3-11. Using Trigonometry to Calculate Distance and Direction 73
Problem 73
Solution 73
How it Works 73

Recipe 3-12. Working with Complex Numbers 74
Problem 74
Solution 74
How it Works 75

■Chapter 4: Working with Arrays 77

Recipe 4-1. Creating Arrays 77
Problem 77
Solution 77
How it Works 78

Recipe 4-2. Changing Arrays 79
Problem 79
Solution 79
How it Works 80

Recipe 4-3. Adding Arrays..**81**

Problem..81

Solution...82

How it Works..82

Recipe 4-4. Arrays of Arrays..**86**

Problem..86

Solution...86

How it Works..86

Recipe 4-5. Traversing Arrays **88**

Problem..88

Solution...88

How it Works..88

Recipe 4-6. Sorting Arrays **90**

Problem..90

Solution...90

How It Works..90

Recipe 4-7. Using Arrays as Stacks **100**

Problem..100

Solution...101

How it Works..101

Recipe 4-8. Slicing and Splicing Arrays **102**

Problem..102

Solution...102

How it Works..102

Recipe 4-9. Debugging Arrays..**105**

Problem..105

Solution...105

How it Works..106

Recipe 4-10. Storing Arrays 107

Problem 107

Solution.. 107

How it Works.. 107

■**Chapter 5: Dates and Times**.. **109**

Recipe 5-1. Working with Time Zones... 109

Problem 109

Solution.. 109

How it Works.. 110

Recipe 5-2. Creating a Timestamp 110

Problem 110

Solution.. 110

How it Works.. 111

Recipe 5-3. Working with Dates 112

Problem 112

Solution.. 112

How it Works.. 112

Recipe 5-4. Displaying Timestamps 113

Problem 113

Solution.. 113

How it Works.. 113

Recipe 5-5. Using ISO Formats 116

Problem 116

Solution.. 116

How it Works.. 116

Recipe 5-6. Working with Week Numbers... 117

Problem 117

Solution.. 117

How it Works.. 118

Recipe 5-7. The DateTime Class 118

Problem 118

Solution.. 118

How it Works.. 118

Recipe 5-8. Storing Date and Time Values 122

Problem 122

Solution.. 122

How it Works.. 122

Recipe 5-9. Calculating Elapsed Time.. 123

Problem 123

Solution.. 123

How it Works.. 123

■Chapter 6: Strings.. 125

Recipe 6-1. Creating Strings 125

Problem 125

Solution.. 125

How it Works.. 125

Recipe 6-2. Working with the Characters in a String 126

Problem 126

Solution.. 126

How it Works.. 126

Recipe 6-3. Replacing Characters.. 127

Problem 127

Solution.. 127

How it Works.. 127

Recipe 6-4. Creating Long Strings with Heredoc and Newdoc 128

Problem 128

Solution.. 128

How it Works.. 128

Recipe 6-5. Escaping Strings 130

    Problem 130

    Solution.. 131

    How it Works.. 131

Recipe 6-6. Reformatting Strings... 132

    Problem 132

    Solution.. 132

    How it Works.. 132

Recipe 6-7. Trimming Whitespace... 133

    Problem 133

    Solution.. 133

    How it Works.. 133

Recipe 6-8. Finding Strings in Strings 133

    Problem 133

    Solution.. 134

    How it Works.. 134

Recipe 6-9. Dividing Strings into Substrings.. 135

    Problem 135

    Solution.. 135

    How it Works.. 135

Recipe 6-10. Displaying HTML Entities 137

    Problem 137

    Solution.. 137

    How it Works.. 137

Recipe 6-11. Generating Hash Values for Files 139

    Problem 139

    Solution.. 139

    How it Works.. 139

Recipe 6-12. Storing Passwords 141

    Problem 141

    Solution 141

    How it Works 141

■ **Chapter 7: Files and Directories** **143**

Recipe 7-1. Include and Require 143

    Problem 143

    Solution 143

    How it Works 144

Recipe 7-2. Reading Files 145

    Problem 145

    Solution 145

    How it Works 146

Recipe 7-3. Writing Files 147

    Problem 147

    Solution 147

    How it Works 148

Recipe 7-4. Copy, Rename, and Remove Files 148

    Problem 148

    Solution 149

    How it Works 149

Recipe 7-5. File Properties 150

    Problem 150

    Solution 150

    How it Works 150

Recipe 7-6. Permissions 152

    Problem 152

    Solution 152

    How it Works 152

Recipe 7-7. Symbolic Links 153

Problem 153

Solution 153

How it Works 153

Recipe 7-8. Directories 155

Problem 155

Solution 155

How it Works 155

Recipe 7-9. CSV Files 156

Problem 156

Solution 156

How it Works 156

Recipe 7-10. Streams 159

Problem 159

Solution 159

How it Works 159

Recipe 7-11. Stream Context 160

Problem 160

Solution 160

How it Works 160

Recipe 7-12. File Iterators 162

Problem 162

Solution 162

How it Works 162

Recipe 7-13. Download Files 164

Problem 164

Solution 164

How it Works 164

Recipe 7-14. Upload Files **165**

    Problem 165

    Solution.. 165

    How it Works.. 165

Recipe 7-15. Zipped Files **166**

    Problem 166

    Solution.. 166

    How it Works.. 167

■Chapter 8: Dynamic Imaging **169**

Recipe 8-1. Creating Images **169**

    Problem 169

    Solution.. 169

    How it Works.. 170

Recipe 8-2. Image Resize **171**

    Problem 171

    Solution.. 171

    How it Works.. 171

Recipe 8-3. Image Crop **173**

    Problem 173

    Solution.. 173

    How it Works.. 173

Recipe 8-4. Image Rotate **176**

    Problem 176

    Solution.. 176

    How it Works.. 176

Recipe 8-5. Image Flip **177**

    Problem 177

    Solution.. 177

    How it Works.. 177

Recipe 8-6. Adding a Watermark 178
    Problem 178
    Solution 178
    How it Works 179

Recipe 8-7. Changing Colors 180
    Problem 180
    Solution 180
    How it Works 180

Recipe 8-8. Draw on Images 182
    Problem 182
    Solution 182
    How it Works 182

Recipe 8-9. Transparency 190
    Problem 190
    Solution 190
    How it Works 190

Recipe 8-10. Adding Text 191
    Problem 191
    Solution 191
    How it Works 191

Recipe 8-11. Caching Images 193
    Problem 193
    Solution 193
    How it Works 193

■Chapter 9: Regular Expressions 197

Recipe 9-1. Format Validation 200
    Problem 200
    Solution 200
    How it Works 200

Recipe 9-2. Sub Patterns 203

    Problem 203

    Solution.. 203

    How it Works... 203

Recipe 9-3. String Replacement 205

    Problem 205

    Solution.. 205

    How it Works... 206

■Chapter 10: Variables 209

Recipe 10-1. Converting Variable Type.. 209

    Problem 209

    Solution.. 209

    How it Works... 210

Recipe 10-2. Allocating Memory 210

    Problem 210

    Solution.. 210

    How it Works... 211

Recipe 10-3. Determining Memory Use 212

    Problem 212

    Solution.. 212

    How it Works... 212

Recipe 10-4. Taking Advantage of Variable Scope 213

    Problem 213

    Solution.. 213

    How it Works... 213

Recipe 10-5. Avoiding Global Variable Problems with Super Globals 214

    Problem 214

    Solution.. 214

    How it Works... 214

Recipe 10-6. Determining Variable Type 215

    Problem 215

    Solution 215

    How it Works 215

Recipe 10-7. Reducing Memory Use with References 216

    Problem 216

    Solution 216

    How it Works 216

Recipe 10-8. Using Constants 219

    Problem 219

    Solution 219

    How it Works 219

Recipe 10-9. Variable Variables 220

    Problem 220

    Solution 220

    How it Works 220

Recipe 10-10. Comparing Variables 221

    Problem 221

    Solution 221

    How it Works 222

Recipe 10-11. Working with Strings 223

    Problem 223

    Solution 223

    How it Works 223

Recipe 10-12. Handling Floating Point Numbers 224

    Problem 224

    Solution 224

    How it Works 224

Recipe 10-13. Special Language Constructs 225
Problem 225
Solution 225
How it Works 225

Recipe 10-14. Iterating Over Array Values 228
Problem 228
Solution 228
How it Works 229

Recipe 10-15. Generating Output 229
Problem 229
Solution 229
How it Works 230

■Chapter 11: Functions 231
Recipe 11-1. Calling Functions 231
Problem 231
Solution 231
How it Works 232

Recipe 11-2. Variable Scope 232
Problem 232
Solution 232
How it Works 233

Recipe 11-3. Passing Parameters 234
Problem 234
Solution 234
How it Works 234

Recipe 11-4. Optional Parameters 236
Problem 236
Solution 236
How it Works 236

Recipe 11-5. Type Declarations 238

Problem 238

Solution 238

How it Works 238

Recipe 11-6. Return Values 239

Problem 239

Solution 239

How it Works 239

Recipe 11-7. Check if Function Exists 241

Problem 241

Solution 241

How it Works 241

Recipe 11-8. Calculated Function Names 242

Problem 242

Solution 242

How it Works 242

Recipe 11-9. Anonymous Functions 243

Problem 243

Solution 243

How it Works 243

Recipe 11-10. Variable Parameter List 246

Problem 246

Solution 246

How it Works 246

■Chapter 12: Web Fundamentals 249

Recipe 12-1. Headers 249

Problem 249

Solution 249

How it Works 250

Recipe 12-2. $_GET and $_POST 250

Problem 250

Solution 251

How it Works 251

Recipe 12-3. Cookies 253

Problem 253

Solution 253

How it Works 254

Recipe 12-4. Server Variables 255

Problem 255

Solution 255

How it Works 255

Recipe 12-5. Session Data 257

Problem 257

Solution 257

How it Works 258

Recipe 12-6. Content Type and Disposition 259

Problem 259

Solution 259

How it Works 259

Recipe 12-7. Caching 261

Problem 261

Solution 261

How it Works 261

Recipe 12-8. Remote Content 262

Problem 262

Solution 262

How it Works 263

Recipe 12-9. The HTTPS Protocol 265

    Problem 265

    Solution 265

    How it Works 265

Recipe 12-10. AJAX Requests 266

    Problem 266

    Solution 266

    How it Works 266

Recipe 12-11. Web Sockets 267

    Problem 267

    Solution 267

    How it Works 267

■Chapter 13: Creating and Using Forms 271

Recipe 13-1. Form Elements 271

    Problem 271

    Solution 271

    How it Works 274

Recipe 13-2. Default Values 276

    Problem 276

    Solution 276

    How it Works 277

Recipe 13-3. Form Validation 280

    Problem 280

    Solution 280

    How it Works 280

Recipe 13-4. Form Generation 283

    Problem 283

    Solution 283

    How it Works 284

Recipe 13-5. File Upload 288

    Problem 288

    Solution... 288

    How it Works.. 289

Recipe 13-6. Form Data 290

    Problem 290

    Solution... 290

    How it Works.. 291

■Chapter 14: XML, RSS, WDDX, and SOAP 293

Recipe 14-1. Exchanging Data with XML 293

    Problem 293

    Solution... 293

    How it Works.. 294

Recipe 14-2. Generating XML Response 300

    Problem 300

    Solution... 300

    How it Works.. 300

Recipe 14-3. Sharing Data with RSS... 303

    Problem 303

    Solution... 304

    How it Works.. 304

Recipe 14-4. Consuming RSS Feeds... 306

    Problem 306

    Solution... 307

    How it Works.. 307

Recipe 14-5. Standard Data Exchange... 308

    Problem 308

    Solution... 308

    How it Works.. 309

Recipe 14-6. SOAP Server and Client... 311

Problem 311

Solution... 311

How it Works.. 311

Chapter 15: Data Exchange with JSON.. 317

Recipe 15-1. Fetching Data with AJAX.. 317

Problem 317

Solution... 317

How it Works.. 317

Recipe 15-2. Returning JSON.. 319

Problem 319

Solution... 319

How it Works.. 320

Recipe 15-3. Consuming a JSON API 321

Problem 321

Solution... 321

How it Works.. 321

Recipe 15-4. JSON API 324

Problem 324

Solution... 324

How it Works.. 325

Recipe 15-5. Calling API's 327

Problem 327

Solution... 327

How it Works.. 327

Recipe 15-6. API Authentication 330

Problem 330

Solution... 330

How it Works.. 330

■**Chapter 16: Using MySQL Databases**... **333**

Recipe 16-1. Connecting to MySQL... 333

Problem 333

Solution.. 333

How it Works... 334

Recipe 16-2. Persistent Connections 337

Problem 337

Solution.. 337

How it Works... 338

Recipe 16-3. Fetching Data.. 338

Problem 338

Solution.. 339

How it Works... 339

Recipe 16-4. Inserting Data... 341

Problem 341

Solution.. 341

How it Works... 341

Recipe 16-5. Updating Data 348

Problem 348

Solution.. 348

How it Works... 349

Recipe 16-6. Deleting Data 351

Problem 351

Solution.. 351

How it Works... 351

Recipe 16-7. Schema Information.. 355

Problem 355

Solution.. 355

How it Works... 356

Index... 357

About the Author

Frank M. Kromann has spent more than 30 years solving business problems using software and technology. Since the introduction of the first web browser he has developed systems with web technology on Unix, Linux, Windows, and Mac platforms, with the primary focus on PHP, JavaScript, C/C++, and other languages.

He has contributed several PHP extensions over the years and has been a member of the PHP development team since 1997. Previous publications included several articles in *PHP Magazine* and he was the coauthor of *PHP 5 Recipes* (Apress, 2005).

Frank M. Kromann has held managing positions for more than 20 years, leading both smaller and larger teams in development and implementation of business systems and processes utilizing databases and programming. Currently he is an Engineering Manager at Panasonic Avionics and the CEO and cofounder of Web by Pixel, Inc.

Kromann holds a Master of Science degree in Electrical Engineering from the Technical University of Denmark.

About the Technical Reviewer

Massimo Nardone holds a Master of Science degree in Computing Science from the University of Salerno, Italy. He has worked as a Project Manager, Software Engineer, Research Engineer, Chief Security Architect, Information Security Manager, PCI/SCADA Auditor, and Senior Lead IT Security/Cloud/SCADA Architect for many years. He currently works as Chief Information Security Office (CISO) for Cargotec Oyj. He has more than 22 years of work experience in IT including Security, SCADA, Cloud Computing, IT Infrastructure, Mobile, Security, and WWW technology areas for both national and international projects. He worked as visiting lecturer and supervisor for exercises at the Networking Laboratory of the Helsinki University of Technology (Aalto University). He has been programming and teaching how to program with Android, Perl, PHP, Java, VB, Python, C/C++, and MySQL for more than 20 years. He holds four international patents (PKI, SIP, SAML, and Proxy areas).

Nardone is the coauthor of *Pro Android Games* (Apress, 2015).

Introduction

PHP 5 Recipes: A Problem-Solution Approach was released in 2005. At that time there were still many sites using the older PHP 4 version of the scripting language, and PHP 5 introduced many new features and a totally redesigned model for object-oriented programming. Since then PHP has seen many releases, and it's time to upgrade the contents and recipes that cover some of the new features that have been added to the language in the eleven years since the first book. The current version of PHP is 5.6.x and the development team recently released version 7.0 that promises double the performance and half the memory use compared to PHP 5.6. The jump from PHP 5 to PHP 7, skipping the major version 6 has to do with a research project that was labeled PHP 6. This project was abandoned because of complexity and performance problems.

PHP is a scripting language most commonly used to create dynamic web content; in fact about 80 percent of the web servers have PHP installed in some form. PHP can also be used as a general purpose scripting language for shell scripts, and it's even possible to create desktop applications with the help of the PHP-GTK extension. This book is going to focus on web and shell scripting and it is intended for beginners as well as advanced users.

PHP is a loosely typed scripting language. There is no need to declare variables before using them and variables can change types as the content changes. As a scripting language there is no need to compile or otherwise process the code before execution. When the interpreter is instructed to execute a script it will load the content of the file, perform the compilation, and execute the code if no compilation errors are found. Various forms of caching can bypass the compilation stage and move directly to execution.

CHAPTER 1

■ ■ ■

Installation and Configuration

It has been about 10 years since *PHP 5 Recipes – A Problem-Solution Approach* was published and PHP, and web technology in general, has come a long way since then. It's time to update some of the recipes.

The example code in this book is designed to work with the current versions (PHP 5.6 and PHP 7) but in many cases the examples will work with older versions of PHP 5. PHP 7 is still fairly new and many site owners have not yet upgraded. For the most part PHP 7 is compatible with PHP 5.6 but it does include a few new features and a couple of backwards compatibility issues. Not all extensions have been updated to work with the new Zend Engine (the internal workings of PHP).

It is highly recommended to use the very latest version of PHP. This will ensure the best performance and security, and it will provide access to the latest features.

PHP was designed as a scripting language for generating dynamic web content in the form of responses to requests from a client (usually a browser) to a web server using the HTTP protocol. The browser is no longer the only type of client for these scripts. In a world where more and more data is accessed through web services that return JSON, XML, or other structured formats, we are seeing clients being anything: from applications on a smart phone, other applications, and even servers talking to other servers to exchange data.

Recipe 1-1. Installing PHP

Problem

PHP is an open source scripting language that has been ported to many different platforms. It can run on anything from a Raspberry PI to a big IBM mainframe. Installing PHP used to require the user to compile the interpreter from source code, but today many operating systems provide packages that make it easy to install. No matter which operating system and web server you choose to use, the problem is the same: how do I get the web server to execute a script and return the response?

Solution

The number of supported operating systems, web servers, and server API's is quite large and the number of different combinations is even bigger. Most of the web servers on the Internet that use PHP as a scripting language are running some form of Linux and some are running Windows. When it comes to development environments there are Windows, Mac OSX, and Linux systems that are common. In addition to this there are at least three types of web servers: Apache, Nginx, and Internet Information Server (IIS) on Windows.

Electronic supplementary material The online version of this chapter (doi:10.1007/978-1-4842-0605-8_1) contains supplementary material, which is available to authorized users.

The common problem that all these configurations is solving is the injecting of a script parser into the web server so requests for certain files will result in invoking of a script and returning the output generated by the script. Other types of requests to the web server such as static HTML, images, JavaScript, and CSS files, etc., are handled by the web server directly as the server will resolve the request to a file on the file system and return the file unchanged to the requester.

The usual configuration is to tell the web server that files with a certain file extension (.php) are to be interpreted by PHP. When a request comes in for such a file the web server will pass the request to PHP and wait for the output.

How it Works

With the large number of possible combinations of operating systems, web servers, and ways to link PHP to the web server, I have chosen a few combinations that are described in the following few examples. The first example covers how to install Apache and PHP on a clean CentOS 7 operating system using the package management tool yum. A later example will show how to do the same on Windows.

The package manager yum is used to install, update, or remove packages from the CentOS repository. It can also be used to list the available packages. It is always a good idea to make sure the system is fully up to date before installing new packages. This is done by running the following command:

```
yum update
```

This will ensure all kernel and application packages are updated to the latest version. After installing a new kernel the system must be rebooted.

The name of the apache package is called httpd, so to list all the packages related to the Apache web server we could issue the following command:

```
# yum list httpd*
Available Packages
httpd.x86_64                    2.4.6-40.el7.centos              base
httpd-devel.x86_64              2.4.6-40.el7.centos              base
httpd-manual.noarch             2.4.6-40.el7.centos              base
httpd-tools.x86_64              2.4.6-40.el7.centos              base
```

Note that many of the yum commands should be run as the root user. Either use su - to switch to the root account or use sudo in front of each command to execute that command as the root user.

The output shows that there are five packages available in this environment. It is only necessary to install the first package. It can be done with the command.

```
yum install httpd
```

This will install all packages needed to get the basic web server installed. The Apache web server depends on the packages apr, apr-util, httpd-tools, and mailcap. After installation the server can be configured to start automatically by calling.

```
systemctl enable httpd
```

And started with this command:

```
systemctl start httpd
```

This will provide you with a standard Apache 2.4 configuration. It is ready to serve static html files, but there are still a few steps to do before it can serve requests to PHP scripts. To test the new web server configuration it is necessary to create the first HTML document. The default configuration places the document root at /var/www/html. In addition the default configuration is set to default to a document called index.html. This is used if the request is made without a specific document. Use VI or your preferred editor to create index.html in the folder /var/www/html. The content could look like this:

```
<!DOCTYPE html>
<html>
<head>
  <title>Apache</title>
</head>
<body>
  <h1>It works!</h1>
</body>
</html>
```

Testing of the web server as responding can be done with the wget command or by pointing a web browser to the host name or IP address of the server. Depending on the configuration of the operating system you might have to install the wget command first. If you have a firewall installed you might also have to configure that to allow tcp traffic on port 80 to the server.

Instead of a static HTML document we can now create the first simple PHP script. This will not do much until PHP is installed, but it will showcase how PHP scripts work on a server that's not configured to handle requests for PHP scripts. The very first PHP script could be a simple one like this:

```
<?php
// 1_1.php
phpinfo();
?>
```

The last closing tag ?> is not necessary unless the file contains any content after the closing tag that is going to be sent directly to the client as is, without PHP interpreting the content. In fact it is a common standard to exclude the closing ?> on scripts that only contain PHP code.

If the browser is pointed to the web server (in my case the address is http://192.168.23.148/phpinfo.php), the output will show the content of the file.

```
<?php
phpinfo();
?>
```

The next step is to install one or more PHP packages. To get a list of the available packages use the yum command:

```
# yum list PHP*
Available Packages
php.x86_64                    5.4.16-36.el7_1         base
php-bcmath.x86_64             5.4.16-36.el7_1         base
php-cli.x86_64                5.4.16-36.el7_1         base
php-common.x86_64             5.4.16-36.el7_1         base
php-dba.x86_64                5.4.16-36.el7_1         base
```

3

php-devel.x86_64	5.4.16-36.el7_1	base
php-embedded.x86_64	5.4.16-36.el7_1	base
php-enchant.x86_64	5.4.16-36.el7_1	base
php-fpm.x86_64	5.4.16-36.el7_1	base
php-gd.x86_64	5.4.16-36.el7_1	base
php-intl.x86_64	5.4.16-36.el7_1	base
php-ldap.x86_64	5.4.16-36.el7_1	base
php-mbstring.x86_64	5.4.16-36.el7_1	base
php-mysql.x86_64	5.4.16-36.el7_1	base
php-mysqlnd.x86_64	5.4.16-36.el7_1	base
php-odbc.x86_64	5.4.16-36.el7_1	base
php-pdo.x86_64	5.4.16-36.el7_1	base
php-pear.noarch	1:1.9.4-21.el7	base
php-pecl-memcache.x86_64	3.0.8-4.el7	base
php-pgsql.x86_64	5.4.16-36.el7_1	base
php-process.x86_64	5.4.16-36.el7_1	base
php-pspell.x86_64	5.4.16-36.el7_1	base
php-recode.x86_64	5.4.16-36.el7_1	base
php-snmp.x86_64	5.4.16-36.el7_1	base
php-soap.x86_64	5.4.16-36.el7_1	base
php-xml.x86_64	5.4.16-36.el7_1	base
php-xmlrpc.x86_64	5.4.16-36.el7_1	base

Note that the version is 5.4.16 although the custom version is 5.6.20 or 7.0.5. This is the case with many Linux distributions. They do backport security updates but they might not backport new features or new versions. It is possible to get PHP from other repositories other than the official CentOS one, but if a newer version is needed, I recommend compiling it from source as described in Recipe 1-3.

The basic package is all that's needed, but installing the php-cli, php-common, and one or more database packages is most likely going to work for most people. The packages can be installed one by one or you can choose to install all the packages. The first example shows how to install a few packages.

```
yum install php php-cli php-common php-mysql
```

This will also install libzip and php-pdo.

Installing all packages is done with `yum install php*`.

After installation of the PHP packages it is necessary to restart the Apache server. This will make sure the installed Apache module is loaded.

```
systemctl restart httpd
```

Pointing the browser to the web server (`http://192.168.23.148/phpinfo.php` or `http://localhost/ phpinfo.php`) will now yield this output:

PHP Version 5.4.16

System	Linux localhost.localdomain 3.10.0-327.13.1.el7.x86_64 #1 SMP Thu Mar 31 16:04:38 UTC 2016 x86_64
Build Date	Jun 23 2015 21:18:22
Server API	Apache 2.0 Handler
Virtual Directory Support	disabled
Configuration File (php.ini) Path	/etc
Loaded Configuration File	/etc/php.ini
Scan this dir for additional .ini files	/etc/php.d
Additional .ini files parsed	/etc/php.d/curl.ini, /etc/php.d/fileinfo.ini, /etc/php.d/json.ini, /etc/php.d/mysql.ini, /etc/php.d/mysqli.ini, /etc/php.d/pdo.ini, /etc/php.d/pdo_mysql.ini, /etc/php.d/pdo_sqlite.ini, /etc/php.d/phar.ini, /etc/php.d/sqlite3.ini, /etc/php.d/zip.ini
PHP API	20100412
PHP Extension	20100525
Zend Extension	220100525
Zend Extension Build	API220100525,NTS
PHP Extension Build	API20100525,NTS
Debug Build	no
Thread Safety	disabled
Zend Signal Handling	disabled
Zend Memory Manager	enabled
Zend Multibyte Support	disabled
IPv6 Support	enabled
DTrace Support	disabled
Registered PHP Streams	https, ftps, compress.zlib, compress.bzip2, php, file, glob, data, http, ftp, phar, zip
Registered Stream Socket Transports	tcp, udp, unix, udg, ssl, sslv3, sslv2, tls
Registered Stream Filters	zlib.*, bzip2.*, convert.iconv.*, string.rot13, string.toupper, string.tolower, string.strip_tags, convert.*, consumed, dechunk

This program makes use of the Zend Scripting Language Engine: Zend Engine v2.4.0, Copyright (c) 1998-2013 Zend Technologies

Powered By

The actual output will show much more data but this shows that PHP is now working on the server.

It is not that common to have Linux installed on a desktop or laptop computer. If you want to be able to test the PHP code locally before deploying it to a server you will need a local web server that supports PHP. It is also possible to do all the development remotely, but that will require Internet access.

Use the following commands to show the actual version of Apache and PHP that's installed on the system:

```
# httpd -v
Server version: Apache/2.4.6 (CentOS)
Server built:   Nov 19 2015 21:43:13
```

And for PHP

```
# php -v
PHP 5.4.16 (cli) (built: Jun 23 2015 21:17:27)
Copyright (c) 1997-2013 The PHP Group
Zend Engine v2.4.0, Copyright (c) 1998-2013 Zend Technologies
```

And to get a list of the installed PHP extensions use the php –m command:

```
# php -m
[PHP Modules]
bz2
calendar
Core
ctype
curl
date
ereg
exif
fileinfo
filter
ftp
gettext
gmp
hash
iconv
json
libxml
mhash
mysql
mysqli
openssl
pcntl
pcre
PDO
pdo_mysql
pdo_sqlite
Phar
readline
Reflection
```

```
session
shmop
SimpleXML
sockets
SPL
sqlite3
standard
tokenizer
xml
zip
zlib

[Zend Modules]
```

On the Mac OSX platform, PHP comes preinstalled. On my version of Mac OSX (El Capitain) the installed versions can be listed with the same commands as above:

```
$ httpd -v
Server version: Apache/2.4.16 (Unix)
Server built:   Jul 31 2015 15:53:26
$ php -v
PHP 5.5.30 (cli) (built: Oct 23 2015 17:21:45)
Copyright (c) 1997-2015 The PHP Group
Zend Engine v2.5.0, Copyright (c) 1998-2015 Zend Technologies
```

The default-installed modules are the following:

```
$ php -m
[PHP Modules]
bcmath
bz2
calendar
Core
ctype
curl
date
dba
dom
ereg
exif
fileinfo
filter
ftp
gd
hash
iconv
json
ldap
libxml
mbstring
mysql
```

```
mysqli
mysqlnd
openssl
pcre
PDO
pdo_mysql
pdo_sqlite
Phar
posix
readline
Reflection
session
shmop
SimpleXML
snmp
soap
sockets
SPL
sqlite3
standard
sysvmsg
sysvsem
sysvshm
tidy
tokenizer
wddx
xml
xmlreader
xmlrpc
xmlwriter
xsl
zip
zlib

[Zend Modules]
```

Getting PHP to run on Windows is almost as easy. Please note that PHP no longer supports older versions of Windows (XP/2003 etc.). The first step is to install a web server: IIS or Apache. These days there is not much difference in performance or features between the two. If you are going to deploy the PHP scripts on IIS on a Windows server it's recommended to do the development on a similar platform. The same goes for Apache deployments.

When developing on Windows and deploying on Linux it is important to note a few key differences between the two operating systems. First of all, file names on Windows are case insensitive. If your script refers to a file called MyFile.php but the actual file name is myfile.php, it will work on Windows but break when you deploy to the Linux platform. Secondly there is the matter of directory separator. This is a slash (/) on Linux and Unix environments and a backslash (\) on windows. PHP can use both when referencing local files but always use slashes in URL's. It is recommended to always use the slash as a directory separator on Windows because there is no need to escape that character when it's written as part of a double quoted string.

To install Internet Information Services (IIS version 7 or later) on a Windows 10 system, launch the control panel and click on "Programs and Features." In the left bar there is a link to "Turn Windows features on or off." This will bring up a window with Windows Features. Simply enable the option for Internet Information Services and click on the Ok button, as shown in the image below.

Make sure to expand the World Wide Web Services folder, then expand Application Development Features and select the CGI option.

This will install the web server, the CGI module needed for PHP, and the management tools. Be aware that other processes (like Skype and Plex) installed on the computer might already be using the default web port (80). If that is the case you can either disable these services or use a different port for the web server. Using different ports for each web site you are working on will allow you to host multiple sites. It will also allow concurrent use of Apache and IIS on the same system.

It is possible to have multiple web sites (on the same server) share a single port. Using different host names for each web site does that. These host names can be managed locally in a hosts file. This file is located in c:\Windows\System32\Drivers\etc on a Windows system and in /etc on a Mac or Linux system.

The default IIS configuration creates a web server that listens on port 80 and uses %SystemDrive%\inetpub\wwwroot as the document root. %SystemDrive% normally resolves to C:\. It is not necessary to use this directory structure for the web site.

The next step is to start the web site. In my case I had to use a different port as port 80 is used for Skype. Use the IIS manager application to make changes to the site. The Internet Information Services (IIS) manager can be found in the control panel under administrative tools or by typing IIS in the search bar. The application looks like this:

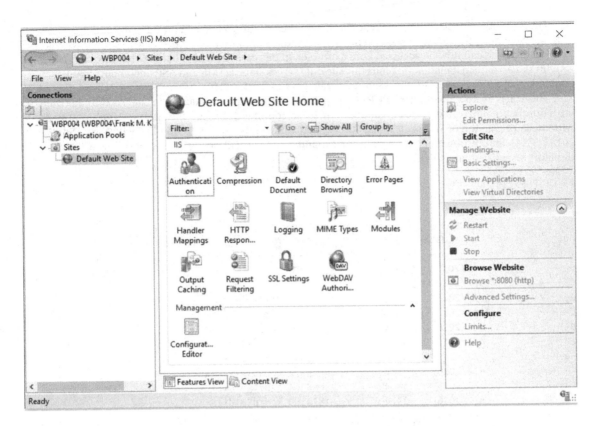

Right-click on the Default Web Site and select the Edit Bindings option and double-click on the line to change the configuration. Only the port number is changed from 80 to 8080. It's also possible to limit the IP address or host name, and it's possible to add additional bindings to bind the same web site to different port numbers and/or host names if needed.

The final step is to start the site. Right-clicking on the Default Web Site in the left pane and then the Manage Website option to expand the menu and select the Start option does this.

The web site can now be accessed from a browser. In this case the URL is http://localhost:8080. As with the Apache installation on Linux this site only serves static HTML and ASP documents if ASP is enabled. There are some additional steps needed to get support for PHP.

This starts by downloading the PHP binary package from http://windows.php.net/download. There are a number of different versions to choose from. It is recommended to use the latest version, compiled with the latest version of Microsoft Visual Studio. That is currently PHP 7.0.5 compiled with Visual Studio 2015 (VC14). Simply download the zip file and expand it into C:\PHP, or any other folder. This will give a directory structure that looks like this:

```
PS C:\PHP> ls

    Directory: C:\PHP

Mode                LastWriteTime         Length Name
----                -------------         ------ ----
d-----        4/2/2016     13:48                dev
d-----        4/2/2016     13:48                ext
d-----       2/13/2016     14:52                extras
d-----       2/13/2016     14:52                lib
d-----        4/2/2016     13:48                sasl2
-a----        4/2/2016     13:49          98816 deplister.exe
-a----        4/2/2016     13:49        1175552 glib-2.dll
-a----        4/2/2016     13:49          15872 gmodule-2.dll
-a----        4/2/2016     13:49       25048064 icudt56.dll
-a----        4/2/2016     13:49        1820160 icuin56.dll
-a----        4/2/2016     13:49          41984 icuio56.dll
-a----        4/2/2016     13:49         226816 icule56.dll
-a----        4/2/2016     13:49        1188864 icuuc56.dll
-a----        4/2/2016     13:49          79407 install.txt
-a----        4/2/2016     13:49        1389568 libeay32.dll
-a----        4/2/2016     13:49          36352 libenchant.dll
-a----        4/2/2016     13:49         135168 libpq.dll
-a----        4/2/2016     13:49          77824 libsasl.dll
-a----        4/2/2016     13:49         235008 libssh2.dll
-a----        4/2/2016     13:49           3286 license.txt
-a----        4/2/2016     13:49          51511 news.txt
-a----        4/2/2016     13:49             43 phar.phar.bat
-a----        4/2/2016     13:49          53242 pharcommand.phar
-a----        4/2/2016     13:49          52736 php-cgi.exe
-a----        4/2/2016     13:49          30720 php-win.exe
-a----        4/2/2016     13:49          98304 php.exe
-a----        4/2/2016     13:49           2523 php.gif
-a----        4/2/2016     13:49          70752 php.ini-development
-a----        4/2/2016     13:49          70784 php.ini-production
-a----        4/2/2016     13:49        7088640 php7.dll
-a----        4/2/2016     13:49         869002 php7embed.lib
-a----        4/2/2016     13:49         197632 php7phpdbg.dll
-a----        4/2/2016     13:49         214528 phpdbg.exe
-a----        4/2/2016     13:49          20183 readme-redist-bins.txt
-a----        4/2/2016     13:49          12722 snapshot.txt
-a----        4/2/2016     13:49         274944 ssleay32.dll
```

In most cases it's also necessary to install the redistribution libraries provided by Microsoft. It is important to install the right version of these but you can install them all and some of them might be installed already from other programs and tools installed on the system. The links to the different versions can be found in the left pane on the site `http://windows.php.net`.

The final step is to enable PHP in the web server. This is similar to how it was done for Apache on Linux. IIS uses the FastCGI interface to communicate between IIS and PHP. On Linux, PHP was installed and loaded as a module under the web server.

Start by clicking on the Default Web Site in the left pane of the IIS Manager. That will bring up a list of icons. Then double-click on the icon called Handler Mappings. Then click on the Add Module Mapping link in the right pane. This opens an input dialog with four input boxes. The first one is where the request path is defined. We want the PHP interpreter to be invoked on all files ending in .php so the value should be *.php. The next box is a drop-down with a number of different modules to choose from. Make sure to select the FastCGIModule and not the CGIModule. The interface between the web server and the module are different and the request will fail if the wrong version is used. In the third box enter the path to php-cgi.exe (or use the browse button to locate the file) and finally enter a name for the Module Mapping. I chose PHP as shown in the screen shot below.

Add Module Mapping   ?   ✕

Request path:

| *.php |

Example: *.bas, wsvc.axd

Module:

| FastCgiModule   ⌄ |

Executable (optional):

| C:\PHP\php-cgi.exe | | ... |

Name:

| PHP| |

[Request Restrictions...]

[OK]   [Cancel]

The IIS Web server is now configured to serve requests to PHP scripts. Restart the web server and place the same phpinfo.php file we used before in the document root (c:\inetpub\wwwroot). If you want to access the server from other computers you will have to turn the firewall off or add a rule for the TCP port 8080 (if that's the one you used).

The sample script will generate output like this:

PHP Version 7.0.5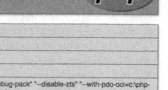

System	Windows NT WBP004 10.0 build 10586 (Windows 10) i586
Build Date	Mar 30 2016 09:57:56
Compiler	MSVC14 (Visual C++ 2015)
Architecture	x86
Configure Command	cscript /nologo configure.js "--enable-snapshot-build" "--enable-debug-pack" "--disable-zts" "--with-pdo-oci=c:\php-sdk\oracle\x86\instantclient_12_1\sdk,shared" "--with-oci8-12c=c:\php-sdk\oracle\x86\instantclient_12_1\sdk,shared" "--enable-object-out-dir=../obj/" "--enable-com-dotnet=shared" "--with-mcrypt=static" "--without-analyzer" "--with-pgo"
Server API	CGI/FastCGI
Virtual Directory Support	disabled
Configuration File (php.ini) Path	C:\WINDOWS
Loaded Configuration File	(none)
Scan this dir for additional .ini files	(none)
Additional .ini files parsed	(none)
PHP API	20151012
PHP Extension	20151012
Zend Extension	320151012
Zend Extension Build	API320151012,NTS,VC14
PHP Extension Build	API20151012,NTS,VC14
Debug Build	no
Thread Safety	disabled
Zend Signal Handling	disabled
Zend Memory Manager	enabled
Zend Multibyte Support	disabled
IPv6 Support	enabled
DTrace Support	disabled
Registered PHP Streams	php, file, glob, data, http, ftp, zip, compress.zlib, phar
Registered Stream Socket Transports	tcp, udp
Registered Stream Filters	convert.iconv.*, mcrypt.*, mdecrypt.*, string.rot13, string.toupper, string.tolower, string.strip_tags, convert.*, consumed, dechunk, zlib.*

This program makes use of the Zend Scripting Language Engine:
Zend Engine v3.0.0, Copyright (c) 1998-2016 Zend Technologies

zend engine

Apache can be installed with binaries provided by Apache Lounge. The links to these can be found on http://windows.php.net. Download the zip file with the version that matches your system and unzip the contents to C:\Apache24. This directory matches the configuration in the httpd.conf file. If you choose to install in a different directory, update the httpd.conf file to match the location.

The default configuration is also using port 80. In order to run both IIS and Apache and possible other applications working on port 80 it is necessary to change the port for Apache. In this example I change the port to 8090 by updating the line in c:\Apache24\conf\httpd.conf

From

```
Listen 80
```

To

```
Listen 8090
```

The final step is to start the web server with this command:

```
C:\Apache24\bin\httpd.exe
```

This command is useful to create a single instance of the server. The server will only be running as long as this process is running. It is also possible to install a service that starts automatically when the computer is started. Adding -k install as an argument to the start command does this:

```
C:\Apache24\bin\httpd.exe -k install
```

As before, pointing a browser to the server, it's now possible to test the web server. In this case the URL is http://localhost:8090.

The final step is to configure the server to support PHP requests. This can be done by using the Apache module that comes with the thread safe version of PHP or by using the FastCGI interface used for the IIS server.

Configuring with the Apache module requires these changes:

Start by creating a file called C:\Apache24\conf\extras\httpd-php.conf and add the following lines:

```
#
LoadModule php7_module "C:/PHP/php7apache2_4.dll"
AddHandler application/x-httpd-php .php

<IfModule php7_module>
  PHPIniDir "C:/PHP"
</IfModule>
```

Then add the following line to the end of C:\Apache24\conf\https.conf

```
Include conf/extra/httpd-php.conf
```

Starting the Apache server will now support PHP requests and the output from phpinfo() looks like this:

PHP Version 7.0.5

System	Windows NT WBP004 10.0 build 10586 (Windows 10) AMD64
Build Date	Mar 30 2016 09:56:03
Compiler	MSVC14 (Visual C++ 2015)
Architecture	x64
Configure Command	cscript /nologo configure.js "--enable-snapshot-build" "--enable-debug-pack" "--with-pdo-oci=c:\php-sdk\oracle\x64\instantclient_12_1\sdk,shared" "--with-oci8-12c=c:\php-sdk\oracle\x64\instantclient_12_1\sdk,shared" "--enable-object-out-dir=../obj/" "--enable-com-dotnet=shared" "--with-mcrypt=static" "--without-analyzer" "--with-pgo"
Server API	Apache 2.0 Handler
Virtual Directory Support	enabled
Configuration File (php.ini) Path	C:\WINDOWS
Loaded Configuration File	(none)
Scan this dir for additional .ini files	(none)
Additional .ini files parsed	(none)
PHP API	20151012
PHP Extension	20151012
Zend Extension	320151012
Zend Extension Build	API320151012,TS,VC14
PHP Extension Build	API20151012,TS,VC14
Debug Build	no
Thread Safety	enabled
Zend Signal Handling	disabled
Zend Memory Manager	enabled
Zend Multibyte Support	disabled
IPv6 Support	enabled
DTrace Support	disabled
Registered PHP Streams	php, file, glob, data, http, ftp, zip, compress.zlib, phar
Registered Stream Socket Transports	tcp, udp
Registered Stream Filters	convert.iconv.*, mcrypt.*, mdecrypt.*, string.rot13, string.toupper, string.tolower, string.strip_tags, convert.*, consumed, dechunk, zlib.*

This program makes use of the Zend Scripting Language Engine:
Zend Engine v3.0.0, Copyright (c) 1998-2016 Zend Technologies

zend·engine

In order to configure Apache to use the FastCGI version of PHP it is necessary to download and install an additional Apache module called mod_fcgid.so. This file should be placed in c:\Apache24\modules and the configuration file for PHP (C:\Apache24\conf\extras\httpd-php.conf) should be changed to this:

```
#
LoadModule fcgid_module modules/mod_fcgid.so
FcgidInitialEnv PHPRC "C:/PHP"
AddHandler fcgid-script .php
FcgidWrapper "C:/PHP/php-cgi.exe" .php
```

The first line can also be placed in the main configuration file (C:\Apache24\conf\httpd.conf). The second line instructs PHP to look for the php.ini file in C:\PHP. The third line instructs Apache to handle requests for .php files via the FastCGI API, and the last line instructs FastCGI to call the php-cgi.exe executable.

In addition it is necessary to add an option called ExecCGI to allow Apache to execute the CGI script. This is either done in the main file by changing the Options in the <Directory> section from "Options Indexes FollowSymLinks" to "Options ExecCGI Indexes FollowSymLinks" or by a similar change for each virtual host that needs the same permissions.

If we load the phpinfo.php file in a browser the output will now show that the server is using the CGI/FastCGI server API instead of the Apache2Handler.

Using the FastCGI interface in Apache and IIS makes it possible to install multiple versions of PHP on the same system. Creating multiple virtual hosts pointing to the same document root but utilizing different CGI handlers makes it very easy to test the application code with different versions of PHP.

Recipe 1-2. Configuring PHP

Problem

The focus in the previous section was to install and perform basic configuration of a web server to be used with PHP. There are a large number of configuration options for PHP that works independently of the web server. What is the best approach to configuring PHP?

Solution

The basic configuration is done through a file called php.ini. It can be located in a number of different places depending on how PHP is compiled and installed and which operating system of PHP it is installed on. In addition it's possible to have different php.ini files based on which server API is used to execute the PHP script. This makes it possible to have one php.ini file that's used by the web server and a different file that is used when the CLI version of PHP is used to execute a script as a cron job or command line.

A common location of the php.ini file(s) is in /etc/php.ini on most Linux and Mac OSX systems, and on Windows it's common to place these files in the C:\Windows folder but it can be placed in other locations based on environment variables or other configuration options.

If php.ini is the only file that's found it will be used by all server API's. There is a special naming convention that makes it possible to have files specific to each server API. The name of each of these can be used as the replacement for ASPI in the name of the php-SAPI.ini file. Common names for SAPI's are cli, apache, apache2handler, cgi-fcgi, isapi, and many more.

Some of the settings in php.ini can be set or overwritten at runtime. This is done with the ini_set() function. Some settings have an impact on resources and security, and these can only be defined in the main php.ini file (system administrator), and others can be set in per directory bases and some can be set by the script at runtime (ini_set()).

It is common practice to use one configuration for the development environment and another for the production environment. In the development environment it's often helpful to get error and warnings shown directly in the web page, and in the production environment it's preferred not to show any errors or warnings that might expose vulnerabilities or simply confuse the visitor.

If the server is hosting multiple virtual hosts it can be necessary to overwrite certain values on the php.ini file for one or more of these virtual hosts. That way it's possible to have one set of error reporting for the development instance and a different set for the production instance even though both sites are installed on the same web server, sharing a single php.ini file. These overwrites can be defined in Apache configuration where the virtual host is defined or in a .htaccess file in a specific directory.

It is recommend to minimize the use of .htaccess files. These files are parsed on every request and this can have an impact on performance. Using the Apache configuration or a php.ini file will cause the settings to be read once, when the server is started.

If the display_errors option is set to off in php.ini and it is decided to set a different value for a single host it can be done by adding a php_flag to the <VirtualHost></VirtualHost> section of the Apache configuration. This can either be in the main httpd.conf file or in a file specific to the host as shown in the following sample.

```
<VirtualHost *:80>
  ServerName www.example.com
  DocumentRoot /var/www/example.com/root
  DirectoryINdex index.html index.php
  php_flag display_errors on
</VirtualHost>
```

The option php_flag is used for Boolean options. Other php.ini values can be set or overwritten with the php_value option. To set the value for error_reporting to E_ALL (showing all errors, warnings, and notices, etc.), you will have to use the integer value for E_ALL. When configured in the php.ini file it's possible to use the names (E_ALL, E_ERROR, E_NOTICE etc.). These values are not known within the Apache configuration and we have to use the corresponding integer value. Finding the value of the E_ALL constant can be done with the following command-line script:

```
# php -r 'echo E_ALL;'
```

Using the -r option when running the CLI version of PHP is an easy way to run a simple one-line PHP script. The script will show that the value is the sum of the 15 first bits of an integer or 32767. So to set the error_reporting to E_ALL in the Apache configuration use the following line:

```
php_value error_reporting 32767
```

How it Works

When PHP is installed from source it includes two different versions of the php.ini file called php.ini-development and php.ini-production. These two files can be used as a recommended baseline for the two different environments. In most cases these contain a good starting point for configuration of PHP, but in most cases and as new features are added to the web site it's necessary to add or change certain values. At the top of these files there is a Quick Reference section, a list of options that would normally be different in the two environments or different from the default value if no setting is provided:

```
;;;;;;;;;;;;;;;;;;;;
; Quick Reference ;
;;;;;;;;;;;;;;;;;;;;
; The following are all the settings that are different in either the production
; or development versions of the INIs with respect to PHP's default behavior.
; Please see the actual settings later in the document for more details as to why
; we recommend these changes in PHP's behavior.

; display_errors
;   Default Value: On
;   Development Value: On
;   Production Value: Off
```

```
;  display_startup_errors
;    Default Value: Off
;    Development Value: On
;    Production Value: Off

;  error_reporting
;    Default Value: E_ALL & ~E_NOTICE & ~E_STRICT & ~E_DEPRECATED
;    Development Value: E_ALL
;    Production Value: E_ALL & ~E_DEPRECATED & ~E_STRICT

;  html_errors
;    Default Value: On
;    Development Value: On
;    Production value: On

;  log_errors
;    Default Value: Off
;    Development Value: On
;    Production Value: On

;  max_input_time
;    Default Value: -1 (Unlimited)
;    Development Value: 60 (60 seconds)
;    Production Value: 60 (60 seconds)

;  output_buffering
;    Default Value: Off
;    Development Value: 4096
;    Production Value: 4096

;  register_argc_argv
;    Default Value: On
;    Development Value: Off
;    Production Value: Off

;  request_order
;    Default Value: None
;    Development Value: "GP"
;    Production Value: "GP"

;  session.gc_divisor
;    Default Value: 100
;    Development Value: 1000
;    Production Value: 1000

;  session.hash_bits_per_character
;    Default Value: 4
;    Development Value: 5
;    Production Value: 5
```

```
;  short_open_tag
;    Default Value: On
;    Development Value: Off
;    Production Value: Off

;  track_errors
;    Default Value: Off
;    Development Value: On
;    Production Value: Off

;  url_rewriter.tags
;    Default Value: "a=href,area=href,frame=src,form=,fieldset="
;    Development Value: "a=href,area=href,frame=src,input=src,form=fakeentry"
;    Production Value: "a=href,area=href,frame=src,input=src,form=fakeentry"

;  variables_order
;    Default Value: "EGPCS"
;    Development Value: "GPCS"
;    Production Value: "GPCS"
```

If you are installing from a precompiled distribution you might see default standards, and the php.ini file might be split into multiple files for easier management.

In addition to the display_errors and error_reporting there is an option called log_errors. When it's turned on all the errors that are encountered based on the error_reporting flag will be written to a log file. This is very useful when trying to track down errors on a development or production server after they happened. As a developer you might not have access to the browser where the error occurred so being able to read through the errors after the fact can be a helpful debugging tool. Along with the log_errors option there is also an option (error_log) to specify the name of the error log file. If it's not specified the errors will go into Apaches error log.

The error_log option can be set to a file name or a full path. When it's configured as just a file name the file will be placed in the same directory as where the main PHP script of the request was found. If you use a full path the error file is written at a specific location and it can even be shared among multiple hosts on the same server.

If the E_NOTICE option is turned on the error log file can grow very fast. It is recommended to clear these files from time to time.

The option register_argc_argv is used to define whether the variables $argc and $argv are defined. These values are commonly used with the CLI version of PHP to access the number of arguments passed ($argc) and the values of these arguments ($argv). The CLI version will actually overwrite this value in the php.ini and always turn these values on.

The value makes little sense in a web environment where the parameters to the script are stored in $_POST, $_GET, and other super global variables.

The default php.ini files are about 68kb in size. They include quite a bit of descriptive text that is simply ignored when the file is parsed. Big or small versions of the php.ini file do not make any noticeable difference as the file is only read once when the server starts up.

In addition to the values described here it's also important to look at configuration values for memory usage, execution time, size of POST, and upload data. If the max memory limit is set too high it could be possible to run out of resources in a high traffic situation. On the other hand the memory limitation must be high enough to handle the data. It is important to code the site in way that makes it possible to stay within reasonable limits. If you are running into a memory problem you could just go ahead and increase the configured value, but that might be an indication that you need to refactor the script to be more efficient with the resources.

Memory allocation can only be configured in php.ini (or in the apache configuration). That is not the case for the max_execution_time. It is set to 30 seconds by default and that should be enough for most of the requests on any site. In fact any request that takes more than 4 seconds should be optimized if possible to give the user the best possible experience. It can however be necessary to increase the execution time on certain request. If you have a query that analyzes a large data set and needs additional time you can specify the time needed with the use of the ini_set() function. The syntax to extend the max execution time to 90 seconds look like this:

```
ini_set('max_execution_time', 90);
```

The web server might have its own timeout values that will interrupt the execution of a PHP script if this value is exceeded. The max_execution_time only affects the actual PHP runtime. If the PHP script contains system calls the 'clock' is stopped while these calls are running.

One important configure option is the default time zone. Without this configuration the system will generate a warning each time one of the date functions are used. The setting is called date.timezone and can be set to any of the supported time zone values. Setting it to UTC will cause all the date/time functions to work the same way as the once prefixed with gm. The function date() and gmdate() will return the same value. Setting it to any other value like 'Americal/Los_Angels' will cause the two functions to return values with an eight hour offset.

The script when needed can change the default time zone. If a user's time zone is stored in a database the script can use that value to set the time zone. That way all representation of data/time values can be done according to each user's time zone. The function to set the time zone dynamically is called date_default_timezone_set() and it takes a string as the only parameter.

Most of the configuration options apply to both Windows and Linux, but a few of them are specific to Windows. The big difference is things like naming of extensions. On linux the names end in .so and on Windows they are prefixed with php_ and end in .dll (mysqli.so vs. php_mysqli.dll).

Extensions can be loaded by the following configurations:

```
extension=mysqli.so
```

or on Windows

```
extension=php_mysqli.dll
```

Extensions can also be compiled in so there is no need to load them in php.ini. This is the case with the standard extension (Core, ctype, date, etc.).

Recipe 1-3. Compiling PHP

Problem

Using a precompiled version of PHP is most likely going to be good enough for most PHP developers, but if the operating system doesn't provide the latest version or you want to create your own extensions or perhaps even contribute to the PHP project, you will have to compile PHP from source code. How is this done?

Solution

There are two basic ways to get the source code for PHP. The first is to download a preconfigured and officially released version of PHP, and the other is to get the source code from the git repository. The first option provides all the files matching a specific version and when a new version is released the developer must download that package and compile everything again.

Using the git repository makes it very easy to switch between versions and also very easy to always have the latest version. It is not recommended to run a production server on the current development branch. It might contain untested features. Production servers should be run on the officially released versions, as these have been through religious QA testing.

In order to compile PHP from sources it's necessary to have a few tools installed. On a Linux environment these include automake, autoconf, libtool, and the compiler (gcc). On windows you will need a version of Microsoft Visual Studio. In addition to these there are a number of open source libraries that PHP depends on. Most of these can be detected during installation and quickly installed from the package manager (on Linux). On Windows there is no package manager that makes this easy, but it's still doable to download the source packages for these libraries and compile them as needed.

How it Works

The main difference between using an official release of PHP and compiling from the git repository is the use of the 'buildconf' utility. On the official releases this was done when the source files were packaged, and if you try to run the command it will generate a warning. The basic functionality of the buildconf script is to scan through all the directories in the source tree and generate the configure file. The configure file is then used to generate the Makefile, the input to the compiler that describes all the files and dependencies needed to compile the configured options. This section will demonstrate building PHP 7 from a cloned git repository.

On a clean install of CentOS 7 the first step will be to a version of git. Use the package manager to do this:

```
$ yum install git
```

Make sure you are running this command as root or remember to prefix it with sudo. Depending on the packages installed on the system already, this might install a number of other packages that git depends on.

In the home directory create a folder called Source and change to that folder and then use the git command to clone the git repository:

```
$ mkdir Source
$ cd Source
$ git clone http://git.php.net/repository/php-src
```

This will create a directory called php-src with a copy of all the source files. If you need a specific version of PHP use the git checkout command to switch to the specific branch. The command git branch -a will give a list of all available branches. The list is quite long as the repository contains versions going back to PHP 4.0.

By default the master branch is checked out. This branch contains the latest and greatest code. As of today that corresponds to the unreleased PHP 7.1 version. To get the latest released version (PHP 7.0) uses this command:

```
$ git checkout PHP-7.0
Branch PHP-7.0 set up to track remote branch PHP-7.0 from origin.
Switched to a new branch 'PHP-7.0'
```

Before the buildconf command is executed it's necessary to make sure the toolchain is complete.

```
$ yum install gcc autoconf automake libtool
```

This will install enough tools to run the buildconf command:

```
$ ./buildconf
buildconf: checking installation...
buildconf: autoconf version 2.69 (ok)
rebuilding aclocal.m4
rebuilding configure
rebuilding main/php_config.h.in
```

This will generate the configure script that is used to specify the operation to use when compiling PHP. Running this command at this time will result in a long output that ends with an error:

```
$ ./configure
checking for grep that handles long lines and -e... /usr/bin/grep
checking for egrep... /usr/bin/grep -E
...
configure: WARNING: This bison version is not supported for regeneration of the Zend/PHP
parsers (found: none, min: 204, excluded: ).
checking for re2c... no
configure: WARNING: You will need re2c 0.13.4 or later if you want to regenerate PHP parsers.
configure: error: bison is required to build PHP/Zend when building a GIT checkout!
```

This error indicates that the system is missing some functionality required to compile PHP. In this case it's the bison library. This can be installed with the following command:

```
$ yum install bison
```

After that we can run the configure script again and look for more errors. This will be the missing libxml2 library. By default PHP includes support for SimpleXML and other XML extensions. Installing the library alone is not quite enough. The system require both the library and the header and other files needed to link against so the command to install looks like this:

```
$ yum install libxml2-devel
```

In this example the configure script was used without any options. If options to include various extensions were used, other dependencies could show up and you will have to install these and repeat the configure option until all the dependencies are installed.

When the configure script completes successfully the output will end with these lines:

```
Generating files
configure: creating ./config.status
creating main/internal_functions.c
creating main/internal_functions_cli.c
+--------------------------------------------------------------------+
| License:                                                           |
| This software is subject to the PHP License, available in this     |
| distribution in the file LICENSE.  By continuing this installation |
| process, you are bound by the terms of this license agreement.     |
| If you do not agree with the terms of this license, you must abort |
| the installation process at this point.                            |
+--------------------------------------------------------------------+
```

```
Thank you for using PHP.

config.status: creating php7.spec
config.status: creating main/build-defs.h
config.status: creating scripts/phpize
config.status: creating scripts/man1/phpize.1
config.status: creating scripts/php-config
config.status: creating scripts/man1/php-config.1
config.status: creating sapi/cli/php.1
config.status: creating sapi/cgi/php-cgi.1
config.status: creating ext/phar/phar.1
config.status: creating ext/phar/phar.phar.1
config.status: creating main/php_config.h
config.status: executing default commands
```

The configuration is now ready to build by running the make command. This takes a few minutes depending on the number of enabled extensions. The make command will produce many lines of output ending with these lines:

```
Build complete.
Don't forget to run 'make test'.
```

It is always a good idea to run the test suite before installing. It will provide valuable feedback to the QA team by sending a list of failed tests.

The new version of PHP is now ready to be installed. The default install location in in /usr/local because no other location was provided to the configure script. This will actually allow the installation of this newly compiled version alongside the version installed with the CentOS package manager. To install this version run this command:

```
$ sudo make install
```

After installation check the version of PHP:

```
$ php -v
PHP 7.0.6-dev (cli) (built: Apr  2 2016 20:05:26) ( NTS )
Copyright (c) 1997-2016 The PHP Group
Zend Engine v3.0.0, Copyright (c) 1998-2016 Zend Technologies
```

So far it's only the CLI and CGI versions of PHP that were compiled. In order to compile the Apache module version it's necessary to add at least one option to the configure command:

```
$ ./configure --with-apxs2
```

This command will most likely fail, as the apxs script is not installed by default with the apache package from CentOS. The apxs script is installed with the httpd-devel package.

```
$ sudo yum install httpd-apxs2
$ ./configure --with-apxs2
$ make
$ sudo make install
```

This will install the php module into the httpd.conf file located in /etc/httpd. Because the PHP 5.4 version was installed earlier there is now a conflict between the two and it's no longer possible to start the Apache server without errors. To resolve these errors it's necessary to edit the file to disable the PHP 5 version of the module. The install script installs the new module in /etc/httpd/conf/httpd.conf and the CentOS installation created a modules configuration file /etc/httpd/conf.modules.d/10-php.conf. First edit the file /etc/httpd/conf/httpd.conf and locate the line

```
LoadModule php7_module          /usr/lib64/httpd/modules/libphp7.so
```

This line should be removed and added to the file /etc/httpd/conf.modules.d/10-php.conf. The file will now look like this:

```
#
# PHP is an HTML-embedded scripting language which attempts to make it
# easy for developers to write dynamically generated webpages.
#
<IfModule prefork.c>
#  LoadModule php5_module modules/libphp5.so
   LoadModule php7_module          /usr/lib64/httpd/modules/libphp7.so
</IfModule>
```

The Apache server can now be started and pointing a browser to the phpinfo.php script will show the following information:

PHP Version 7.0.6-dev

System	Linux localhost.localdomain 3.10.0-327.13.1.el7.x86_64 #1 SMP Thu Mar 31 16:04:38 UTC 2016 x86_64
Build Date	Apr 2 2016 20:34:15
Configure Command	'./configure' '--with-apxs2'
Server API	Apache 2.0 Handler
Virtual Directory Support	disabled
Configuration File (php.ini) Path	/usr/local/lib
Loaded Configuration File	(none)
Scan this dir for additional .ini files	(none)
Additional .ini files parsed	(none)
PHP API	20151012
PHP Extension	20151012
Zend Extension	320151012
Zend Extension Build	API320151012,NTS
PHP Extension Build	API20151012,NTS
Debug Build	no
Thread Safety	disabled
Zend Signal Handling	disabled
Zend Memory Manager	enabled
Zend Multibyte Support	disabled
IPv6 Support	enabled
DTrace Support	disabled
Registered PHP Streams	php, file, glob, data, http, ftp, phar
Registered Stream Socket Transports	tcp, udp, unix, udg
Registered Stream Filters	convert.iconv.*, string.rot13, string.toupper, string.tolower, string.strip_tags, convert.*, consumed, dechunk

This program makes use of the Zend Scripting Language Engine:
Zend Engine v3.0.0, Copyright (c) 1998-2016 Zend Technologies

zend engine

The list of modules installed can be shown by running the CLI version of php with the parameter –m.

```
$ php -m
[PHP Modules]
Core
ctype
date
dom
fileinfo
filter
hash
iconv
json
libxml
mysqli
mysqlnd
pcre
PDO
pdo_sqlite
Phar
posix
Reflection
session
SimpleXML
SPL
sqlite3
standard
tokenizer
xml
xmlreader
xmlwriter

[Zend Modules]
```

Recipe 1-4. Installing MySQL

Problem

We now have a system with a web server that supports executing PHP scripts and returning the output of the script instead of the raw source file. In order to complete the installation of a fully functional development stack we need to install the MySQL database server.

Solution

The basic installation of a MySQL compatible database on CentOS 7 is called MariaDB. The official MySQL database is owned by Oracle. It is still kept as an open source and they have a few community-based versions. When Oracle purchased Sun Microsystems and thereby acquired the MySQL source code the original development team created a new version. They have been developing new features and improved performance. So far the two products provide a feature set that is compatible but as time goes by we might see the two products develop features that are not compatible.

To install the MariaDb Server and all its dependencies, run these commands as the root user:

```
$ yum install mariadb-server
$ systemctl enable mariadb
$ systemctl start mariadb
```

After that it is recommended to run the command mysql_secure_installation. This is a script that will set a root password, disable remote root login, and perform other changes that will enhance security. With the exception of setting a root password it is safe to answer yes to all questions. The name of the script is the same for both MySQL and MariaDb installations.

How it Works

This completes the installation of the database sever but there is no support in PHP for this database. In order to get the MySQLi extension installed it is necessary to reconfigure PHP to add the extension, recompile, and reinstall:

```
$ ./configure --with-apxs2 --with-mysqli
$ make
$ sudo make install
```

In this environment it is necessary to re-edit the /etc/httpd/conf/httpd.conf file and remove the entry added for the php7_module.

The PHP installation is now complete. If other extensions are needed the steps above can be repeated.

To install MariaDB on Windows is equally easy. The latest installation packages can be found at https://mariadb.org/download/, or if you prefer the MySQL version you can download the installation files from http://www.mysql.com/downloads/.

Recipe 1-5. Virtual Machines

Problem

When development is done on a Windows or Mac OSX computer and deployment is done on a Linux environment it is easy to run into issues that are related to differences in the operating systems, or there could be issues with lack of support for specific extensions on one of the platforms. Is there a way to minimize these problems?

Solution

There are a number of cloud-based services that offer relatively cheap virtual Linux environments. Many of these can be configured and launched in a few minutes and the user only pays for the time the configuration is active. The cost is as low as $10 per month.

Having a virtual server in the cloud requires an Internet connection to use with the server. If work is done offline it is more convenient to install a Virtual Machine on the development environment. A Virtual Machine is a system that allows the primary operating system on a computer to be the host for one or more client systems. This is supported on Windows, Mac OSX, and Linus systems, either with native software, third-party freeware (VirtualBox), or commercial products (VM-Ware or Parallels).

How it Works

VirtualBox is supported by Oracle and can be downloaded for free at `https://www.virtualbox.org/`. After installation of the software you can create as many virtual machines as you have space on the hard drive. Each virtual machine requires 10-100Gb of disk space. It is possible to install both Windows and Linux guests. The guests can be installed from an ISO image that can be downloaded from the preferred Linux distributions web site. Windows even provides distributions of prebuilt systems that can be downloaded and launched. Most of these can be used for up to 90 days for testing purposes. If you have a valid Windows license you can also create an installation that doesn't expire.

CHAPTER 2

■ ■ ■

Classes and Objects

Object-oriented programming provides many advantages over procedural programming. It helps with encapsulation when code is shared within a team or between teams and it can help protect elements of the code from being abused. This is especially the case when code is shared in compiled form but the same mechanisms can be applied to a scripting language like PHP. This chapter describes how object-oriented programming works in PHP.

Recipe 2-1. Writing a Simple Class

Problem

PHP can be used as a procedural programming language, but you want to make use of the many features of object-oriented programming with classes and objects to create advanced libraries and applications that make collaboration and encapsulation easy.

Solution

A class is the foundation of object-oriented programming. A class is a collection of properties and methods that goes together and so this is where to start when writing an object-oriented PHP application.

Like most other object-oriented programming languages the keyword class is used to define classes that consist of class variables, class constants, and methods. The class is used to define all the data and all the functionality associated with the object that can be instantiated from the class. In other words, the class is the definition and the object is the live instance and multiple instances can be created from the same class where each instance exists as a value in a variable.

How it Works

The first example is a simple class definition where the class foo has a single method called a(). Methods are defined as any regular function but because it's defined within a class it becomes a method that belongs to that class.

```php
<?php
// 2_1.php
class foo {
  function a() {
    echo "Method foo::a()\n";
  }
}
```

© Frank M. Kromann 2016
F.M. Kromann, *PHP and MySQL Recipes*, DOI 10.1007/978-1-4842-0605-8_2

Recipe 2-2. Writing a Base Class

Problem

PHP supports different types of classes that serve various purposes. These are called base, abstract, and interface classes. You want to use a base class to include functionality that is shared by multiple subclasses that all share the same base functionality.

Solution

A base class is usually a simple class that can be used to instantiate objects that store member data and can perform actions on the data. A base class can also be extended to add additional or changed functionality. This principle can be repeated so extended classes can be extended further and so on.

How it Works

In the following example we have a class with one member function and a second class that extends the first one and adds a second member.

```php
<?php
// 2_2.php
class foo {
  function a() {
    echo "Method foo::a()\n";
  }
}

class bar extends foo {
    function b() {
        echo "Method bar::b()\n";
    }
}
```

Classes, as defined in the above example, act as a definition of data and behavior. They do not do anything by themselves and must be instantiated before they can be used. If methods are defined as static they can be used without instantiation, and this is described later in this chapter. Instantiation is done by assigning a variable that is the result of calling the new operator followed by the name of the class and any parameters that might be required by the constructor. The constructor is a special function that can be defined to automatically initiate the object. The constructor method does not have to exist, but it does allow passing of parameters the same way as functions do. This is also described later in the section about magical methods.

It is possible to instantiate as many objects of a class as the available memory permits.

The next example is based on reusing the previous script file that defined the class's foo and bar. The variable $foo will be an instance of the class foo and $bar will be an instance of the class bar. Although the bar class only contains one method called b(), it inherits all the methods from foo as it's extended from that class. Therefore it's also possible to call the method a() on the instance of the class bar.

```php
<?php
// 2_3.php
include "./2_2.php";
$foo = new foo();
$foo->a();
```

```
$bar = new bar();
$bar->b();
$bar->a();
```

Access to member variables and methods is done with the use of the dereferencing symbol ->. The instance of a class or object can be used as any other variable. It can be copied to other variables and passed as parameters to functions.

Recipe 2-3. Writing an Abstract Class

Problem

PHP supports different types of classes that serve various purposes. These are called base, abstract, and interface classes. You want to use an abstract class definition to define functions that are common for one or more subclasses. Each subclass will define the specific behavior of each function but all classes that extend an abstract base class must implement all of the methods. When a class is defined as an abstract class it must contain at least one abstract function, and abstract classes cannot be instantiated directly, only through a class that extends the abstract class.

Solution

An abstract class cannot be instantiated as objects but serves the sole purpose of providing basic method definitions for derived classes, and it can include abstract methods that provide a method definition without any functionality or fully defined methods that can be overwritten or left as is. All the abstract methods must be declared and defined in full by the derived classes. Abstract classes are useful when building a system of classes that all have the same set of functionality but with different implementations. An example of this can be a set of database access classes. They all need connect, disconnect, and other functions but they all implement these in a slightly different way.

By defining an abstract base class with all the common functions, any derived class will have to implement the exact same functions and thereby make it easier to switch between the databases by simply instantiating a different class.

■ **Note**   To compare abstract classes with base classes, see Recipe 2-2 for details of using base classes.

How it Works

Let's see an example of this: a database abstraction system. The root class is an abstract class that defines all the methods needed (connect, disconnect, query, etc.) and each of the derived classes will then implement the logic to each type database. There might even be functionality that is shared among all the databases and that would then be defined once in the abstract class.

```php
<?php
// 2_4.php
abstract class MyDB {
  protected $link = null;
  abstract function connect($database, $host = null, $user = null, $password = null);
```

```php
    abstract function disconnect();
    abstract function query($sql);
    function escape($str) {
      return str_replace("'", "\'", $str);
    }
}

class MySQL extends MyDB {
    function connect($database, $host = null, $user = null, $password = null) {
      $this->link = mysql_connect($host, $user, $password);
      mysql_selectdb($database, $this->link);
    }

    function disconnect() {
      mysql_disconnect($this->link);
      $this->link = null;
    }

    function query($sql) {
      $rs = mysql_query($sql);
    }
}

class sqLite extends MyDB {
    function connect($database, $host = null, $user = null, $password = null) {
      $this->link = sqlite_open($database);
    }

    function disconnect() {
      sqlite_close($this->link);
      $this->link = null;
    }

    function query($sql) {
      $rs = sqlite_query($sql);
    }
}
```

In the example above the abstract class MyDB is extended to the classes MySQL and sqLite. The two extended classes have the exact same methods so if the same schema is defined in the MySQL and SQLite databases the developer could choose to implement the business logic to work with both systems, and it could be a simple configuration parameter to decide on which database to use in production. It would be easy to extend this system to include support for other database systems. This simple system does not provide abstraction for differences in the query language used by each database system but that can also be included in the database abstraction. So instead of passing query strings to the query method it would be necessary to create methods to access specific types of data and perform joins, etc.

Recipe 2-4. Writing an Interface

Problem

Although PHP supports extending classes, each class can only extend a single class. PHP does not support multiple inheritance. Sometimes it is necessary to define a set of functions that must be implemented in addition to the functionality provided by the base class or abstract class. This is useful when classes need a predefined set of behaviors to solve specific functionality like sorting of member data.

Solution

The solution is to use interface classes to define additional functionality with a predefined set of functions. Interface classes act more as a definition of a contract and PHP allows any class to implement as many interfaces as needed. If a class implements one or more interfaces it must implement all of the methods required by each interface. Interface classes only contain the definition of methods but no actual code. They can be compared to a collection of abstract methods from an abstract class.

How it Works

Each interface class is usually a collection of methods that defines behavior as in the next example where the class records implement the interface sort with the methods ascending(), descending(), and shuffle().

```php
<?php
// 2_5.php
interface sort {
  function ascending();
  function decendding();
  function shuffle();
}

class records implements sort {
  private $data = array();
  function add($title) {
    $this->data[] = $title;
  }
  function ascending() {
    sort($this->data);
  }
  function decendding () {
    rsort($this->data);
  }
  function shuffle() {
    shuffle($this->data);
  }
  function get() {
    return $this->data;
  }
}
```

```
$beatles = new records();
$beatles->add("Yellow Submarine");
$beatles->add("Sgt. Pepper's Lonely Hearts Club Band");
$beatles->add("Help");
$beatles->add("Abbey Road");

echo "Ascending\n";
$beatles->ascending();
print_r($beatles->get());

echo "Decending\n";
$beatles->decendding();
print_r($beatles->get());

echo "Random\n";
$beatles->shuffle();
print_r($beatles->get());
```

In the example the variable $beatles is an instance of the class records and the title of four famous albums from The Beatles is added to the object. Then the object is used to sort and print the data ascending, descending, and in random order. The output will look like this:

```
Ascending

Array
(
    [0] => Abbey Road
    [1] => Help
    [2] => Sgt. Pepper's Lonely Hearts Club Band
    [3] => Yellow Submarine
)

Decending

Array
(
    [0] => Yellow Submarine
    [1] => Sgt. Pepper's Lonely Hearts Club Band
    [2] => Help
    [3] => Abbey Road
)

Random

Array
(
    [0] => Yellow Submarine
    [1] => Help
    [2] => Sgt. Pepper's Lonely Hearts Club Band
    [3] => Abbey Road
)
```

Recipe 2-5. Class Members as Regular Functions

Problem

PHP supports two different contexts for using classes. These are called static context and object context.

In object context the class is used to instantiate an object: in essence that means creating a variable with a copy of the class and the class constructor method is executed if it is defined. This copy can then be used to interact with class variables and methods.

In the static context it is not necessary to instantiate the class as an object before using it and the constructor is not executed. Calling methods statically work almost like a plain function call but with the benefit of encapsulation provided by the objects.

In some cases it can be useful to call class members as if they were regular functions. Normally this is only possible by instantiating an object based on the class, and then executing the member function on that object.

Solution

By using the keyword static in front of a function definition, this makes that method accessible in the static context. It can still be used as a regular member function.

How it Works

In the next example we show how a member can be used in both static and object contexts.

```php
<?php
// 2_6.php
class foo {
    static function a() {
    echo "Test\n";
    }
}
foo::a();
$foo = new foo();
$foo->a();
```

In this case the method a() is called directly/statically as if it was a regular function just by prefixing it with the name of the class and two colons. The same function is also called by instantiating an object $foo from the class foo and then calling the method on the object.

When member functions are called statically it's not possible to reference member variables by using $this but it is possible to reference statically defined variables with the use of self::. Referencing $this is only allowed when classes are used in the object context.

```php
<?php
// 2_7.php
class foo {
    static private $b = 5;
    static function a() {
        foo::$b++;
        echo foo::$b;
    }
}
foo::a();
```

Note that the member variable is defined with the private keyword. That prevents accessing the variable from outside any of the member functions. Referencing foo::$b from the global scope will cause a runtime error. If the variable was defined using the public keyword it would be possible to access it with foo::$b.

It is possible to have classes that contain both static and non-static variables and methods but they will have to be used within the correct context. If a static function access a member variable with the $this reference the script will produce a runtime error.

When a class is used in a static context each of the member variables will exist in memory only once. When used in the object context the member variables will be copied to each object and manipulating a member variable in one object will not affect any of the member variables in other objects even if they are instantiated from the same class and defined as static.

Recipe 2-6. Protecting Data and Methods

Problem

When working with class properties and methods it's often needed to protect the data from being manipulated outside of the class scope. In doing so it's only the class itself or derived classes that have access to class variables and member functions.

Solution

Using the visibility keywords when defining class variables and member functions restricts how these can be accessed. There are three keywords available: public, protected, and private. If no keyword is used the default visibility will be set to public.

Any class property or method that is declared as public can be accessed directly. If declared as protected they can be accessed by the object itself or by any object that is instantiated from a derived class, and finally a private class property or method can only be accessed by the object where it is defined.

How it Works

In the example below a class with a single member variable is used to instantiate an object.

```php
<?php
// 2_8.php
class foo {
  $a = 5;
}
$foo = new foo();
$foo->a = 7;
```

Because no visibility keyword was used the variable $a can be manipulated as soon as the object is instantiated.

Using the private keyword will make the variable invisible and it will no longer be possible to manipulate it:

```php
<?php
// 2_9.php
class foo {
  private $a = 5;
```

```
}
$foo = new foo();
$foo->a = 7;
```

Trying to manipulate the variable will cause the following fatal error:

```
Fatal error: Cannot access private property foo::$a in 2_x.php on line 6
```

When member variables are protected or private it's necessary to provide functions to set or get the values if these variables should be accessed outside of the class, as shown in the next example where a special function __construct() is used to set the value when the object is instantiated.

```php
<?php
// 2_10.php
class foo {
  private $type = null;
  function __construct($type) {
    $this->type = $type;
  }
  function getType() {
    return $this->type;
  }
}
$t = new foo('Book');
echo $t->getType() . "\n";
```

In some cases it's necessary to provide access to private members. Declaring them with the use of the public keyword can do this, but that would provide both read and write access to the variable. In order to restrict the access to read only the member can be declared as private and a method can be provided to return a copy of the data as shown in the previous example. The property $type is declared as private and the method getType() is used to access the value. The property can only be set by the constructor that could include validation before setting the value.

Recipe 2-7. Mixed Static and Object Context

Problem

When a class is used in both static and object context and it's necessary to reference member variables and methods, we can't use the $this keyword.

Solution

In this case the self:: prefix will make it possible to access variables and members independent of the context the class is used in.

How it Works

Member variables or methods that are declared as static can be accessed with the self:: prefix, which means to access the class variable that is declared static. Using self:: will work when the class is used in both static and object context, but only if the variable is declared as static.

```php
<?php
// 2_11.php
class foo {
  static private $value = 6;
  function getValue() {
      return self::$value;
  }
}
echo foo::getValue() . "\n";
$bar = new foo();
echo $bar->getValue() . "\n";
```

Recipe 2-8. Referencing Class Members

Problem

Accessing public or protected properties or methods of a parent class is normally done by referencing them as if they were direct members of the child class. In some cases, methods are overwritten in a child class and a different access method is needed.

Solution

The use of the prefix parent:: will give explicit access to the variables or methods of the parent class. In addition it's also possible to access members of a class higher in the class hierarchy simply by prefixing the variable with the name of the class and two colons (::).

How it Works

When working with classes and object there are a few keywords of interest. These are used to reference member variables and methods within the object tree. When a class is instantiated to an object it's possible to reference member variables or methods with the use of $this. The use of $this will give access to all members and methods in the current object and protected and public members and methods of parent objects.

Along the same lines we have the prefix parent:: to access members of a parent class. This can be used to access any non-private member variable or methods, even if the extended class overwrites methods from the parent.

```php
<?php
// 2_12.php
class foo {
  protected $value = 6;
  function method() {
    echo "foo::method()\n";
  }
}
```

```php
class bar extends foo {
  function method() {
    parent::method();
    echo "bar::method()\nvalue = {$this->value}\n";
  }
}
$a = new bar();
$a->method();
```

It is also possible to use the name of a class further up in the class hierarchy to access public or protected members. In the following example foo:: is used to reference a member of the parent class. This is done on a method with the same name. This causes the method to be overwritten so the original version will have to be called explicitly with foo:: or parent::. Using $this-> would only work in the object context and only if the method was not overwritten in the derived class.

```php
<?php
// 2_13.php
class foo {
  protected $value = 6;
  function method() {
    echo "foo::method()\n";
  }
}
class bar extends foo {
  function method() {
    foo::method();
    echo "bar::method()\nvalue = {$this->value}\n";
  }
}
$a = new bar();
$a->method();
```

Recipe 2-9. Instantiation of Classes

Problem

When objects are instantiated or destroyed it's sometimes necessary to run code to perform the initialization of the object or to clean up connections to resources, etc.

Solution

Classes in PHP have two special functions called __construct() and __destruct(). Note the two underscores before the name. These functions are optional. If they are defined they will be executed when the new operator or when the object is removed with the unset() function, when the variable that contains the object is assigned a new value or when it is destroyed automatically when the script ends.

Constructors can take any number of parameters but destructors can't have any parameters.

How it Works

Each time a class is instantiated to an object the system will call the constructor method of the class to initialize the object. It is not required for a class to have a constructor, if no special initialization is needed. The constructor is defined with the special method name __construct().

```php
<?php
// 2_14.php
class foo {
  private $type = null;
  function __construct($type) {
    $this->type = $type;
  }
}
$t = new foo('Book');
```

In this case the constructor method takes a parameter so when objects are instantiated the parameter must be passed.

Classes can also define a __destruct() method that's called when the object is destroyed. In most cases destruction of objects will happen automatically when the script terminates, but it can also happen programmatically by setting the value of the variable to null or using the unset() function on the object variable. In the next example the class logger is used to write events to a logfile. The constructor takes the name of the file as a parameter, the log() method will add a line to the file containing a timestamp and the text passed to the function, and when the object is destroyed it will add a line and close the file.

```php
<?php
// 2_15.php
class logger {
  private $fp;
  function __construct($file_name) {
    $this->fp = fopen($file_name, "at");
  }
  function __destruct() {
    $this->log('Log file closed');
    if ($this->fp) {
      fclose($this->fp);
    }
  }
  function log($message) {
    if ($this->fp) {
      $t = date("c");    //ISO 8601 timestamp
      fwrite($this->fp, "{$t} {$message}\n");
    }
  }
}
$logger = new logger('log.txt');
$logger->log('Event');
```

Besides __construct() and __destruct() there are a couple of special method names that can make life easier for the developer. These are called magic methods and will provide predefined functionality if used on classes. All the magic methods have names that start with two underscore characters. The PHP manual has a section that describes all the magic methods here: http://php.net/manual/en/language.oop5.magic.php.

Recipe 2-10. Printing Objects

Problem

When debugging objects it can be necessary to print an object or some representation of an object. In other instances it is necessary to convert an object to a string as part of the application flow of returning values to the client.

Solution

There are a number of predefined methods that can be implemented on a class. These are commonly known as magic methods. These methods add specific behaviors to a class. This includes getters, setters, constructors, destructors, etc.

By using the magic method __toString() it's possible to define how an object behaves when it is used in a string context, either as a parameter to print() or echo or embedded directly in a double quoted string. The __toString() method does not take any parameters.

How it Works

The method __toString() defines how the object will be handled when used in a string context. An object is handled in a string context if compared to a string, embedded in a string, or printed. The __toString() method must always return a string and if it's not defined on an object that's used as a string the result will be the word object. The __toString() method can be used to generate output from objects in a structured form. A simple html class that can be used to generate HTML elements of various types is shown in the next example.

```php
<?php
// 2_16.php
class html {
  private $type;
  private $c = '';
  function __construct($type = 'div') {
    $this->type = $type;
  }
  function content($c) {
    $this->c .= $c;
  }
  function __toString() {
    return "<{$this->type}>{$this->c}</{$this->type }>";
  }
}
$div = new html();
$span = new html('span');
$span->content('place some text here');
$div->content($span);
echo $div;
```

In this example there are two instances of the html class() called $div and $span. The $span object gets a string added as the content and the $div object gets the $span object added. When the $div object is used in the echo statement the __toString() method is called. That will cause the __toSting() method to be called on the $span object when it's used as a variable embedded in the string.

41

Recipe 2-11. Variable Overloading

Problem

When class properties are declared as private they can only be accessed by the methods of the class. Creating a function to get and set each of these private member variables can end up creating a long list of methods on the class. Can this be done in an easier way?

■ **Note** Recipe 2-5 covers property visibility.

Solution

With the help of a special set of overloading functions it's possible to create access to private variables as if they were public and at the same time provide validation on setting these variables. The magic methods to manage variable overloading are __get(), __set(), __isset(), and __unset().

How it Works

The following example shows how to use these.

```php
<?php
// 2_17.php
class car {
  private $type;
  private $properties = array();

  function __construct($type) {
    $this->type = $type;
  }

  function __set($name, $value) {
    switch($name) {
      case 'type' :
        $this->type = $value;
        break;
      case 'wheels' :
        if (in_array($value, array(3,4,6))) {
          $this->properties[$name] = $value;
        }
        else {
          trigger_error(
            "Property wheels must be 3,4 or 6",
            E_USER_NOTICE
          );
        }
        break;
      case 'seats' :
```

```php
      if (in_array($value, array(2,4,5,7,8))) {
        $this->properties[$name] = $value;
      }
      else {
        trigger_error(
          "Property seats must be 2,4,5,7 or 8",
          E_USER_NOTICE
        );
      }
      break;
    default :
      $this->properties[$name] = $value;
      break;
    }
  }

  function __get($name) {
    if (array_key_exists($name, $this->properties)) {
      return $this->properties[$name];
    }
    else if($name == 'type') {
      return $this->type;
    }
    trigger_error(
      "Undefined property $name",
      E_USER_NOTICE
    );
    return null;
  }

  function __isset($name) {
    return array_key_exists($name, $this->properties);
  }

  function __undet($name) {
    unset($this->properties[$name]);
  }

  function __toString() {
    $prop = array();
    foreach ($this->properties as $k => $v) {
      $prop[] = "$v $k";
    }
    return "The {$this->type} has " . implode(", ", $prop) . "\n";
  }
}

$c1 = new car('truck');
$c1->wheels = 4;
$c1->seats = 2;
$c1->color = 'white';
```

```
$c2 = new car('big truck');
$c2->wheels = 6;
$c2->seats = 5;
$c2->color = 'blue';

echo $c1;
echo $c2;

$c2->seats = 9; // This will trigger a notice.
```

Running this script will generate the following output:

```
The truck has 4 wheels, 2 seats, white color
The big truck has 6 wheels, 5 seats, blue color

Notice: Property seats must be 2,4,5,7 or 8 in /source/2_15.php on line 35
```

The class car has two private members called $type and $properties. The variable $type is set when an object is instantiated from the class. In the example $c1 is instantiated with the type 'truck' and $c2 is instantiated with 'big truck'. There is no validation on the type so any value can be used. The example also allows the setting of other properties: wheels, sets, color, etc. These are all stored in the $properties array and the values are handled by the __get() and __set() magic method. The code allows any property to be added but provides special handling for wheels and seats. If a value is set outside of the valid ranges the code will use the trigger_error() function to print a notice. The property will not be set but the code will continue.

Recipe 2-12. Serializing Types and Object

Problem

Serializing PHP variables is used to convert integers, strings, and arrays into a string representation that can be written to a file or database and later on retrieved and deserialized to get back to its original value. Serializing objects is a bit trickier as these can contain connections to resources and other values that require special handling on serialization and deserialization.

Solution

When working with the serialize() and unserialize() functions on objects it might be necessary to perform special actions on the object to handle correct initialization of member variables. The methods __sleep() and __wakeup() are used in this context. The __sleep() function is called, if it exists, when an object is serialized. The function should return an array of member variable names that should be serialized. The function __wakeup() is called when the object is re-created with the unserialize() function. This can be used to handle things like disconnect and reconnect to databases or other forms of cleanup and initialization needed for proper use of the objects.

How it Works

The following example shows how an object instance of a database class can be serialized and unserialized. When the object is created the parameters to the constructor is stored in private variables and a connection is created to the database. When the object is serialized the name of the three private variables is returned by the __sleep() function and when it is unserialized the __wakeup() function will automatically reconnect to the same database.

```php
<?php
// 2_18.php
class Database {
  protected $pdo;
  private $dsn, $username, $password;

  public function __construct($dsn, $username, $password) {
    $this->dsn = $dsn;
    $this->username = $username;
    $this->password = $password;
    $this->connect();
  }

  private function connect() {
    $this->pdo = new PDO($this->dsn, $this->username, $this->password);
  }

  public function __sleep() {
    return array('dsn', 'username', 'password');
  }

  public function __wakeup() {
    $this->connect();
  }
}

$db = new Database('sqlite:mydb', 'user', 'password');

$a = serialize($db);
echo $a;
```

This script will produce a single line of output that describes the serialized object:

```
O:8:"Database":3:{s:13:"Databasedsn";s:11:"sqlite:mydb";s:18:"Databaseusername";
s:4:"user";s:18:"Databasepassword";s:8:"password";}
```

Recipe 2-13. Copying an Object

Problem

If an object is created by instantiating a class with the new operator and later on is assigned to a second variable, PHP only creates a reference to the object instead of copying the object. Manipulating the object stored in the first variable will also affect the object stored in the second variable as they both reference the same object.

Solution

The magic function __clone() is used to perform special actions on a newly created copy of an object. As with any of the magical methods these cannot be called directly but they are invoked by special actions. The __clone() method is called when an object is created with the use of the clone keyword. Cloning the object provides a true copy of the object compared to assigning the object to a new variable, which will produce a reference to the object.

How it Works

The next example shows the difference between assigning an object to a new variable and cloning the object.

```php
<?php
// 2_19.php
class foo {
  public $a = 5;
}

$b = new foo();

$c = $b;
$c->a++;
echo $b->a . "\n";

$d = clone $b;
$d->a++;
echo $b->a . "\n";
echo $d->a . "\n";
```

In the first part the object $b is assigned to a new variable and the member variable a is incremented by 1. This will cause both $b->a and $c->a to become 6 as both variables $b and $c references the same object. In the second part the object $b is cloned and stored in the variable $d. Changing the values of the member variable a in $d will not affect the value of a in $b as $b and $d are referencing two different objects. This was done without the use of the __clone() method. Adding this magic method will make it possible to perform actions on the object () after it is cloned, as shown next:

```php
<?php
// 2_20.php
class foo {
  public $a = 5;
```

```php
    function __clone() {
        $this->a = 0;
    }
}

$b = new foo();

$c = $b;
$c->a++;
echo $b->a . "\n";

$d = clone $b;
$d->a++;
echo $b->a . "\n";
echo $d->a . "\n";
```

Now the code will call the __clone() method after all the member variables are copied so in the case the member of a of $d will be set to 0 after the clone and then incremented to 1, and there is still no effect on the original object.

Recipe 2-14. Using Objects as Functions

Problem

PHP supports the use of variable function names. This makes it possible to store the name of a function in a string $a = "MyFunction"; and have the function executed with the $a(); syntax. If the variable contains an object PHP will generate a runtime error.

Solution

Defining the magic method __invoke() on a class will cause that method to be executed when the object is used as a function.

How it Works

In the example below the object will use the var_dump() function on itself when invoked as a function.

```php
<?php
// 2_21.php
class foo {
  private $a = 5;
  function __invoke() {
    var_dump($this);
  }
}

$a = new foo();
$a();
```

The output of this script looks like this:

```
object(foo)#1 (1) {
  ["a":"foo":private]=>
  int(5)
}
```

Recipe 2-15. Overloading Methods

Problem

PHP does not support method overloading the same way as other languages where the same method name can be used multiple times in the same class but with a different argument list.

Solution

The same way as variables or properties can be overloaded with the __get() and __set() magic methods it's also possible to overload methods. This is done with __call() and __callStatic().

If these functions are defined and an object is used to call a nonexisting member function one of these will be called instead. If the member is called in the object context __call() will be used and __callStatic() will be used when the method is called in the static context. The following example shows how the method overload can be implemented. It also demonstrates that the method names of overloaded methods will be handled as is (case sensitive) and not like functions and methods normally act as case insensitive names.

How it Works

In the next example we create a class called MethodOverload and define the functions to handle method overloading.

```php
<?php
// 2_22.php
class MethodOverload {
  private function call($name, $param, $context) {
    switch ($name) {
      case 'f1' :
      case 'f2' :
        echo "You called $name in $context context\n";
        break;
      default :
        trigger_error("Undefined method '$name'", E_USER_NOTICE);
        break;
    }
  }
  function __call($name, $param) {
    $this->call($name, $param, 'object');
```

```
  }
  static function __callStatic($name, $params) {
   self::call($name, $param, 'static');
  }
  static function abc() {
    echo "abc() called\n";
  }
}

$a = new MethodOverload();
$a->f1();

MethodOverload::f2();
MethodOverload::F2();
MethodOverload::ABC();
```

The class is instantiated and the function f1() is called in the object context. This method does not exist but because it's defined in the call method() it's still possible to get the method executed without errors. The same way the object has support for calling the methods in the static context. The output of this script is shown below.

```
You called f1 in object context
You called f2 in static context

Notice: Undefined method 'F2' in /source/02/2_22.php on line 11
abc() called
```

Recipe 2-16. Debugging Objects

Problem

When objects are passed to functions like var_export() or var_dump() they might expose database credentials or other configuration options that should be hidden from the user of the class/object.

Solution

Using the magic methods __set_state() and __debugInfo()() makes it possible to change how the objects are handled by the debugging functions. The method __set_state() must be declared static and takes a single parameter that will be an array with all properties defined on the object and it should return the value var_export() should process. This can be any type so it is possible to simply return an array with some of the input parameters removed. If __set_state() is undefined when an object is passed to var_export() the system will generate a fatal error and stop execution.

The method __debugInfo() was introduced in PHP 5.6 and can be used to overwrite the properties dumped by var_dump(). If __debugInfo() is undefined var_dump() will dump all private, protected, and public members.

How it Works

This can be used to hide content like database credentials in debug output as shown in the next example.

```php
<?php
// 2_23.php
class database {
  protected $host;
  protected $user;
  protected $password;

  function __construct($host, $user, $password) {
    $this->host = $host;
    $this->user = $user;
    $this->password = $password;
  }
}

$db = new database('localhost', 'user', 'secret');
var_dump($db);

class database2 {
  protected $host;
  protected $user;
  protected $password;

  function __construct($host, $user, $password) {
    $this->host = $host;
    $this->user = $user;
    $this->password = $password;
  }
  function __debugInfo() {
    return array(
      'host' => $this->host,
    );
  }
}

$db = new database2('localhost', 'user', 'secret');
var_dump($db);
```

When this script is executed with PHP 5.6 or newer it will produce the following output where the first section is from the object with no __debugInfo() method and the second section only contains the properties that were elected to export.

```
object(database)#1 (3) {
  ["host":protected]=>
  string(9) "localhost"
  ["user":protected]=>
  string(4) "user"
  ["password":protected]=>
```

```
    string(9) "secret"
}
object(database2)#2 (1) {
  ["host"]=>
  string(9) "localhost"
}
```

Recipe 2-17. Using Objects without a Class

Problem

Converting an associated array to an object makes it possible to access the member data as if they were defined in a regular object.

Solution

PHP has a built-in class called stdClass. It is used when typecasting arrays to objects or it can be used to create an object without defining a class first.

How it Works

The stdClass does not have any member variables or methods but it will turn all the elements of an associative array into public members when the array is cast to an object as shown in this next example:

```php
<?php
// 2_24.php
$a = [
  'host' => 'localhost',
  'database' => 'mydb',
  'user' => 'user'
];
$o = (object)$a;
echo $o->host;
```

The stdClass can also be used to create an empty object and manually add public member variables to it.

```php
<?php
// 2_25.php
$a = new stdClass();
$a->host = 'localhost';
```

In this example the default setter will cause a public member variable called host to be created on the object.

Recipe 2-18. Directory Iteration

Problem

Iterating over files and directories can be done with the functions opendir(), readdir(), and closedir() that works in a procedural setting. Would it be possible to do the same with an object-oriented approach?

Solution

Some of the built-in functions will also return objects. One example of this is the dir() function that will return an instance of the built-in Directory() class. It takes a directory path as the first parameter. This class provides methods for read() and close().

How it Works

The next example shows how to use these functions to iterate over a directory and output the name and type of all the files.

```php
<?php
// 2_26.php
$path = "./";

// Open a known directory, and proceed to read its contents
if (is_dir($path)) {
  if ($dh = opendir($path)) {
    while (($file = readdir($dh)) !== false) {
      echo "filename: $file : filetype: " . filetype($path . $file) . "\n";
    }
    closedir($dh);
  }
}
```

The same code written with the use of the object-oriented interface and the Directory class could look like this.

```php
<?php
// 2_27.php
$path = "./";

// Open a known directory, and proceed to read its contents
if (is_dir($path)) {
  $dir = dir($path);
  while (($file = $dir->read()) !== false) {
    echo "filename: $file : filetype: " . filetype($path . $file) . "\n";
  }
  $dir->close();
}
```

The dir() function sets the two public properties, path and handle, so the same functionality can be obtained by creating an instance of the Directory class and setting the property values manually.

```php
<?php
// 2_28.php
$path = "./";

// Open a known directory, and proceed to read its contents
if (is_dir($path)) {
  $dir = new Directory();
  $dir->path = $path;
  $dir->handle = opendir($path);
  while (($file = $dir->read()) !== false) {
    echo "filename: $file : filetype: " . filetype($path . $file) . "\n";
  }
  $dir->close();
}
```

Finally there is a predefined class Exception that's used with handling of runtime errors through the try, catch, finally pattern that will be discussed in a later chapter.

Recipe 2-19. Writing Reusable Code

Problem

PHP only allows extending classes from a single base class. It does allow the use of interface classes but that requires the user to type the functionality of each interface each time it's used.

When working with classes and objects it's often needed to have the exact same functionality in multiple classes. This can be private methods to perform validation or public methods that provide access to private members etc. In many cases this is handled by creating the methods in the base class but when the classes are derived from different base classes that's not possible.

Solution

PHP version 5.4 and newer supports the use of traits to handle this situation. Traits are named code blocks that can be reused in many different classes. The code block is written and maintained in one place and used in many places. Making a change will affect all places where it is used.

How it Works

The definition of a trait works almost as a class definition. The keyword trait is used along with a name and a set of member variables and/or functions.

The following example shows how a trait can be used to define protected variables that are used in a single class.

```php
<?php
// 2_29.php
trait A {
  protected $var;
}
```

```php
class B {
  use A;
  function Get() {
    return $this->var;
  }
  function Set($var) {
    $this->var = $var;
  }
}
$o = new B();
$o->Set(15);
echo $o->Get();
```

In this example there is only a single variable and a single class that uses the trait, but in the case of multiple variables and many classes using the same set of variables this would save some typing and it would make code maintenance easier.

The real save comes when the trait also include functions as in the next example where the Get() and Set() functions are moved to the trait and the trait is used in two different classes.

```php
<?php
// 2_30.php

trait A {
  protected $var;
  function Get() {
    return $this->var;
  }
  function Set($var) {
    $this->var = $var;
  }
}

class B {
  use A;
}

class C {
  use A;
}

$o = new B();
$o->Set(15);
echo $o->Get();
```

Trait works as a copy and paste function at compile time. That means a copy of the trait is inserted in all places where it's used as if the code was written the exact same way in all places. If the trait is used in classes used in the static context the notion of copying the code will act slightly different from static object declared from the same base class. If member variables or functions are declared as static and used in two different classes they will become different instances. This is only the case when the classes are used in the static context. The next two examples show the difference between extending a base class and using a trait to define a member variable.

```php
<?php
// 2_31.php

class A {
  public static $var;
}

class B extends A {}
class C extends A {}

B::$var = 15;
echo B::$var . "\n";
echo C::$var . "\n";
```

In this case the output will be the number 15 on two lines.

```php
<?php
// 2_32.php

trait A {
  public static $var;
}

class B {
  use A;
}
class C {
  use A;
}

B::$var = 15;
echo B::$var . "\n";
echo C::$var . "\n";
```

And in this case the output will be the number 15 on the first line followed by an empty line.

To avoid naming conflicts the methods from a base class, a trait and members from the current class. The precedence order is that members from the current class override Trait methods, which in turn overrides inherited methods. This makes it possible to define a trait that contains functions that will overwrite functions inherited from a base class or to overwrite functions inserted from a trait in the current class. So that case where a function is the same in 9 out of 10 instances is handled by overwriting one or more methods in the trait when needed.

Traits can also include abstract functions. In that case it is a requirement that the class where the trait is used defines the function.

Just like classes traits can be extended to include other traits. These can be easier to work with as the developer can include a simple trait, a list of traits, or the trait that combines all the traits needed as show in his next example where two traits for addition and subtraction are added to a single trait called math. Note that the name of the trait is the same as the function in the trait. This works the same way as for classes where it is possible to have a member method with the same name as the class.

```php
<?php
// 2_33.php
trait add {
  function add($a, $b) {
    return $a + $b;
  }
}
trait subtract {
  function subtract($a, $b) {
    return $a - $b;
  }
}
trait math {
  use add, subtract;
}
class calc {
  use add, subtract;
}
class calc2 {
  use math;
}

$o = new calc2();
echo $o->add(4,5) . "\n";
```

Inserting multiple traits in a class might cause conflicts if the same method names are used in more than one of the traits. This can be resolved by specifying exactly which of the methods to use by using the keyword instead of and by renaming the conflicting method when using the trait. In the following example the two traits A and B both have the same function f1(). By adding B::f1 instead of A to the use statement the parser will use the f1() function from the B thread. The second line renames the f1() function from trait A to func1() allowing its use in the class C.

```php
<?php
// 2_34.php
trait A {
  function f1() {}
}
trait B {
  function f1() {}
}
class C {
  use A, B {
    B::f1 insteadof A;
    A::f1 as func1;
  }
}
```

Recipe 2-20. Avoiding Name Collisions

Problem

A common problem for authors of libraries that are included in other projects is collisions of names. It is not possible to define a function or class more than once with the same name. Early on, adding prefixes to the function and class names solved this problem, but that often creates a less readable code base.

Solution

The concept of namespaces was introduced in PHP 5.3, and is considered one of the most important improvements to the language, in that release. With the introduction of the keywords namespace and use it is possible to define and use functions within a namespace and thereby allow the same function name to be used in multiple places. The definition of namespaces must be the first statement in a script. If it's defined in any other place the interpreter will stop the script with a fatal error. If multiple namespaces are needed in the same file they can be defined by using the namespace keyword again. This will not result in an error as the first part of the script already belongs to a namespace.

Although any script code is allowed after the definition of a namespace it only applies to functions, classes, and constants. Everything else will appear in the global space.

The namespace called PHP is reserved for internal functions, other than that the names follow the same rules as variable names. They must start with a letter or underscore and the following characters can be letters, numbers, and underscores.

The backslash character is also allowed but it does not really become part of the name. It acts as a separator for sub-namespaces. These are useful on larger projects where multiple parts of the project can have functions or classes with the same names.

How it Works

The following example shows a simple declaration of a namespace.

```php
<?php
// 2_35.php
namespace Test;

function t1() {
}
```

In many ways namespaces works like a file system where file names or paths can be relative to the current directory or subdirectory of the current directory or they can be specified absolutely with reference to the root of the file system.

The same principle applies to namespaces where the current namespace is set by the namespace keyword and constants, functions, and classes are referred to relative to the current namespace or absolutely. This is illustrated with the following two sample scripts.

```php
<?php
// 2_36.php
namespace Test\Utilities;

function f1($a) {
  return $a * 2;
}
```

57

```php
<?php
// 2_37.php
namespace Test;
include "2_36.php";

function f1($a) {
  return $a * 3;
}

echo "Relative\n";
echo f1(5) . "\n";
echo Utilities\f1(5) . "\n";

namespace MyProject;

echo "Absolute\n";
echo \Test\f1(5) . "\n";
echo \Test\Utilities\f1(5) . "\n";
```

The function f1() is defined in the first script file and it belongs to the namespace Test\Utilities. The function f1() is also defined in the second script file but this time under the namespace Test so the two functions will not have a conflict. Accessing the two functions is done either relatively where f1(5) will call the version of the function in the Test namespace (current namespace) and Utilities\f1(5) is calling the version from the included file that is defined in the sub-namespace.

Then the namespace is changed to MyProject and the only way to reference the two copies of the f1() function is to use the absolute path starting from the root.

Sometimes when long namespaces with sub-namespaces are used it can be useful to create an alias for the full name as shown in the next example where the file from before 2_35.php is included and the namespace used in that file is aliased to a namespace called U.

```php
<?php
// 2_38.php
include "2_36.php";

use Test\Utilities as U;

echo U\f1(3) . "\n";
```

This script does not define a namespace and although one is defined in the included file the current namespace is still the root or global space. Functions in the namespace Test\Utilities can now be accessed from the alias U. Instead of aliasing namespaces it's also possible to import or use classes and interfaces in the current namespace. This functionality was extended in PHP version 5.6 to allow inclusion of functions and constants. This is done with use function or use constant where the use keyword alone works on classes.

```php
<?php
// 2_39.php
include "2_36.php";

use function Test\Utilities\f1;

echo f1(3) . "\n";
```

The example above will produce a parse error if used with PHP 5.5 or older.

Recipe 2-21. Autoloading Classes on First Use

Problem

Working with many classes and remembering to include the right class definition files is tedious.

Solution

Autoloading is a concept that allows automatic inclusion of files that defines classes the first time a class is used.

How it Works

There are a couple of different methods to implement this functionality. The simple way is to give each file the same name as the class it defines and define a the magic function __autoload().

```php
<?php
// 2_40.php
function __autoload($class_name) {
  include $class_name . '.php';
}
```

Using this will reduce the need to have a long list of include statements at the beginning of each file and it will ensure that only the classes that are needed by the script are included. The content of the function can be a simple include as in the example above or it can be a more elaborate statement that figures out which file is needed through a lookup table.

Alternatively the function spl_autoload_register(), from the SPL extension, can be used to register a function or a class method that can resolve the class name into a specific file name based on a lookup table or other method. The SPL extension is enabled by default on most PHP installations.

An example of how to use the spl_autoload_register() function is shown below:

```php
<?php
// 2_41.php
function autoload($class) {
  include "../classes/{$class}.inc";
}
spl_autoload_register("autoload");
```

When this code is used and a class not currently defined within PHP and the current script is instantiated the autoloader will execute the autoload() function. If the file is not found or it doesn't define the class there will be an error, otherwise the class will be included and the class defined.

CHAPTER 3

■ ■ ■

Performing Math Operations

A large number of math functions are built in to the core of PHP and additional functionality is available through extensions including arbitrary precision numbers, statistics, and linear algebra.

The built-in functions cover exponential, logarithmic, trigonometric, hyperbolic functions as well as rounding and random number generators.

PHP supports integer and float data types that can be used to perform the basic math operations: addition (+), subtraction (-), multiplication (*), and division (/). No special functions are needed to perform these actions and the logic can be written directly into the code.

```php
<?php
// 3_1.php
$i = 5;
$j = 5 * $i;
```

The order in which math operations are executed follows the same standard as most other programming languages where multiplication and division are performed before addition and subtraction. In the next example the calculation is performed as 3 × $i, in this case 15 and then 5 is added so the content of $j will be 20.

```php
<?php
// 3_2.php
$i = 5;
$j = 5 + 3 * $i;
```

If it's needed to add 3 and 5 before multiplying with $i, that operation must be isolated with parentheses.

```php
<?php
// 3_3.php
$i = 5;
$j = (5 + 3) * $i;
```

In this case 5 and 3 are added before the multiplication so the result in $j is 8 × 5 or 40.

PHP version 5.6 introduces a new math operator (**) as a simple way of creating an exponential expression. Before version 5.6 the use of the pow() function was the only way to perform this math operation.

```php
<?php
// 3_4.php
$k = 2 ** 10;
```

© Frank M. Kromann 2016

F.M. Kromann, *PHP and MySQL Recipes*, DOI 10.1007/978-1-4842-0605-8_3

The old way of writing this with the pow() function is

```php
<?php
// 3_5.php
$k = pow(2, 10);
```

The result of this will be an integer if both base and exponent are non-negative integers and the result can be represented by an integer (less than PHP_INT_MAX). In all other cases the result will be a float value.

PHP also support the modulus (%) operator that is used to find the reminder of an integer division.

Recipe 3-1. Changing the Base Values for Numbers

Problem

By default PHP uses base 10 to represent numbers when numbers are printed as output or numbers are used to assign values to variables or used in calculations it is assumed that base 10 is used. In various situations it makes the code more readable to use other base values for numbers.

Solution

PHP supports 3 other base values (2, 8, 16) binary, octal, and hexadecimal. In order to tell PHP that the number written in a formula is not a base 10 number is to add a qualifier to the number 0b for binary, 0 for octal, and 0x for hexadecimal numbers.

How it Works

In the next example the number 100 is used without qualifier and with each of the three special qualifiers to turn the number into binary, octal, and hexadecimal values. The output does not do the same conversion so the program will show the base 10 value of the number 100 in each of the representations.

```php
<?php
// 3_6.php
$i = 100;
$b = 0b100;
$o = 0100;
$h = 0x100;
echo $i . "\n";
echo $b . "\n";
echo $o . "\n";
echo $h . "\n";
```

The output of this example is the following:

```
100
4
64
256
```

When using the base qualifiers on numbers the valid digits are these:

- 0b or binary only allow 0 and 1,

- 0 or octal only allow 0 to 7,

- 0x or hexadecimal allow 0-9 and the letters a-f or A-F.

Using invalid digits will produce a parse error.

Allowing these qualifiers makes certain types of values more readable. Consider the file permissions on a Linux file system. These are normally represented with three octal digits for owner, group, and other permission where 4 represents read, 2 represents write, and 1 represents execute permissions. The number 0750 means the owner has read, written, and executed permissions; and that the group has read and executed and everyone else has no access. If this number would have been represented in the decimal number system it would be 488 and it would not be easy to read the access.

Recipe 3-2. Converting to a Different Base Value

Problem

Using qualifiers on numbers is only an option when the numbers are written as part of the PHP code. If the number comes from a database or an API call and when numbers are written as output from the program, we need other methods to convert between different base values.

Solution

PHP comes with a few functions that make this easy. The function dechex() converts an integer value in base 10 to the corresponding value in base 16. The opposite operation of converting a hexadecimal string to an integer is handled by the hexdec() function. Similarly the functions decbin() and bindec() convert between base 10 and base 2 and finally the functions decoct() and octdec() convert between base 10 and base 8.

In addition to the base qualifiers and conversion functions PHP also comes with a built-in function that can be used to convert numbers between arbitrary bases. The function base_convert() takes three arguments called value, from base, and to base.

```
base_convert(number, frombase, tobase);
```

The value can be either an integer or a string representing an integer. If an integer is used PHP will convert the number to a string before making the conversion. The return value is always a string. If the return value is in base 10 the resulting string can be used as a numerical string in calculations and PHP will convert it to a number when the calculation is performed.

How it Works

The example below will print the value 4.

```
<?php
// 3_7.php
echo base_convert(100, 2, 10);
```

Note that the input value of 100 is given as an integer and the function will convert that into a string, using the conventional base 10 representations, before performing the operation. If the number was written in binary representation (0b100) the system would convert that value to a string (4) and in that case the function will return 0 as 4 is not a valid number in base 2.

```php
<?php
// 3_8.php
echo base_convert(0b100, 2, 10);
```

Converting numbers to a different base can be useful to compact the size of number strings. The valid bases are any integer between 2 and 36. The 26 characters in the English alphabet and the 10 digits define this limitation.

Recipe 3-3. Storing Binary Values in Integers

Problem

Programming often use bit values to store flags or options that only have two possible values (On and Off or True and False). This allows the storage of 32 or 64 values in a single integer value. Using base 10 values to check, set or clear any of these flags is a bit cumbersome as the numbers (1, 2, 4, 8, 16, 32, 64, etc.) are difficult to remember and work with.

Solution

In addition to the basic math operations PHP also handles binary operations. These can be used to change single bits in a number, shift bits left or right, etc. Depending on the operating system and how PHP was compiled the number of available bits in an integer value is either 32 or 64. That gives $2 ** 32$ or $2 ** 64$ different values of an integer. Because all of PHP's integers are signed the first bit is used to handle the sign and that leaves $2 ** 31$ or $2 ** 63$ positive and negative values when the binary string is converted to a decimal number.

How it Works

We can use the base_convert() function to print out a binary representation of an integer value. On a 64-bit version of PHP the following code will produce 63 1's

```php
<?php
// 3_9.php
echo base_convert(PHP_INT_MAX, 10, 2);
```

```
111111111111111111111111111111111111111111111111111111111111111
```

This is the binary representation of 9223372036854775807. There are only 63 1's because the first bite is 0 and that's not printed by the base_convert() function although it's still part of the 64 bits.

With the use of the binary not operator (~) all the bits in the number can be flipped so in the next example we get a 1 followed by 63 0's.

```php
<?php
// 3_10.php
echo base_convert(~PHP_INT_MAX, 10, 2);
```

```
1000000000000000000000000000000000000000000000000000000000000000
```

Recipe 3-4. Setting and Clearing Bits in Binary

Problem

You want to set or clear individual bits in binary representation.

■ **Note** Recipe 3-2 shows how to convert numbers to binary representation for display purposes.

Solution

In addition to the NOT (~) operator PHP also supports bitwise AND (&), OR (|), XOR (^), and shifting left (<<) and right (>>). The bitwise NOT, AND, and OR functions are different from the Boolean NOT (!), AND (&&) and OR (||) operations. In fact the words AND and OR can be used instead of && and || the same ways as it's done in database queries using the SQL92 syntax.

The bitwise OR operator combines the bits from the same location in two variables to form the bit in a new variable using the OR logic. If both bits are 0 the resulting bit will also be 0. If one or both bits are 1 the resulting bit will be 1.

The bitwise AND operator combines the bits from the same location in two variables to form the bit in a new variable using the AND logic. If both bits are 1 the resulting bit will also be 1. If one or both bits are 0 the resulting bit will be 0.

The bitwise XOR operator combines the bits from the same location in two variables to form the bit in a new variable using the XOR logic. If one of the bits is 1 and the other is 0, the resulting bit will be 1. If both bits are 0 or 1 the resulting bit will be 0.

How it Works

If a variable has a value and it is required that certain bits are set to 1, this can be done with the OR operation by adding the value of the exact bits. In the following example the variable $v is assigned the value 12 (0b00). The variable is then combined with 2 (0b10) using the bitwise OR operation and the result is stored in $x. The result is 14 (0b1110) as all the bits in each position are combined staring with the least significant bit. In this example the two numbers have 2 and 4 bits defined but in the internal representation both numbers will have 32 or 64 bits and the once not defined will default to 0. In this case the numbers could be written as 0b1100 and 0b0010. Both representations are valid, and that is also the case for octal and hexadecimal numbers where leading zeros can help readability.

```php
<?php
// 3_11.php
$v = 0b1110;
$x = $v | 0b10;
```

If the opposite operation is required where a specific bit should be cleared the AND operator can be used but we would also need to use the NOT. Consider the following example where $v is assigned the value 14 (0b1110) and the goal is to clear the third bit to create the result 10 (0b1010).

```php
<?php
// 3_12.php
$v = 0b1110;
$x = $v & 0b100;
```

In the case the AND operation will result in the value 4 (0b100) as the third bit is the only location where both bits are 1. If the value is changed to 13 (0b1011) before the AND operation the result would be the expected. Adding the not operator in front of the value will make this happen.

```php
<?php
// 3_13.php
$v = 0b1110;
$x = $v & ~0b100;
```

If ~0b100 is printed it will show the result of -5. That is because the default output is using base 10. This can be illustrated with the use of the printf() function that can format the output to be binary.

```php
<?php
// 3_14.php
printf("%b\n", 0b100);
printf("%b\n", ~0b100);
```

Here is the output:

100

1111111111111111111111111111111111111111111111111111111111111011

In this example all 64 bits are flipped from 0 to 1 or from 1 to 0.

Recipe 3-5. Using Hexadecimal Numbers

Problem

Using integers in a binary way is handy to represent flags but writing long numbers with 0's and 1's is not ideal for readability.

Solution

Using the hexadecimal (base 16) system can help with that. Each digit in a hexadecimal number represents 4 bits of the value. On a 32-bit system the integer can be represented by 8 digits and 16 on a 64-bit system.

How it Works

Changing the binary numbers in the example 14 (0xE) and 8 (0x8) will make the code shorter but still preserve the readability.

```php
<?php
// 3_15.php
$v = 0xE;
$x = $v & ~0x8;
```

This becomes more obvious as more digits are involved.

Recipe 3-6. Increasing Performance with Binary Shift

Problem

Multiplying two numbers used to be hard on computers. Many CPU cycles are needed and with limited resources this was a problem.

Solution

By using binary math it's possible to multiply a number by 2 or divide it by 2 with simple bit shifting. The bitwise shift operations works, as arithmetic, where shifting all bits one place to the left is the same as multiplying by 2 and shifting them one place to the right is the same as dividing by 2. The shift left operator will add 0's to the right side and drop the bit at the left side. The shift right operator will preserve the sign bit and drop the bit at the right.

How it Works

The shift operators can shift any number of bits. The left side of the shift operator is the number that where the bits are going to be shifted and the right side is the number of bits to shift.

```php
<?php
// 3_16.php
$bits = PHP_INT_SIZE * 8;
$v = 1;
for ($i = 0; $i < $bits; $i++) {
  printf("$v << $i = %64b \n", $v << $i);
}
```

Shifting numbers more than the number of bits in an integer (32 or 64) will result in undefined behaviors. The number of bits in an integer can be calculated from the constant PHP_INT_SIZE times 8 (the number of bits in a byte). The output from the example above looks like this:

```
1 << 0 =                                                                 1
1 << 1 =                                                                10
1 << 2 =                                                               100
1 << 3 =                                                              1000
1 << 4 =                                                             10000
1 << 5 =                                                            100000
1 << 6 =                                                           1000000
1 << 7 =                                                          10000000
1 << 8 =                                                         100000000
1 << 9 =                                                        1000000000
1 << 10 =                                                      10000000000
1 << 11 =                                                     100000000000
1 << 12 =                                                    1000000000000
1 << 13 =                                                   10000000000000
1 << 14 =                                                  100000000000000
1 << 15 =                                                 1000000000000000
1 << 16 =                                                10000000000000000
```

```
1 << 17 =                                          100000000000000000
1 << 18 =                                         1000000000000000000
1 << 19 =                                        10000000000000000000
1 << 20 =                                       100000000000000000000
1 << 21 =                                      1000000000000000000000
1 << 22 =                                     10000000000000000000000
1 << 23 =                                    100000000000000000000000
1 << 24 =                                   1000000000000000000000000
1 << 25 =                                  10000000000000000000000000
1 << 26 =                                 100000000000000000000000000
1 << 27 =                                1000000000000000000000000000
1 << 28 =                               10000000000000000000000000000
1 << 29 =                              100000000000000000000000000000
1 << 30 =                             1000000000000000000000000000000
1 << 31 =                            10000000000000000000000000000000
1 << 32 =                           100000000000000000000000000000000
1 << 33 =                          1000000000000000000000000000000000
1 << 34 =                         10000000000000000000000000000000000
1 << 35 =                        100000000000000000000000000000000000
1 << 36 =                       1000000000000000000000000000000000000
1 << 37 =                      10000000000000000000000000000000000000
1 << 38 =                     100000000000000000000000000000000000000
1 << 39 =                    1000000000000000000000000000000000000000
1 << 40 =                   10000000000000000000000000000000000000000
1 << 41 =                  100000000000000000000000000000000000000000
1 << 42 =                 1000000000000000000000000000000000000000000
1 << 43 =                10000000000000000000000000000000000000000000
1 << 44 =               100000000000000000000000000000000000000000000
1 << 45 =              1000000000000000000000000000000000000000000000
1 << 46 =             10000000000000000000000000000000000000000000000
1 << 47 =            100000000000000000000000000000000000000000000000
1 << 48 =           1000000000000000000000000000000000000000000000000
1 << 49 =          10000000000000000000000000000000000000000000000000
1 << 50 =         100000000000000000000000000000000000000000000000000
1 << 51 =        1000000000000000000000000000000000000000000000000000
1 << 52 =       10000000000000000000000000000000000000000000000000000
1 << 53 =      100000000000000000000000000000000000000000000000000000
1 << 54 =     1000000000000000000000000000000000000000000000000000000
1 << 55 =    10000000000000000000000000000000000000000000000000000000
1 << 56 =   100000000000000000000000000000000000000000000000000000000
1 << 57 =  1000000000000000000000000000000000000000000000000000000000
1 << 58 = 10000000000000000000000000000000000000000000000000000000000
1 << 59 = 100000000000000000000000000000000000000000000000000000000000
1 << 60 = 1000000000000000000000000000000000000000000000000000000000000
1 << 61 = 10000000000000000000000000000000000000000000000000000000000000
1 << 62 = 100000000000000000000000000000000000000000000000000000000000000
1 << 63 = 1000000000000000000000000000000000000000000000000000000000000000
```

As an example of that, consider the following example where the value 1 is shifted one bit to the left 64 times and the value one is shifted to the left by 64 bits.

```php
<?php
// 3_17.php
$bits = PHP_INT_SIZE * 8;
$v = 1;
for ($i = 0; $i < $bits; $i++) {
  $v = $v << 1;
}
$vv = 1 << $bits;
echo  "$v, $vv\n";
```

In this case the first value printed is 0, which is correct and the second value is 1, which is incorrect as all bits should be set to 0 after shifting to the left 64 times.

Recipe 3-7. Rounding Floating Point Numbers

Problem

Due to the nature of floating point numbers where the internal representation is binary and most of the places where they are used requires base 10 representation, we often get values with many decimals that are not needed.

Solution

Rounding floating point numbers up or down to the nearest integer is done with ceil() and floor() and rounding to a specific precision is done with the round() function. In addition the function abs() is used to get the absolute value of a number by clearing the sign bit.

How it Works

The next example shows the use of these basic math functions.

```php
<?php
// 3_18.php
$a = -3.2556;
echo abs($a) . "\n";         // 3.2556
echo floor($a) . "\n";       // -4
echo floor(abs($a)) . "\n";  // 3
echo ceil($a) . "\n";        // -3
echo ceil(abs($a)) . "\n";   // 4
echo round($a, 2) . "\n";    // -3.26
```

Note how floor() and ceil() seem to work differently on positive and negative values.

Recipe 3-8. Generating Random Numbers

Problem

Random numbers are often used in games and other programs. Selecting a set of data from a database and presenting it in random order can be used to generate HTML pages that look different for each user visiting.

Solution

There are two sets of randomization functions available in PHP. The rand() function generates a random number between two specified values or between 0 and the maximum available random number as returned by getrandmax(). The random number generator can also be seeded to generate a more random number. This is done with the srand() function. It is no longer needed to call srand() (or mt_srand()) before generating random numbers as this is done automatically.

The other random number generator is called mt_rand() and is based on a generator with known characteristics and it's often much faster than the rand() function. The implementation was created as a drop-in replacement for the rand(), srand(), and getrandmax() functions simply prefixed with mt_. The mt comes from the name of the generator used called Mersenne Twister.

How it Works

The next example shows how to generate a random number between 0 and the maximal random value as well as generating a random number between two boundaries.

```php
<?php
// 3_19.php
$r1 = mt_rand();
$rmax = mt_getrandmax();
$r2 = mt_rand(-5, 5);
echo "$r1\n$rmax\n$r2\n";
```

The random functions will always return integers between the default boundaries or the boundaries provided to the function as parameter. Providing the boundaries makes it possible to generate negative random numbers. The random number can be one of the boundaries or any value between the two, meaning mt_rand(1, 5) can produce values 1, 2, 3, 4, and 5. Generating a random number between 1 and 2 with 3 decimals precision can be done like this:

```php
<?php
// 3_20.php
$r = mt_rand(0, 1000);
$v = 1 + $r / 1000;
echo "Random value between 1 and 2 is $v\n";
```

Recipe 3-9. Expressing Ratios with Logarithmic Functions

Problem

Expressing ratios between two numbers is often done with the Decibel scale (0dB). This is a scale that allows addition instead of multiplication to express changes. As an example, the power level of a transmitter is often given relative to a reference value of 1 mW or 0 dBm. Doubling the power level is the same as adding 3 dB and reducing the power level to half is done by subtracting 3 dB.

Solution

Converting ratios to the Decibel scale requires the use of logarithmic functions. PHP implements both the natural logarithm function `log()` that is based on the natural number e ~ 2.718282 and the `log10()` function that is using base 10. The number e is defined as a constant called `M_E`.

How it Works

The formula for expressing power ratios in db is defined as `10*log10(P2/P1)` where `P1` and `P2` are the power levels. A similar formula is used to express voltage and current rations in db. The formula for that is `20*log10(V2/V1)`. In the next example we calculate the ratio of 1 W compared to 1 mW and expressing it in dB. It is common to use dBm as the unit to indicate that the value is relative to 1 mW.

```php
<?php
// 3_21.php
$ref = 0.001;   // 1 mW.
$p = 1.0;       // 1 W
$r = $p / $ref;
$db = 10*log10($r);
echo $db . " dBm\n";
```

Logarithmic functions only work on positive numbers. Calculating the logarithm of 0 results in negative infinity or `-INF`. All logarithmic functions return 0 for the parameter 1. And finally all logarithmic functions return 1 when the base is provided. `log(e) = 1` and `log10(10) = 1` etc.

The function `log10()` is a convenient function as the `log()` function takes a second argument that defines the base. The base argument defaults to `M_E` if the argument is not passed to the function. So calling `10*log($r, 10);` will provide the same result as `10*log10($r);`.

Recipe 3-10. Calculating Future Values

Problem

Calculating the future value of a principal with a certain interest requires the use of exponential functions. How are these implemented and used in PHP?

Solution

Exponential functions are defined as a base number raised to a power and the `pow()` function is used to calculate the values of a raised to the power of x. The natural exponential function is defined by the natural number e and PHP has a special function to calculate e to the power of x called `exp()`. This function only takes one argument as the base value is given as e.

How it Works

Suppose you want to calculate the compounded interest of a loan of $1000 with an interest of 5 percent per year with the interest added 1, 2, 4, or 12 times a year:

```php
<?php
// 3_22.php
$principal = 1000;
$interest = 0.05;
$periods = array(1, 2, 4, 12);
foreach ($periods as $p) {
        $ci = $principal * pow(1 + $interest / $p, $p);
        echo "Periods: $p, future value = $ci\n";
}
```

The results shown below indicate that even if the annual interest rate is 5 percent the future value after one year depends on how many times the interest is added.

```
Periods: 1, future value = 1050
Periods: 2, future value = 1050.625
Periods: 4, future value = 1050.9453369141
Periods: 12, future value = 1051.1618978817
```

Using the same formula and compounding more and more often we can calculate the value for the continuous compounding or e.

```php
<?php
// 3_23.php
$interest = 1;
$periods = array(1, 2, 4, 12, 52, 365, 8670, 525600, 31536000);
foreach ($periods as $p) {
        $ci = pow(1 + $interest / $p, $p);
        echo "Periods: $p, future value = $ci\n";
}
```

The more often the interest is coumputed the closer the resulting value gets to the natural number (e).

```
Periods: 1, future value = 2
Periods: 2, future value = 2.25
Periods: 4, future value = 2.44140625
Periods: 12, future value = 2.6130352902247
Periods: 52, future value = 2.6925969544372
Periods: 365, future value = 2.714567482022
Periods: 8670, future value = 2.7181250813746
Periods: 525600, future value = 2.7182792426664
Periods: 31536000, future value = 2.718281778469
```

This example shows what happens when the compounding rate is increased every second. If the number of compoundings are increased even further the result will just get closer to the natural exponential e.

Recipe 3-11. Using Trigonometry to Calculate Distance and Direction

Problem

You are creating a web site that provides a list of hotels in the country and you want to provide a service to allow the user find the hotel that's nearest to a given location.

Solution

Trigonometric functions relate an angle of a triangle with the lengths of its sides and are often used to model periodic phenomena and calculate distance and direction between points on a sphere, but they also have many other usages.

There are six basic trigonometric functions that relate to the six possible ratios in a right angle triangle. All the trigonometric functions in PHP operate on angles measured in radians instead of degrees. In order to convert between radians and degrees PHP provides deg2rad() and rad2deg() functions.

You can use Google Maps APIs to find the exact location of each hotel on the list or you can make an approximation by using the zip code and perform a database lookup to convert the zip codes to longitude and latitude.

When you know the coordinates for both locations you can use trigonometric functions to calculate the distance, with the assumption that the earth is almost spherical.

How it Works

The radius of the earth is approximately 6271 km or 3959 miles. These numbers are defined as constants to allow the user to select which unit to use. All the trigonometric functions work on circles defined with a radius of 1 unit. This makes it easy to scale to any sphere.

Longitude and latitude are provided as floating point numbers in degrees so the Pos2Distance() function starts by converting all these to radians used by the trigonometric functions in PHP.

```php
<?php
// 3_24.php
define('RADIUS_KM', 6371);
define('RADIUS_MILES', 3959);

function Pos2Distance($pos1, $pos2, $unit = RADIUS_KM, $precision = 0) {
    $lon1 = deg2rad($pos1['lon']);
    $lat1 = deg2rad($pos1['lat']);
    $lon2 = deg2rad($pos2['lon']);
    $lat2 = deg2rad($pos2['lat']);

    $d = acos(sin($lat1)*sin($lat2) + cos($lat1)*cos($lat2)*cos($lon2-$lon1));

    return round($d * $unit, $precision);

}

$p1 = array('lon' => -74.0059, 'lat' => 40.7128);
$p2 = array('lon' => -118.2437, 'lat' => 34.0522);
```

```
echo "Distance from New York to Los Angeles: " . Pos2Distance($p1, $p2) . " km\n";
```

```
Distance from New York to Los Angeles: 3936 km
```

With similar math it is possible to calculate the bearing it would take to travel in a straight line from New York to Los Angeles.

```php
<?php
// 3_25.php
function Bearing($pos1, $pos2) {
  $lon1 = deg2rad($pos1['lon']);
  $lat1 = deg2rad($pos1['lat']);
  $lon2 = deg2rad($pos2['lon']);
  $lat2 = deg2rad($pos2['lat']);

  $b = rad2deg(atan2(sin($lon2 - $lon1)*cos($lat2), cos($lat1)*sin($lat2) -
sin($lat1)*cos($lat2)*cos($lon2 - $lon1)));

  return $b < 0 ? 360 + $b : $b;

}

$p1 = array('lon' => -74.0059, 'lat' => 40.7128);
$p2 = array('lon' => -118.2437, 'lat' => 34.0522);

echo "Bearing from New York to Los Angeles: " . Bearing($p1, $p2) . "\n";
```

The expected result would be somewhere around southwest (225 degrees) but because the earth is a sphere the result is slightly above the west.

```
Bearing from New York to Los Angeles: 273.68719070573
```

Recipe 3-12. Working with Complex Numbers

Problem

PHP and many other programming languages do not handle complex numbers natively. Working with and calculating impedance of electronic circuits require the use of complex numbers.

Solution

PHP does not support operator overloading and there is no support for complex numbers, but it's still possible to create objects that can be used to handle the various operations of complex math.

How it Works

Complex numbers have two parts and they can be represented as an object with a real and an imaginary part. They are often written as $r + i*j$ where r is the real part, j is the imaginary part, and i is the imaginary number from taking the square root of -1. The following example implements addition, subtraction, and a magic function to handle using the object in a string context.

```php
<?php
// 3_26.php
class Complex {
  public $re;
  public $im;

  function __construct($re, $im) {
    $this->re = $re;
    $this->im = $im;
  }

  static function Add(Complex $c1, Complex $c2) {
    return new Complex($c1->re + $c2->re, $c1->im + $c2->im);
  }

  static function Subtract(Complex $c1, Complex $c2) {
    return new Complex($c1->re - $c2->re, $c1->im - $c2->im);
  }

  function __toString() {
    return $this->re . " + " + $this->im . "i";
  }
}
$c1 = new Complex(1, -2);
$c2 = new Complex(3, 5);
$c3 = Complex::Add($c1, $c2);
$c4 = Complex::Subtract($c2, $c1);
echo "$c1\n$c2\n";
```

```
-1i

8i
```

This is a simple implementation of complex math and it only implements addition and subtraction. For a more complete implementation take a look at the PEAR module Math_Complex at http://pear.php.net/package/Math_Complex/.

MATH EXTENSIONS

By installing the extensions GNU MP (gmp) and/or Binary Calculator Math (bcmath) it will become possible to work on numbers larger than the precision of the PHP version used. The numbers will be represented as stings. The gmp extension is used for arbitrary length integers and bcmath is used for arbitrary precession numbers.

CHAPTER 4

■ ■ ■

Working with Arrays

Arrays play a central role in PHP programming. Many functions return arrays and they are often used to handle configuration. The basic array is a list of key and value pairs where the key can be an integer or a string and the value can be any variable type, including arrays.

Recipe 4-1. Creating Arrays

Problem

Arrays are treated as a fundamental data type in PHP. There are no functions to call or objects that must be instantiated to create variables with array values.

Solution

PHP uses the language construct array() to create arrays. If you assign the value array() to a variable you create an empty array or an array without any elements. It is also possible to include a comma-separated list of key => value pairs between the parentheses to create an array that's already populated with values. If the keys are omitted from the definition PHP will assign numerical values starting at 0 as the keys.

As stated above, the keys can be either integers or strings. If other types of keys are used PHP will perform an automatic type conversion. Floating point and Boolean values will be converted to integers. The null value will be converted to the empty string and valid numerical strings like "7" will be converted to integers as well. The sting "07" will not be converted as 07 is not a valid decimal number.

The keys in an array do not all have to be of the same type. The same goes for the values. These can be mixed as each element in the array is treated as any other variable with no relation to other elements or other variables.

From version 5.3 of PHP it's possible to use shorthand syntax to create arrays. This is done with square brackets [ ] just like it's done in JavaScript.

In order to access a specific element in an array you would need to know the key. The key value is placed in square brackets after the variable name like $b = $a['key'];. This will assign the element value for the key 'key' to the variable $b. If the array element is an array it's possible to access elements in that array by adding a second set of square brackets with a key value $b = $a['key']['key2'];. This can be repeated every time the element is an array.

© Frank M. Kromann 2016
F.M. Kromann, *PHP and MySQL Recipes*, DOI 10.1007/978-1-4842-0605-8_4

How it Works

The following example shows examples of six different arrays.

```php
<?php
// 4_1.php
$a = array();    // Empty array
$b = [];         // Empty array
$c = array(1, 2, 3, 4, 5);
$d = array(5 => 'Orange', 'Apple', 'Banana', 'test' => 5);
$e = array(
  'host' => 'localhost',
  'database' => 'orders',
  'user' => 'root',
  'password' => 'secret',
);
$f = [
  'host' => 'localhost',
  'database' => 'orders',
  'user' => 'root',
  'password' => 'secret',
];
```

The first two arrays are empty with no elements. The third array contains five integer elements and the keys are automatically assigned starting at 0 and ending at 4. In the fourth array the keys are mixed and the first key is defined to be 5 so the following keys will be auto-assigned as 6 and 7 and the last element has a string value as the key.

The last two arrays are identical, and they are just created with the short and the long syntax just as the first two arrays.

When arrays are created the elements are stored in the order of creation. If the values are auto-assigned they will increment from 0 or the last numerical key used.

```php
<?php
// 4_2.php
$a = [1, 2, 5=>3, 4, 5, 10 => 6];
echo "\$a contains\n";
foreach($a as $k => $v) {
  echo "$k = $v\n";
}

$b = [5 => 5, 4 => 4, 3 => 3, 2 => 2];
echo "\$b contains\n";
foreach($b as $k => $v) {
  echo "$k = $v\n";
}
```

This example will produce the following output showing the arrays will be traversed in the order the elements are created and not by the order of the keys or values.

```
$a contains
0 = 1
1 = 2
5 = 3
6 = 4
7 = 5
10 = 6
$b contains
5 = 5
4 = 4
3 = 3
2 = 2
```

Note the output shown is from command-line execution of the script. If the output is shown in a browser the output will not show any line breaks. There is no HTML in the output but the web server still sends the default Content-Type (text/html). Adding a header to set the Content-Type to text/plain will fix this issue.

If the order of the elements is important the values must be created in the order needed or, as described later in this chapter, there are a number of functions available for sorting arrays.

Recipe 4-2. Changing Arrays

Problem

It's very easy to create arrays and assign values though the use of language constructs. The values might not come directly from the programmer, and they might have to be changed over the course of the program execution so there is a need to add, change, and remove elements in the array.

Solution

There are two basic ways to add elements to an array: either by use of a specific index value or by having PHP generate the next available index value. Both methods involve addressing the element in the array by adding square brackets to the variable name.

Changing a value with a specific key is possible by assigning the element in the array a new value. Memory from the old value is automatically released.

Removing an element is done by using() the unset function on the specific element that is to be removed. If unset is used on the arrays itself all elements will be removed. Variables in general can be undefined by assigning them to null. That does not work for arrays where we need to get rid of both the key and the value. It is perfectly fine to have an array element with a null or undefined value.

How it Works

In the next example we take an empty array and values by using a for loop to iterate over a set of values.

```php
<?php
// 4_3.php
$a = array();
for ($i = 1; $i < 10; $i++) {
  $a[] = $i;
}
print_r($a);
```

This will generate the following output:

```
Array
(
    [0] => 1
    [1] => 2
    [2] => 3
    [3] => 4
    [4] => 5
    [5] => 6
    [6] => 7
    [7] => 8
    [8] => 9
)
```

The keys are assigned automatically because they are not provided. In this case the keys will be the values 0 to 8 and the values will be 1 to 9. If specific keys are required the values can be assigned as shown in a modified version of the sample.

```php
<?php
// 4_4.php
$a = array();
for ($i = 1; $i < 10; $i++) {
  $a[$i] = $i;
}
print_r($a);
```

If the key already exists in the array, then it's used to assign a value. The value will be replaced without any warnings.

```php
<?php
// 4_5.php
$a = array(1 => 15, 10 => 20);
for ($i = 1; $i < 10; $i++) {
  $a[$i] = $i;
}
print_r($a);
```

In this example the array is initialized with two key => value pairs. The first one is replaced by the first assignment in the loop but the last one will remain unchanged. The order of the keys will be 1, 10, 2, 3, 4, 5, 6, 7, 8, 9 because that's the order in which they were created.

The arrays used in the examples here are very simple, and instead of using a for loop to populate these arrays it would be more efficient to use the range() function as shown in the next example. The range() function takes two or three parameters. The optional third parameter defines the step between the values created. If it's omitted the step will be 1.

```php
<?php
// 4_6.php
$a = range(1, 9);
print_r($a);
```

Removing elements from the array is done with the unset() function.

```php
<?php
// 4_7.php
$a = range(1, 9);
unset($a[4]);
print_r($a);
```

```
Array
(
    [0] => 1
    [1] => 2
    [2] => 3
    [3] => 4
    [5] => 6
    [6] => 7
    [7] => 8
    [8] => 9
)
```

Recipe 4-3. Adding Arrays

Problem

Numbers can be added to create new values and strings can be concatenated to create longer strings, but what happens if two arrays are added together or combined?

Solution

There are a number of built-in functions to handle combining two arrays into a single array and it's even possible to use the + operator to combine two arrays. The + operator works by combining values from the two arrays and creating the union of the two. Consider $b = $a1 + $a2; Where $a1 and $a2 are both arrays. The resulting array ($b) will contain all the elements from $a1 and all the elements from $a1 where the key doesn't exist in $a1. If the same key is used in both arrays only the element from $a1 (the array on the left side of the + operator) will be included. Given the same two arrays added in the opposite order can give a different result depending on the keys of the two arrays: $c = $a2 + $a1;. The use of the key from the left array does not depend on the key type.

Merging two or more arrays can be done with the array_merge() function. This function acts slightly different than the + operator by overwriting an existing key value with the value of the same key in the right array and by appending elements from numeric keys instead of overwriting the keys.

How it Works

The following example shows the different behavior of the + operator and the array_merge() function on two simple arrays:

```php
<?php
// 4_8.php
$a1 = array('a', 'b');
$a2 = array('c', 'd');
$b1 = $a1 + $a2;
$b2 = $a2 + $a1;
$c1 = array_merge($a1, $a2);
$c2 = array_merge($a2, $a1);
print_r($b1);
print_r($b2);
print_r($c1);
print_r($c2);
```

The two arrays $a1 and $a2 both have two numerical keys (0, 1). When the arrays are added with the + operator the values for the keys from the left array is used and the resulting array only has the same two keys. When the arrays are merged with the array_merge() function the resulting arrays will have four keys (0, 1, 2, 3), and the order of the elements will depend on the order they are used as parameters to the array_merge() function. The output of the script will look like this:

```
Array
(
    [0] => a
    [1] => b
)
Array
(
    [0] => c
    [1] => d
)
```

```
Array
(
    [0] => a
    [1] => b
    [2] => c
    [3] => d
)
Array
(
    [0] => c
    [1] => d
    [2] => a
    [3] => b
)
```

Changing the keys from numerical to strings will change the behavior slightly as seen in the next example where they keys (0, 1) are changed to strings ('x', 'y').

```php
<?php
// 4_9.php
$a1 = array('x' => 'a', 'y' => 'b');
$a2 = array('x' => 'c', 'y' => 'd');
$b1 = $a1 + $a2;
$b2 = $a2 + $a1;
$c1 = array_merge($a1, $a2);
$c2 = array_merge($a2, $a1);
print_r($b1);
print_r($b2);
print_r($c1);
print_r($c2);
```

The same logic still applies but because there are no numerical keys the resulting arrays will only have two keys but using the + operator will preserve the value of the left array and the array_merge() function will overwrite the values of the same keys as shown in the output of the code.

```
Array
(
    [x] => a
    [y] => b
)
```

```
Array
(
    [x] => c
    [y] => d
)
Array
(
    [x] => c
    [y] => d
)
Array
(
    [x] => a
    [y] => b
)
```

If there is no overlap of keys between the arrays the resulting array will contain all values from both arrays and the two methods of combining arrays will give the same result.

```php
<?php
// 4_10.php
$a1 = array('a', 'b');
$a2 = array('x' => 'c', 'y' => 'd');
$b1 = $a1 + $a2;
$b2 = $a2 + $a1;
$c1 = array_merge($a1, $a2);
$c2 = array_merge($a2, $a1);
print_r($b1);
print_r($b2);
print_r($c1);
print_r($c2);
```

In the case the resulting arrays will all have four keys and the values are shown in the order they are added.

```
Array
(
    [0] => a
    [1] => b
    [x] => c
    [y] => d
)
```

```
Array
(
    [x] => c
    [y] => d
    [0] => a
    [1] => b
)
Array
(
    [0] => a
    [1] => b
    [x] => c
    [y] => d
)
Array
(
    [x] => c
    [y] => d
    [0] => a
    [1] => b
)
```

In addition to adding or combining arrays we can also find the intersection between two or more arrays. The function `array_intersect()` will return an array of all the values that are present in the first argument and in all of the additional arguments. The function ignores all the keys if the first array contains 'x' => 'c'; and if the second array contains 'y' => 'c', the value 'c' will be returned in the result.

```php
<?php
// 4_11.php
$a1 = array('x' => 'orange', 'y' => 'grape', 'z' => 'banana');
$a2 = array('grape', 'banana');
$b1 = array_intersect($a1, $a2);
$b2 = array_intersect($a2, $a1);
print_r($b1);
print_r($b2);
```

In this example we show how the returned data keeps the key values from the first array and only retains the values that exists in all the subsequent arrays.

```
Array
(
    [y] => grape
    [z] => banana
)
Array
(
    [0] => grape
    [1] => banana
)
```

Recipe 4-4. Arrays of Arrays

Problem

Most databases work with the concept of rows and columns. SQL databases use queries to select rows of data where every row has the exact same set of columns but different values. How can arrays be used to represent results from database queries?

Solution

Most of the database APIs in PHP provides a function that can fetch a single row as an indexed or associated array. If a query is performed to select all rows from a table and a defined set of columns it's easy to create a structure that will look over all the rows and create an array of arrays. The other array will correspond to the rows and each element in the array will be an array with all the columns.

How it Works

In this example we use a table called person that has three columns called first_name, last_name, and date_of_birth. The table contains four rows, one for each member of the pop group The Beatles.

```
-- 4_12.sql
create database samples;
use samples;
create table person (
  first_name varchar(50),
  last_name varchar(50),
  date_of_birth int
);
insert into person (first_name, last_name, date_of_birth)
      values ('John', 'Lenon', -922406400);
insert into person (first_name, last_name, date_of_birth)
      values ('Paul', 'McCartney', -869097600);
insert into person (first_name, last_name, date_of_birth)
      values ('Ringo', 'Star', -930528000);
```

```
insert into person (first_name, last_name, date_of_birth)
        values ('George', 'Harrison', -847324800);
```

The code to query this table and store all values in an array would look something like this.

```php
<?php
// 4_12.php
$con = mysqli_connect("127.0.0.1", "root", "secret", "book");
$rs = mysqli_query($con, "select * from person");
if ($rs) {
  $persons = array();
  while($row = mysqli_fetch_assoc($rs)) {
    $persons[] = $row;
  }
  mysqli_free_result($rs);
}
mysqli_close($con);
print_r($persons);
```

The date of birth column is represented by a Unix timestamp. The values are negative as they indicate the number of seconds before January 1, 1970. The output of this sample will look something like this.

```
Array
(
    [0] => Array
        (
            [first_name] => John
            [last_name] => Lenon
            [date_of_birth] => -922406400
        )

    [1] => Array
        (
            [first_name] => Paul
            [last_name] => McCartney
            [date_of_birth] => -869097600
        )

    [2] => Array
        (
            [first_name] => Ringo
            [last_name] => Star
            [date_of_birth] => -930528000
        )
```

```
[3] => Array
    (
        [first_name] => George
        [last_name] => Harrison
        [date_of_birth] => -847324800
    )

)
```

This show a two-level array structure where the outer array represents the selected rows and each of the inner arrays represents a single record, all showing the same three key values. The outer array uses numerical keys where the inner arrays are using string keys where the keys values represent the column names of the query. If mysqli_fetch_row() function was used instead of the mysqli_fetch_assoc() function the inner arrays would also use numerical keys, in the order of the column names in the querys' string. Both of these functions can be called multiple times. As long as there is data in the result set the functions will return a row. When there are no more rows in the result the function will return NULL.

Recipe 4-5. Traversing Arrays

Problem

Accessing individual elements and values of an array require knowledge about the key names.

Solution

There are a number of ways to traverse an array with or without using the key names. If all the keys are numerical and in order starting at 0, it's possible to use a simple for loop to traverse the array. If the values are out of order or a mix of numerical and string keys are used, we can use the each() function to return the value at the current index. The index is an internal pointer that keeps track of the current elements in an array. Each time the each() function is called the current element is returned and the internal pointer is incremented. If the internal pointer is incremented above the last element the each() function will return false, indicating that no more elements exists. If it is necessary to iterate over the same array again the reset() function must be called to reset the internal pointer back to the beginning of the array.

In addition to the each() and reset() functions there are functions to return the current, next, previous, last element and the key of the current element of the array. These are called current(), next(), previous(), key(), and end(). The functions current() and key() do not change the internal pointer. All the other functions change the internal pointer. Use of these functions is typically associated with the use of a while loop.

If you don't care about the internal pointer and you want to iterate over an array multiple times and have easy access to the keys and values, the simplest way is to use the foreach() language construct.

How it Works

In this example we use the array from the previous example to create a list of formatted strings that shows the full name and date of birth for each of the members of The Beatles. We use all three methods of iteration.

```php
<?php
// 4_13.php
$con = mysqli_connect("127.0.0.1", "root", "secret", "book");
$rs = mysqli_query($con, "select * from person");
if ($rs) {
  $persons = array();
  while($row = mysqli_fetch_assoc($rs)) {
    $persons[] = $row;
  }
  mysqli_free_result($rs);
}
mysqli_close($con);

for ($i = 0; $i < sizeof($persons); $i++) {
  echo "{$persons[$i]['first_name']} {$persons[$i]['last_name']} " .
    gmdate("M j Y", $persons[$i]['date_of_birth']) . "\n";
}
```

The result of the MySQL query is an array of arrays so in order to access the names and birthdays we need to provide keys for both the first- and second-level arrays. That is still the case if we use the each() function as it returns an array with four keys. The keys 0 and 1 will point to the key and value and in addition we also get the keys 'key' and 'value' returned.

```php
<?php
// 4_14.php
$con = mysqli_connect("127.0.0.1", "root", "secret", "book");
$rs = mysqli_query($con, "select * from person");
if ($rs) {
  $persons = array();
  while($row = mysqli_fetch_assoc($rs)) {
    $persons[] = $row;
  }
  mysqli_free_result($rs);
}
mysqli_close($con);

reset($persons);
while ($person = each($persons)) {
  echo "{$person['value']['first_name']} {$person['value']['last_name']} " .
    gmdate("M j Y", $person['value']['date_of_birth']) . "\n";
}
```

The last method is to use the foreach() construct. This function will iterate over all elements of the array and it is not necessary to remember to reset the internal pointer in the array. We can also work directly on the keys and elements so the code becomes a bit simpler.

```php
<?php
// 4_15.php
$con = mysqli_connect("127.0.0.1", "root", "secret", "book");
$rs = mysqli_query($con, "select * from person");
if ($rs) {
```

```
  $persons = array();
  while($row = mysqli_fetch_assoc($rs)) {
    $persons[] = $row;
  }
  mysqli_free_result($rs);
}
mysqli_close($con);

foreach ($persons as $person) {
  echo "{$person['first_name']} {$person['last_name']} " .
    gmdate("M j Y", $person['date_of_birth']) . "\n";
}
```

If the key of each element was needed we can change the statement to foreach ($persons as $key => $person), and if we need to make updates to the values in the array we can change this to foreach ($persons as $key => &$person) and have $person be a reference to each of the elements in the array so if $person['date_of_birth'] is assigned a new value it is updated in the array and not in the copy of the element. In addition we could also add new values to the array by assigning $person['new_key'] a value.

Recipe 4-6. Sorting Arrays

Problem

As we saw in the beginning of this chapter the elements of an array will appear in the order the elements are added. When an array is traversed the keys and values are handled in the order they appear in the array and not in a logical order of increased index value alphabetically.

Solution

There are many ways to sort an array. It can be done by the keys or by the values and in increasing or decreasing orders. Sorting by the value is done by the functions sort() and rsort(). Both of these will return an array where the keys are replaced with numerical values starting at 0. Any string keys or spacing between the keys will be lost. If you want to preserve the key association you can use the asort() or arsort() functions that will move the values around but keep the key association.

It is also possible to sort an array by the value of the keys using the ksort() and krsort() functions.

How it Works

The simplest array is one that uses numerical keys to store some values. This array can be sorted by the values in normal or reverse order.

```
<?php
// 4_16.php
$fruit = array('pear', 'apple', 'orange', 'banana', 'kiwi');
sort($fruit);
print_r($fruit);
rsort($fruit);
print_r($fruit);
```

Note that the sort functions work directly on the array variable as it is passed by reference. This example will produce the following output:

```
Array
(
    [0] => apple
    [1] => banana
    [2] => kiwi
    [3] => orange
    [4] => pear
)
Array
(
    [0] => pear
    [1] => orange
    [2] => kiwi
    [3] => banana
    [4] => apple
)
```

In this case all the values were lowercase strings. If the strings had mixed case values the sorting would be done according to the ASCII table where all uppercase letters come before the lowercase letters and the sorting would look incorrect. The sort functions allow for a second parameter that can be used to indicate a case insensitive string sorting like sown in this next example.

```php
<?php
// 4_17.php
$fruit = array('pear', 'apple', 'Orange', 'Banana', 'kiwi');
sort($fruit);
print_r($fruit);
sort($fruit, SORT_FLAG_CASE | SORT_STRING);
print_r($fruit);
```

The output from this script will show the arrays sorted first case sensitive, where all the fruits that begin with an uppercase letter is listed first, and then case insensitive.

```
Array
(
    [0] => Banana
    [1] => Orange
    [2] => apple
    [3] => kiwi
    [4] => pear
)
```

```
Array
(
    [0] => apple
    [1] => Banana
    [2] => kiwi
    [3] => Orange
    [4] => pear
)
```

Another wrinkle on sorting is when the strings contain numbers. The expectation would be that item1, item2 comes before item11 and item12, but because the sorting is done character by character the computer will order these items as item1, item11, item12 and item2. To get around this there is an additional flag SORT_NATURAL that can be added to the second parameter.

```php
<?php
// 4_18.php
$items = array('item1', 'Item11', 'Item12', 'item2', 'item20', 'item21');
sort($items);
print_r($items);
sort($items, SORT_FLAG_CASE | SORT_NATURAL | SORT_STRING);
print_r($items);
```

The array is first sorted with the standard sorting function causing the elements that begins with an uppercase character to show up first. Adding the flags to sort case insensitive and natural will cause the array to be sorted as expected.

```
Array
(
    [0] => Item11
    [1] => Item12
    [2] => item1
    [3] => item2
    [4] => item20
    [5] => item21
)
Array
(
    [0] => item1
    [1] => item2
    [2] => Item11
    [3] => Item12
    [4] => item20
    [5] => item21
)
```

Instead of using the flags to the sort() function it's also possible to use natsort() and natcasesort() to accomplish the same result.

Sorting an array that uses strings as keys will cause the keys to be lost if we use sort() or rsort(). In order to preserve the strings we would have to use the asort() and arsort() functions. If we expand the fruit example from before and turn the fruit values into keys and add inventory values (number of each fruit in stock) the example would look something like this:

```php
<?php
// 4_19.php
$fruit = array('pear' => 10, 'apple' => 3, 'orange' => 15, 'banana' => 5, 'kiwi' => 2);
sort($fruit);
print_r($fruit);

$fruit = array('pear' => 10, 'apple' => 3, 'orange' => 15, 'banana' => 5, 'kiwi' => 2);
asort($fruit);
print_r($fruit);
```

Note that the array fruit is defined twice because the sort() function will replace the keys with numerical keys. The sorting of the array will cause the items to be sorted by inventory count, but by using the sort() function we lose the keys so we no longer know what each item is. In the second half of the example we use asort() that keeps the keys and we can still tell what the items are.

```
Array
(
    [0] => 2
    [1] => 3
    [2] => 5
    [3] => 10
    [4] => 15
)
Array
(
    [kiwi] => 2
    [apple] => 3
    [banana] => 5
    [pear] => 10
    [orange] => 15
)
```

If instead of getting the items sorted by inventory count we wanted to get them in alphabetical order we can sort by the keys by the use of the ksort() function.

```php
<?php
// 4_20.php
$fruit = array('pear' => 10, 'apple' => 3, 'orange' => 15, 'banana' => 5, 'kiwi' => 2);
ksort($fruit);
print_r($fruit);
```

And the elements would appear like this:

```
Array
(
    [apple] => 3
    [banana] => 5
    [kiwi] => 2
    [orange] => 15
    [pear] => 10
)
```

So far the sorting has worked on simple arrays. If we return to the example of retrieving data from a database where we get rows and columns and try to sort the resulting array directly, we would get a result that is based on comparing arrays. This is done by comparing all the elements of each of the arrays to determine which one is "bigger" and then using that to set the order of the elements.

```php
<?php
// 4_21.php
$con = mysqli_connect("127.0.0.1", "root", "Wbp2Theworld", "book");
$rs = mysqli_query($con, "select * from person");
if ($rs) {
  $persons = array();
  while($row = mysqli_fetch_assoc($rs)) {
    $persons[] = $row;
  }
  mysqli_free_result($rs);
}
mysqli_close($con);
sort($persons);
print_r($persons);
```

In this example we have added a call to the sort() function to the code from example 4_9.php and instead of the records showing up in the order of John, Paul, Ringo, and George they will now show up in alphabetically order based on the first element of each record.

```
Array
(
    [0] => Array
        (
            [first_name] => George
            [last_name] => Harrison
            [date_of_birth] => -847324800
        )
```

```
    [1] => Array
        (
            [first_name] => John
            [last_name] => Lenon
            [date_of_birth] => -922406400
        )

    [2] => Array
        (
            [first_name] => Paul
            [last_name] => McCartney
            [date_of_birth] => -869097600
        )

    [3] => Array
        (
            [first_name] => Ringo
            [last_name] => Star
            [date_of_birth] => -930528000
        )

)
```

If we wanted this example to sort by the last name column we could change the order of the columns in the query.

```php
<?php
// 4_22.php
$con = mysqli_connect("127.0.0.1", "root", "Wbp2Theworld", "book");
$rs = mysqli_query($con, "select  last_name, first_name, date_of_birth from person");
if ($rs) {
  $persons = array();
  while($row = mysqli_fetch_assoc($rs)) {
    $persons[] = $row;
  }
  mysqli_free_result($rs);
}
mysqli_close($con);
sort($persons);
print_r($persons);
```

In this case the order of the columns has changed so when the sort() function is called the comparison will start with the last name column and thus produce the following result.

```
Array
(
    [0] => Array
        (
            [last_name] => Harrison
            [first_name] => George
            [date_of_birth] => -847324800
        )

    [1] => Array
        (
            [last_name] => Lenon
            [first_name] => John
            [date_of_birth] => -922406400
        )

    [2] => Array
        (
            [last_name] => McCartney
            [first_name] => Paul
            [date_of_birth] => -869097600
        )

    [3] => Array
        (
            [last_name] => Star
            [first_name] => Ringo
            [date_of_birth] => -930528000
        )

)
```

The sort() function has an optional second parameter called sort_flags. This parameter is used to define how the sorting is done. The default value is SORT_REGULAR and it will use the standard PHP compare functions to determine is one value is greater or less than another value. There are four other flags that can be used:

- SORT_NUMERIC will convert the values to numbers. This is useful if the values are numerical strings.

- SORT_STRING will convert the values to strings before comparing.

- SORT_LOCALE_STRING will convert to strings but use the locale setting on the system to sort.

- SORT_NATURAL will use the string comparison method but numerical strings.

In addition there is a flag to make the sorting case insensitive. This flag can be combined with any of the other flags.

It is of course more efficient to use the sorting functionality of the database and return the records in the order they should be used, but there can be times where a different order is needed. Changing the query to change the order of the columns could have an impact on presentation so that route might not be optimal either.

This is where the usort() function becomes handy. The usort() function takes two parameters, the first being the array to sort and the second the name of a user-defined callback function that will be used to compare two elements of the array. If we want to expand on example 3_9.php and define functions to sort the array of persons by first name, last name, or date of birth it could look something like this.

```php
<?php
// 4_23.php

function SortFirstName($a, $b) {
  if ($a['first_name'] == $b['first_name']) {
    return 0;
  }
  elseif ($a['first_name'] > $b['first_name']) {
    return 1;
  }
  else {
   return -1;
  }
}

function SortLastName($a, $b) {
  if ($a['last_name'] == $b['last_name']) {
    return 0;
  }
  elseif ($a['last_name'] > $b['last_name']) {
    return 1;
  }
  else {
   return -1;
  }
}

function SortDOB($a, $b) {
  if ($a['date_of_birth'] == $b['date_of_birth']) {
    return 0;
  }
  elseif ($a['date_of_birth'] > $b['date_of_birth']) {
    return 1;
  }
  else {
   return -1;
  }
}
```

```php
$con = mysqli_connect("127.0.0.1", "root", "Wbp2Theworld", "book");
$rs = mysqli_query($con, "select * from person");
if ($rs) {
  $persons = array();
  while($row = mysqli_fetch_assoc($rs)) {
    $persons[] = $row;
  }
  mysqli_free_result($rs);
}
mysqli_close($con);
usort($persons, 'SortFirstName');
print_r($persons);
usort($persons, 'SortLastName');
print_r($persons);
usort($persons, 'SortDOB');
print_r($persons);
```

In this case we have defined three callback functions, each one to sort on a specific column. The code calls each of the sorting functions and the output is shown below.

```
Array
(
    [0] => Array
        (
            [first_name] => George
            [last_name] => Harrison
            [date_of_birth] => -847324800
        )

    [1] => Array
        (
            [first_name] => John
            [last_name] => Lenon
            [date_of_birth] => -922406400
        )

    [2] => Array
        (
            [first_name] => Paul
            [last_name] => McCartney
            [date_of_birth] => -869097600
        )
```

```
        [3] => Array
            (
                [first_name] => Ringo
                [last_name] => Star
                [date_of_birth] => -930528000
            )
)

Array
(
    [0] => Array
        (
            [first_name] => George
            [last_name] => Harrison
            [date_of_birth] => -847324800
        )

    [1] => Array
        (
            [first_name] => John
            [last_name] => Lenon
            [date_of_birth] => -922406400
        )

    [2] => Array
        (
            [first_name] => Paul
            [last_name] => McCartney
            [date_of_birth] => -869097600
        )

    [3] => Array
        (
            [first_name] => Ringo
            [last_name] => Star
            [date_of_birth] => -930528000
        )
)
```

```
Array
(

    [0] => Array
        (
            [first_name] => Ringo
            [last_name] => Star
            [date_of_birth] => -930528000
        )

    [1] => Array
        (
            [first_name] => John
            [last_name] => Lenon
            [date_of_birth] => -922406400
        )

    [2] => Array
        (
            [first_name] => Paul
            [last_name] => McCartney
            [date_of_birth] => -869097600
        )

    [3] => Array
        (
            [first_name] => George
            [last_name] => Harrison
            [date_of_birth] => -847324800
        )
)
```

Sorting by first or last name does not make any difference in the case of the four members of The Beatles but sorting by date of birth shows the records in a different order.

Recipe 4-7. Using Arrays as Stacks

Problem

A stack is a commonly used structure where elements can be added and removed from the open end of the stack. Stacks are considered as last-in first-out structures.

Solution

With the use of the functions `array_pop()`, `array_push()`, `array_shift()`, and `array_unshift()` it is possible to use arrays as a stack. Shift and unshift works on the beginning of the array where push and pop works on the end of the array. These functions will return the first or last element of the array. If the array is empty or the variable is not an array these functions will return NULL.

How it Works

The function `array_push()` will add an element to the end of an array. The key will be the next available numerical value. If the array is empty the first key will be 0. The function `array_pop()` will remove the last value from the array and return it so it can be assigned to a value or used in a comparison.

```php
<?php
// 4_24.php
$stack = array();
array_push($stack, 'orange');
array_push($stack, 'apple');
array_push($stack, 'banana');
print_r($stack);
$fruit = array_pop($stack);
print_r($stack);
```

In this case we have added three fruits to the stack and printed all the values of the array. Then we use `array_pop()` to remove the element that was added last and print the contents of the array again. This time only two values are left in the array.

```
Array
(
    [0] => orange
    [1] => apple
    [2] => banana
)
Array
(
    [0] => orange
    [1] => apple
)
```

We can accomplish the same functionality with the use of `array_unshift()` and `array_shift()`.

```php
<?php
// 4_25.php
$stack = array();
array_unshift($stack, 'orange');
array_unshift($stack, 'apple');
array_unshift($stack, 'banana');
```

```
print_r($stack);
$fruit = array_shift($stack);
print_r($stack);
```

The fruits will show up in the reverse order and each time we add or remove an element all keys of the existing elements will have to be shifted up or down in order to make room for the new element. This will cause the shift and unshift functions to be a bit slower than push and pop.

```
Array
(
    [0] => banana
    [1] => apple
    [2] => orange
)
Array
(
    [0] => apple
    [1] => orange
)
```

Recipe 4-8. Slicing and Splicing Arrays

Problem

You need to get a section of an array or insert an array into the middle of another array.

Solution

There are two functions to handle these operations. The function array_slice() can be used to cut a portion of an array and assign it to a new array. The function array_splice() can be used to insert an array anywhere in another array.

How it Works

The array_slice() function takes two to four parameters. The first is the source array, the second is the offset. This is the number of elements to skip from the beginning of the array. The optional third parameter is the length of the slice or number of elements to copy. Finally the optional fourth element defines if the numerical array keys are going to be preserved. The default is false. The following example shows how a small section of two elements can be copied from a larger array. The example also demonstrates the difference between preserving the keys or not.

```
<?php
// 4_26.php
$a = array(
  'apple',
```

```
    'orange',
    'banana',
    'animal' => 'horse',
    'vechicle' => 'truck'
);

print_r(array_slice($a, 2, 2));
print_r(array_slice($a, 2, 2, true));
```

The output looks like this:

```
Array
(
    [0] => banana
    [animal] => horse
)
Array
(
    [2] => banana
    [animal] => horse
)
```

It is a small difference but in the first part of the output the index from the banana is changed from 2 to 0 and in the second part its position/key is preserved.

The `array_splice()` function also takes four parameters. The first is the source array, the second is the offset, the third is a length, and the fourth is the array to inset. The function can be used in three distinct ways. The first is to remove a section of an array, the second is to insert a new array into the array, and the third is a combination of both of these things.

This first parameter (the source array) is passed by reference. This causes the value of the array to be changed by the function. In addition the function will return an array with all the elements that were replaced.

The second parameter can be positive or negative. If it's positive the offset is counted from the beginning of the array and if it's negative it's counted from the end of the array.

If the length parameter is omitted then all elements from the offset to the end of the array will be removed. If it is positive the function will remove that number of elements from the offset position. If length is negative the end of the removed elements will be found by counting that number of elements from the end of the array. These calculations are similar to the substr() function that can have positive and negative values for both offset and length.

In the following example there are two arrays being spliced. Because the array_splice() function works directly on the source array it is necessary to create a copy of the array before calling the function (only because the same array is being used in all three samples.

```
<?php
// 4_27.php
$a = array(
    'apple',
    'orange',
```

```php
    'banana',
    'animal' => 'horse',
    'vechicle' => 'truck'
);
$b = array(
    'kiwi',
    'grape'
);

// Remove all but two elements from the array
$a1 = $a;
$r = array_splice($a1, 2, 2);
print_r($r);
print_r($a1);

// instert $b into $a
$a1 = $a;
$r = array_splice($a1, 2, 0, $b);
print_r($r);
print_r($a1);

// remove one element and inster $b
$a1 = $a;
$r = array_splice($a1, 2, 1, $b);
print_r($r);
print_r($a1);
```

The output of this example gives the following six arrays:

```
Array
(
    [0] => banana
    [animal] => horse
)

Array
(
    [0] => apple
    [1] => orange
    [vechicle] => truck
)

Array
(
)
```

```
Array
(
    [0] => apple
    [1] => orange
    [2] => kiwi
    [3] => grape
    [4] => banana
    [animal] => horse
    [vechicle] => truck
)

Array
(
    [0] => banana
)

Array
(
    [0] => apple
    [1] => orange
    [2] => kiwi
    [3] => grape
    [animal] => horse
    [vechicle] => truck
)
```

Recipe 4-9. Debugging Arrays

Problem

Arrays are printed directly as output so knowing the exact value of a super global or an array variable that is generated from a database query or an API call requires the use of other outputting methods.

Solution

PHP has three functions that make debugging of array variables easy. These are print_r(), var_dump(), and var_export(). The print_r() function walks through the array recursively and prints the keys and values in a nice readable way. The var_dump() and var_export() functions will also print information the data type and size of the elements

How it Works

In this example we use an array with mixed numerical and string keys to show how the debug information looks when the three output methods are used.

```php
<?php
// 4_28.php
$a = array(
  'apple',
  'orange',
  'banana',
  'animal' => 'horse',
  'vechicle' => 'truck'
);
print_r($a);
var_dump($a);
var_export($a);
```

The output from this code looks like this:

```
Array
(
    [0] => apple
    [1] => orange
    [2] => banana
    [animal] => horse
    [vechicle] => truck
)
array(5) {
  [0]=>
  string(5) "apple"
  [1]=>
  string(6) "orange"
  [2]=>
  string(6) "banana"
  ["animal"]=>
  string(5) "horse"
  ["vechicle"]=>
  string(5) "truck"
}
array (
  0 => 'apple',
  1 => 'orange',
```

```
  2 => 'banana',
  'animal' => 'horse',
  'vechicle' => 'truck',
)
```

The first and the third example are the easiest to read but they do not contain any type info. Only the var_export() function produces output that can be used in an eval statement or written directly to a php script file to be included or executed at a later time. This can be useful for writing config files.

Note that these outputs should be included in a <pre>..</pre> tag when they are used in a browser context in order for the formatting to be as shown above.

Recipe 4-10. Storing Arrays

Problem

Arrays are defined differently in different languages and are often not supported natively by file systems or databases, so how can the values of arrays be stored?

Solution

With the use of serialize() and unserialize() or json_encode() and json_decode() it's possible to stringify any array (and other types of PHP variables) so they can be written to a file or saved as a value in a varchar column in a database. The json_* functions are also useful to convert arrays to a structure that can be interpreted by the JavaScript engine in a browser.

JSON is short for JavaScript Object Notation and it is commonly used to write and exchange data in JavaScript code or between other systems like PHP and JavaScript. It can also be used as a serialization format within PHP.

How it Works

Let's first consider the format of an array that is serialized and the same array as a JSON encoded string. Both of them are string values that have enough information to describe each element in a form where it can be regenerated.

```php
<?php
// 4_29.php
$a = array(
  'apple',
  'orange',
  'banana',
  'animal' => 'horse',
  'vechicle' => 'truck'
);
echo serialize($a) . "\n";
echo json_encode($a) . "\n";
```

The two outputs will look like this:

```
a:5:{i:0;s:5:"apple";i:1;s:6:"orange";i:2;s:6:"banana";s:6:"animal";s:5:"horse";s:8:"vehi
cle";s:5:"truck";}
```

```
{"0":"apple","1":"orange","2":"banana","animal":"horse","vechicle":"truck"}
```

In the serialized version we see information about the type and length. The a:5: indicates an array with five elements, i: means integer and s:6: indicates a string with six characters. Using serialized data between 64-bit and 32-bit versions of PHP can lead to overflows as integers can hold much larger values in 64-bit versions.

The serialized data can be written to a database or a file and retrieved again later.

```php
<?php
// 4_30.php
$a = array(
  'apple',
  'orange',
  'banana',
  'animal' => 'horse',
  'vechicle' => 'truck'
);
file_put_contents('serialize.dat', serialize($a));
```

In this example we write the serialized array to a file called serialize.data and in the follow example the file is read, unserialized, and the result is printed with the print_r() function

```php
<?php
// 4_31.php
$a = unserialize(file_get_contents('serialize.dat'));
print_r($a);
```

And the output will look like this:

```
Array
(
    [0] => apple
    [1] => orange
    [2] => banana
    [animal] => horse
    [vechicle] => truck
)
```

CHAPTER 5

■ ■ ■

Dates and Times

PHP does not have a variable type dedicated to storing date or time values. Instead, integers are used to indicate the number of seconds before or since January 1st, 1970, also called Epoc. When dates and times are treated as a single value they are called a timestamp. The use of integers makes it easy to calculate differences between two timestamps as ordinary math applies.

Recipe 5-1. Working with Time Zones

Problem

All the date and time functions in PHP assume the timestamps to be in Coordinated Universal Time (UTC). It is necessary to configure PHP to use a specific time zone to convert all input and output of date values so they show up in the right order.

Solution

PHP can be configured with a setting in the php.ini file. The setting is called date.timezone and the allowable values include names such as CET for Central European Time and PST for Pacific Standard Time. In addition you can also configure it by region and city such as America/Los_Angeles or Europe/Amsterdam. For a full list of supported time zones please see http://php.net/manual/en/timezones.php.

Having a single time zone configured for the web server works fine when the users of the web site are local and all share the same time zone. In cases where users come from different time zones it is necessary to be able to define the time zone for each user. This can be done by defining a preference where the user can select the time zone and use the function date_default_timezone_set() to set the current time zone before any date functions are used. Anonymous users will not have a preference defined, and they will get all date/time values presented as if they were in the time zone defined by the server.

If the time zone is undefined when one of the date/time functions are called the system will print a warning and fall back to the UTC time zone.

```
Warning: date(): It is not safe to rely on the system's time zone settings. You are
*required* to use the date.timezone setting or the date_default_timezone_set() function.
In case you used any of those methods and you are still getting this warning, you most
likely misspelled the time zone identifier. We selected the time zone 'UTC' for now, but
please set date.timezone to select your time zone.
```

In older versions of PHP the warnings might vary or no warning is given at all. Anyone using versions older than PHP 5.3 is strongly encouraged to upgrade for both security and performance reasons and to get the benefit of all the new functionality.

How it Works

The easy way to ensure a time zone is configured is by setting the date.timezone value in `php.ini`. Remember to restart the web server when you make changes to `php.ini`. Setting the time zone programmatically makes it possible to overwrite the value in `php.ini` when needed.

```php
<?php
// 5_1.php
$ts = time();
echo date("Y m d H:i:s", $ts) . "\n";
date_default_timezone_set("UTC");
echo date("Y m d H:i:s", $ts) . "\n";
```

With `date.timezone` defined to `America/Los_Angeles` this code will produce output that looks like this:

```
2015 03 25 11:36:12

2015 03 25 18:36:12
```

If the output is shown in a browser the whitespace generated by "\n" is not shown as a line break. Either use HTML (<br/>) or add a header to set the content type to text/plain.

The time difference shows as 7 hours although the normal difference between UTC time and the time in Los Angeles is 8 hours. This is caused by daylight savings time in Los Angeles. Daylight savings time never applies to UTC.

In the example above the date function is passed two variables. The first one is the format string and the second is a timestamp. The second parameter is optional and if it's not passed the date function will use the current time when generating the string.

Recipe 5-2. Creating a Timestamp

Problem

Timestamps are useful when ordering data. They do not have the sorting problems as date time strings do where the ordering depends on the format of the string. In Europe the dates are typically formatted as day, month, and year; and in the United States it's common to use month, day, and year. An easy is to use a format of year, month, and day. This will provide a way to sort correctly by date but that does not present well.

Solution

There are a number of ways to create a timestamp in PHP. The simplest way is to use the `time()` function to return the timestamp for the current date and time. If you need to get a timestamp for a specific date and time you can use the `mktime()` function. This function takes a number of parameters. All the parameters are optional and can be left out from the right. Any parameter that is left out will be set to the current value based on the system time and the selected time zone. The parameters are Hour, Minute, Second, Month, Day, Year, and Is DST, which indicates whether or not daylight savings time should be taken into account.

Having the date and time split up into individual parts is not always practical so for those instances there are a couple of functions that can help. The function strtotime() creates a timestamp based on parsing of a string. The function works without a specific format. This makes it difficult to interpret 03 01 2015 as it can mean both March 1st and January 3rd depending on where in the world you are. The strtotime() function also allows more creative strings to be passed in like "+1 month," which will take the current day and time and add 1 month, or "January 5th 2015 + 15 weeks," or "first Monday of April 2016."

How it Works

In the next example we look at the various ways of creating timestamps.

```php
<?php
// 5_2.PHP
// Get timestamp for current day and time
$ts = time();
echo $ts . "\n";
echo date("M j Y H:i:s", $ts) . "\n";

// Get timestamp for March 1st 2015 at 00:00:00
$ts = mktime(0, 0, 0, 3, 1, 2015);
echo $ts . "\n";
echo date("M j Y H:i:s", $ts) . "\n";

// Use strtotime() to get a timestamp for a specific day time
$ts = strtotime("first Monday of April 2016");
echo $ts . "\n";
echo date("M j Y H:i:s", $ts) . "\n";
```

In these three examples the time portion is defaulting to 00:00:00 for the last two dates. This is because no time value is specified as part of the string. The sample first prints the integer value of each timestamp and then converts it back to a string value with the date() function.

```
1427317600

Mar 25 2015 14:06:40

1425196800

Mar 1 2015 00:00:00

1459753200

Apr 4 2016 00:00:00
```

Although Epoc is set to start on January 1st, 1970, it is still possible to use timestamps that represent dates before that. This is done with the use of negative values for the timestamp. On older versions of PHP for Windows this was not possible. It was fixed in PHP 5.1.

On a 32-bit system the range of the timestamp goes from -2147483648 to 2147483647 these values correspond to the dates 1901/12/13 20:45:51 and 2038/01/19 03:14:08. On a 64-bit system the corresponding values are -292277022657/01/27 08:29:52 and 292277026596/12/04 03:30:07.

Recipe 5-3. Working with Dates

Problem

Using timestamps to store date values can cause some undesired results when the data is used across multiple time zones.

This happens for birthdays and other dates like that. If you create a web site where users from all over the world can enter their birthdate and you store that as an integer timestamp and then use the date() function with a different user's time zone, you might get wrong dates.

Solution

There are two special versions of mktime() and date() that ignore the time zone and always operates on UTC values. These are called gmmktime() and gmdate(). These are convenient when you want to store date values as timestamps.

How it Works

In this example we have a user who enters his birthday as October 10th, 1980, using the time zone of Europe/Copenhagen. A second user looks at the birthday from the America/Los_Angeles time zone.

```php
<?php
// 5_3.php
// User 1 born on October 10th 1980 in Copenhagen Denmark
date_default_timezone_set("Europe/Copenhagen");
$dob = mktime(0, 0, 0, 10, 10, 1980);

// User 2 looks at the birthday from Los Angeles
date_default_timezone_set("America/Los_Angeles");
echo date("M j Y", $dob). "\n";
```

It now looks like the birthday is on October 9th. If we replace the date() and mktime() functions with the gmdate() and gmmktime() this problem will go away.

```php
<?php
// 5_4.php
// User 1 born on October 10th 1980 in Copenhagen Denmark
date_default_timezone_set("Europe/Copenhagen");
$dob = gmmktime(0, 0, 0, 10, 10, 1980);

// User 2 looks at the birthday from Los Angeles
date_default_timezone_set("America/Los_Angeles");
echo gmdate("M j Y", $dob). "\n";
```

Not all months include the same number of data and PHP provides a quick way to verify if the combination of day, month, and year corresponds to a valid date. This function is called checkdata() and it takes three parameters: month, day, and year. The function returns true if the parameters correspond to a valid date and returns false otherwise.

Recipe 5-4. Displaying Timestamps

Problem

Dates and times are used in many different ways around the world. Using an integer to represent a UNIX timestamp for any date, time, or date/time value makes it easy to sort and calculate date and time differences but they are not very practical for showing actual dates.

Solution

The date() functions is used to convert a UNIX timestamp into a readable sting format based an a formatting string with a long range of options. In addition to the date() function that uses English names for months and weekdays the function strftime() provides the same functionality but uses the settings for setlocale() to provide names, and the formatting strings are slightly different than the values used for the date() function.

How it Works

The formatting string for the date() function is a combination of upper- and lowercase letters. Any character that is not recognized as a formatting character will remain as is in the returned string. This is useful for adding periods, slashes, dashes, or colons to separate values.

In this next example we take the timestamp for the current time and format it as a European and U.S. date time string. The timestamp will represent the date and time in the time zone that is configured on the server.

```php
<?php
// 5_5.php
$ts = time();
// European
echo date("d/m/Y H:i:s", $ts) . "\n";

// US
echo date("m/d/Y h:i:s a", $ts) ."\n";
```

The output of this program will look something like this.

```
27/03/2015 16:46:28

03/27/2015 04:46:28 pm
```

The two major differences here are the swapping of day and month and the use of a 24-hour vs. a 12-hour representation of time. As you can see, spaces, slashes, and colons are not converted but all other characters are converted to a portion of the date time string that is returned. The full list of the supported characters can be found at http://php.net/date.

Because the strftime() function relies on underlying operating system functions to format the string and translate names for months and week days the system expects the formatting placeholders to be % followed by a single upper- or lowercase letter.

Let's take a look at the same example but this time we include the name for the day of week and the full name of the month.

```php
<?php
// 5_6.php
$ts = time();

echo date("l F d Y h:i:s a", $ts) ."\n";
```

This will output the date time string as shown below.

```
Friday March 27 2015 04:54:36 pm
```

In order to use the `strftime()` function we would have to change the formatting string as seen in this next example.

```php
<?php
// 5_7.php
$ts = time();

echo strftime("%A %B %e %Y %I:%M:%S %P ", $ts) ."\n";
```

This example will generate output that looks like this:

```
Friday March 27 2015 05:03:40 pm
```

In order to get the names for months and weekdays in a different languages we can use the `setlocale()` function to change the behavior to

```php
<?php
// 5_8.php
$ts = time();

setlocale(LC_TIME, 'en_US');
echo "English: ";
echo strftime("%A %B %e %Y %I:%M:%S %P", $ts) ."\n";

setlocale(LC_TIME, 'de_DE');
echo "German: ";
echo strftime("%A %B %e %Y %H:%M:%S", $ts) ."\n";

setlocale(LC_TIME, 'fr_FR');
echo "French: ";
echo strftime("%A %B %e %Y %H:%M:%S", $ts) ."\n";
```

Now we are using the strings from the operating system to show names of workdays and months in the language selected by `setlocale()` and the output will look like this:

```
English: Friday March 27 2015 05:16:32 pm

German: Freitag März 27 2015 17:16:32

French: Vendredi mars 27 2015 17:16:32
```

■ **Note** The language packages for the desired languages must be installed on the system in order for the setlocal() function to be able to utilize them.

If you don't want to rely on setlocale() for translations of names for weekdays and months, the simple solution is to use numeric values for these but it is also possible to write your own formatting function.

```php
<?php
// 5_9.php
$weekdays = array(
  'en' => array(
    'Sunday', 'Monday', 'Tuesday', 'Wednesday',
    'Thursday', 'Friday', 'Saturday', 'Sunday'
  ),
  'da' => array(
    'søndag', 'mandag', 'tirsdag', 'onsdag',
    'torsdag', 'fredag', 'lørdag', 'søndag'
  ),
);

$months = array(
  'en' => array(
    1 => 'January', 'February', 'March', 'April', 'May', 'June',
        'July', 'August', 'September', 'October', 'November', 'December'
  ),
  'da' => array(
    1 => 'januar', 'februar', 'marts', 'april', 'maj', 'juni',
        'juli', 'august', 'september', 'oktober', 'november', 'december'
  ),
);

function FormatDate($ts, $lang = 'en') {
  global $weekdays, $months;

  $d = date('j', $ts);
  $w = date('w', $ts);
  $m = date('n', $ts);
  $y = date('Y', $ts);
  switch($lang) {
    case 'en' :
      return $weekdays[$lang][$w] . ", " . $months[$lang][$m] .
             " {$m} {$y}";
      break;
    case 'da' :
      return $weekdays[$lang][$w] . ", {$m} " . $months[$lang][$m] .
             " {$y}";
      break;
  }
}
```

```
$ts = time();

echo FormatDate($ts) . "\n";
echo FormatDate($ts, 'da') . "\n";
```

This example will produce a two-line output like this:

```
Sunday, March 3 2015

søndag, 3 marts 2015
```

The downside to this is the maintenance of the translation tables but you can do it all within your application without dependencies on the hosting environment.

Recipe 5-5. Using ISO Formats
Problem

In many cases there is a need for a very specific string formatting. When creating e-mail messages it's convenient to have a formatting string, to generate date values for the headers, which follow the standard without having to remember the exact formatting.

Solution

The date() function provides a few specific formatting characters that will convert a timestamp into the string representation according to the specific ISO formatting. Using "c" will generate a string formatted according to the ISO 8601 standard and "r" will generate an RFC 2822-formatted string.

The ISO 8601 standard is intended to make it possible to exchange date and time values between different parts of the world where different formatting is used. The RFC 2822 standard covers exchange of e-mails. There is a commonly used string that looks similar to this and it's used to see the Last-Modified and Expire headers on an HTTP response. The main difference is that the e-mail data includes a time zone offset and the response header is always given in GMT value.

How it Works

If you create your own e-mail client you will have to set headers for to, from, subject, and other parameters in each e-mail message. In addition you would also have to create a header entry for the date and time the e-mail was created. This could look something like this:

```
<?php
// 5_10.php

$msg = "From: mail@example.com\r\n" .
       "To: mail@somedomain.com\r\n" .
       "Subject: ISO date format\r\n";
$msg .= date("c") . "\r\n\r\n";
$msg .= "This is the body of the email message\r\n";

echo $msg;
```

This is just a very simple e-mail message and it is recommended to use one of the many e-mail client classes to handle sending and receiving of e-mail messages. This example will echo the content of the $msg variable.

```
From: mail@example.com

To: mail@somedomain.com

Subject: ISO date format

2015-04-01T12:25:38-07:00

This is the body of the email message
```

Setting the Expires and Last-Modified headers for a HTTP response could look something like this:

```php
<?php
// 5_11.php

$gmt_mtime = gmdate('D, d M Y H:i:s', $last_modified) . ' GMT';
$gmt_etime = gmdate('D, d M Y H:i:s', time() + $ttl) . ' GMT';

header("Pragma: Cache");
header("Cache-Control: max-age=0, must-revalidate");
header("Last-Modified: " . $gmt_mtime);
header("Expires: " . $gmt_etime);

if (!empty($_SERVER['HTTP_IF_MODIFIED_SINCE']) &&
    $_SERVER['HTTP_IF_MODIFIED_SINCE'] == $gmt_mtime) {
  http_response_code(304);
  exit();
}
// Output the rest of the response
```

This will allow the browser to use a cached version of the response if and only if a revalidation sends back the HTTP status 304.

Recipe 5-6. Working with Week Numbers

Problem

In some industries around the world the use of week numbers are quite common. Unfortunately there are multiple different standards for how week numbers are calculated. The week that includes the first Thursday of the year, the week that includes January 4th, the first week with four or more days, or the week that starts with the Monday that falls between December 29th and January 4th.

Solution

The date functions in PHP support the ISO-8601 standard for week numbers, which define the first week to be the week that includes the first Thursday of the year. It is also worth mentioning that week numbering changes between Sunday and Monday and not between Saturday and Sunday as weeks are defined in some parts of the world.

How it Works

In order to get the week number of a given timestamp we use the 'W' formatting character to get week number according to the ISO-8601 standard. Week numbers are often given with the year so the formatting string would be 'Y-W' or 'W-Y'.

```php
<?php
// 5_12.php

$ts = time();
echo date("Y-W", $ts) . "\n";
```

Recipe 5-7. The DateTime Class

Problem

When integer values are used to represent a timestamp as a number of seconds since the reference time, the range of the dates that can be handled is determined by allowed values in an integer variable. On a 32-bit system where an integer is a 4-byte value a timestamp can range from 1901 12 13 20:45:51 to 2038 01 19 03:14:08 in UTC or roughly plus and minus 68 years. How can date and time values beyond this range be represented in PHP?

Solution

On a 64-bit system, where integers are 8-byte values, the timestamp range is between -292277022657 01 28 08:29:52 and 292277026596 12 04 15:30:07 UTC or roughly plus and minus 29 billion years.

Changing the operating system from 32-bit to 64-bit might not always be an option so for that PHP provides a built-in class called DateTime() that allows the same date ranges as on a 64-bit system. The DateTime() class was introduced as experimental with version 5.1 and has been included since version 5.2 of PHP.

How it Works

Instantiating an object from the DateTime() class can be done without parameters. This will create an object with the current time and the current time zone. The date and time can be printed with the use of the same formatting strings as the date() function uses.

```php
<?php
// 5_13.php

$d = new DateTime();
echo $d->format("M d Y h:i:s a") . "\n";
```

which will generate output that looks like this.

```
Mar 29 2015 11:18:36 am
```

If you want the date/time object to contain a specific date and time value rather than the current time you can pass the value as the first argument when the object is instantiated. The format of the date/time value must follow a specific format. The full list of supported formats can be found here: http://php.net/manual/en/datetime.formats.php.

Creating a date/time object with a specific date would look like what is shown in the next example.

```php
<?php
// 5_14.php

$d = new DateTime("2010-10-31 13:15:00");
echo $d->format("M d Y h:i:s a P") . "\n";
```

The first parameter contains both a date part and a time part and the output will show the date and time according to the format string provided.

```
Oct 31 2010 01:15:00 pm -07:00
```

If the date string you pass is from a different time zone you can use the second optional parameter to create the date/time object in a different time zone. When a time zone parameter is used the date/time object will remember that value and use it for all calculations including presentations. If we change the code to include a time zone the output will be the same with the exception of the GMT offset.

```php
<?php
// 5_15.php

$tz = new DateTimeZone("Europe/Copenhagen");
$d = new DateTime("2010-10-31 13:15:00", $tz);
echo $d->format("M d Y h:i:s a P") . "\n";
```

Note that the time zone is passed as an object instantiated from the `DateTimeZone()` class. The output will look like this:

```
Oct 31 2010 01:15:00 pm +01:00
```

The data/time string passed as the first parameter is parsed the same way as the `strtotime()` function. That means you can parse relative dates when you are instantiating the object as shown in the next example where two objects are created. The first one uses the current date and time and the second one calculates a date/time that is two months into the future and at the same time specifies the exact time to 12:00.

```php
<?php
// 5_16.php

$d = new DateTime();
echo $d->format("M d Y h:i:s a P") . "\n";

// Noon in 2 months
$d = new DateTime("+2 months 12:00");
echo $d->format("M d Y h:i:s a P") . "\n";
```

It is a little before noon local time at the time this script was executed so the two times are close but on dates that are two months apart.

```
Mar 29 2015 11:39:46 am -07:00
May 29 2015 12:00:00 pm -07:00
```

Changing the date, time, or time zone after you have created the object is possible with a number of methods on the DateTime() object.

Setting a specific date or time can be done with DateTime::modify(). This method takes a string parameter that works the same as the parameter used in the constructor. You can either change the date/time to a new explicit value or you can modify it relatively.

In the next example the date/time value is instantiated to the current time and then altered with the modify() method to a specific date and then changed relatively to a date that's two months ahead and finally to a date 2000 years ago.

```php
<?php
// 5_17.php

date_default_timezone_set('America/Los_Angeles');
$d = new DateTime();
echo $d->format("M d Y h:i:s a P") . "\n";

$d->modify("2010-10-31");
echo $d->format("M d Y h:i:s a P") . "\n";

// Noon 2 months later
$d->modify("+2 months 12:00");
echo $d->format("M d Y h:i:s a P") . "\n";

$d->modify("-2000 years");
echo $d->format("M d Y h:i:s a P") . "\n";
```

The resulting output shows a change in the GMT offset corresponding to dates where there is no daylight savings time. The first date is because it falls in the wintertime and the second one because daylight savings times didn't exist 2000 years ago.

```
Mar 29 2015 11:56:05 am -07:00

Oct 31 2010 11:56:05 am -07:00

Dec 31 2010 12:00:00 pm -08:00

Dec 31 0010 12:00:00 pm -08:00
```

Although this code was executed on a 64-bit system it would produce the same result on a 32-bit platform.

Another way to work with relative time is to use the add() or sub() methods of the DateTime() object. These methods takes a single parameter that is an object of the class DateInterval(). The DateInterval() constructor uses a string to define the length of the period by specifying a number of years (Y), months (M), weeks (W), days (D), hours (H), minutes (M), and seconds (S). Note that M is used for both months and minutes. This is possible because of two extra letters P and T that designate the period (P) and the time (T) portion of the interval. To create a time interval of 2 years, 3 months, 5 days, and 10 hours you would use the string 'P2Y3M5DT10H'.

```php
<?php
// 5_18.php
date_default_timezone_set('America/Los_Angeles');
$d = new DateTime("Oct 10 1980");
echo $d->format("M d Y h:i:s a P") . "\n";
```

```php
$i = new DateInterval('P2Y3M5DT10H');
$d->add($i);
echo $d->format("M d Y h:i:s a P") . "\n";
```

And the output will look like this where the GMT offset changes because the date moves from a period with daylight savings time to a period without.

```
Oct 10 1980 12:00:00 am -07:00

Jan 15 1983 10:00:00 am -08:00
```

The DateInterval() class is also used when it comes to differences between dates.

```php
<?php
// 5_19.php
// User 1 creates a date
$d1 = new DateTime("Oct 10 1980");
$d2 = new DateTime("March 15 1990");

$i = $d1->diff($d2);

echo $i->format("%Y %M %D %H:%I:%S") . "\n";
```

In this example we have two date and time objects roughly 10 years apart. The output of the script shows 09 05 05 00:00:00, which according to the format indicates 9 years, 5 months, and 5 days. There is no time difference so the two objects have the same time of day.

In the example from earlier where a user enters a date according to a local time zone and another user views the date according to his or her time zone, can be handle by changing the time zone on the date/time object.

```php
<?php
// 5_20.php
// User 1 creates a date
$tz = new DateTimeZone("Europe/Copenhagen");
$d = new DateTime("Oct 10 1980", $tz);
echo $d->format("M d Y h:i:s a P") . "\n";

// User 2 in Los Angeles
$tz = new DateTimeZone("America/Los_Angeles");
$d->setTimezone($tz);
echo $d->format("M d Y h:i:s a P") . "\n";
```

The code shows the same flaw as before where dates stored, as a timestamp, will look like two different dates, caused by the difference in time zone offset.

```
Oct 10 1980 12:00:00 am +01:00

Oct 09 1980 04:00:00 pm -07:00
```

Again the solution for this is to treat dates that shouldn't have a time part, like birthdays, as dates in the same time zone no matter where the user is entering or displaying the dates from. Using the UTC time zone for this is easy but in fact it could be any time zone as long as it does not change between input and output.

The DateTime classes can also be used in a more procedural style by the use of the aliased function names: date_create_immutable() is an alias for DateTimeImmutable::__construct(). I like the object-oriented approach better and I think the names are a bit cleaner. To see the full list of DateTime functions go to http://php.net/manual/en/ref.datetime.php.

Recipe 5-8. Storing Date and Time Values

Problem

Using integers or UNIX timestamps to represent time and date values makes it easy to work with and store. If I create the database schema I tend to simply use an integer or long integer column to store the exact values I use in my PHP scripts. That way I only need to convert to a string when showing dates and times to the user and convert from strings when receiving input from the user.

If you are working on a database where the schema includes native datetime or timestamp columns you might be able to select the value as an integer and use PHP for formatting or you might have to retrieve the textual value of the column and perform the conversion in PHP.

Solution

The MySQL datetime column expects the string to be formatted as a 4-digit year, 2-digit month and day, and 2 digits for hour, minute, and seconds. The time format should be 24 hours. The equivalent formatting string looks like this: date("Y-m-d H:i:s").

How it Works

If we create a simple table with a single datetime column:

```
create table date_time (
  ts datetime;
);
```

We can then create a simple PHP script that can populate the database with random dates between 1970 and now.

```
<?php
// 5_21.php

$now = time();
$dates = [];

for ($i = 0; $i<100; $i++) {
  $dates[] = mt_rand(0, $now);
}
$con = mysqli_connect("127.0.0.1", "root", "seecret", "book");
foreach($dates as $d) {
  $date = date("Y-m-d H:i:s", $d);
  mysqli_query($con, "insert into date_time (ts) values ('{$date}');");
}
mysqli_close($con);
```

If we want to read the same values from the database and convert them into UNIX timestamps using PHP it would look something like this.

```php
<?php
// 5_22.php

$now = time();
$dates = [];

for ($i = 0; $i<100; $i++) {
  $dates[] = mt_rand(0, $now);
}
$con = mysqli_connect("127.0.0.1", "root", "secret", "book");
$rs = mysqli_query($con, "select * from date_time");
while ($row = mysqli_fetch_row($rs)) {
  $dates[] = strtotime($row[0]);
}
mysqli_free_result($rs);
mysqli_close($con);
print_r($dates);
```

Recipe 5-9. Calculating Elapsed Time

Problem

Although PHP has many ways of converting a timestamp to a string representation it does not have a way to show elapsed time.

Solution

In order to get the elapsed time between two timestamps you simply subtract them from each other. This will give the number of seconds between the two timestamps. Using the date function it's possible to create a nice representation of hours, minutes, and seconds between the two timestamps. If the elapsed time were longer than 24 hours we would also need to account for days, weeks, months, and years. Using simple math makes it possible to calculate these values. A day is 86400 seconds long and a week is 7 times that but months are not all the same length and years do vary a bit in length, too, so for those we will have to settle for averages of 30 days or 365 days when the calculations are made.

Instead of trying to convert the number of seconds to its equivalent months, days, hours, etc., it's a bit easier to use the DateTime() class to create two objects from the timestamps and then calculate the diff and use the DateInterval::format() method to represent the elapsed time.

How it Works

In this example we use the timestamp of two events generated with the use of the strtotime() function.

```php
<?php
// 5_23.php
$ts1 = strtotime("2000-06-15 20:30:00");
$ts2 = strtotime("2005-03-18 14:15:30");
```

```
$d1 = new DateTime();
$d1->setTimestamp($ts1);
echo $d1->format("Y-m-d H:i:s") . "\n";
$d2 = new DateTime();
$d2->setTimestamp($ts2);
echo $d2->format("Y-m-d H:i:s") . "\n";

$diff = $d1->diff($d2);
echo $diff->format("Years: %y, Months: %m, days: %d %H:%I:%S") . "\n";
```

The output from the script is a string according to the format string where the formatting characters that start with a % are all replaced with the corresponding value from the time difference.

```
Years: 4, Months: 9, days: 2 17:45:30
```

The strtotime() function can also be used to calculate relative date/time offset. The function supports the GNU date syntax (http://php.net/manual/en/datetime.formats.php). This is a very complex system that allows us to move a number of days, weeks, months, in either direction from the current time or a fixed timestamp.

The following example shows a few use cases of this:

```
<?php
// 5_24.php

date_default_timezone_set("America/Los_Angeles");
// calculate 3 weeks from current time
$ts = strtotime("+3 weeks");
echo date("Y/m/d h:i:s a", $ts) . "\n";

// calculate 5 days back from current time
$ts = strtotime("-5 days");
echo date("Y/m/d h:i:s a", $ts) . "\n";

// calculate a timestamp at 11:30 3 month after a given date
$ref = mktime(0, 0, 0, 12, 15, 2012);
$ts = strtotime("11:30 + 3 month", $ref);
echo date("Y/m/d h:i:s a", $ts) . "\n";
```

This example uses the America/Los_Angeles time zone and the output will look like this:.

```
2016/04/27 12:25:41 pm
2016/04/01 12:25:41 pm
2013/03/15 11:30:00 am
```

CHAPTER 6

■ ■ ■

Strings

Strings are one of the basic variable types in PHP. They are typically used to build the output of a PHP script that is returned as a response to a HTTP request.

A string is a series of characters where each character is defined as a single byte with ordinal values form 0 to 255. The single byte limitation makes it impossible to have native Unicode support for strings. The mb_string extension makes it possible to work with Unicode (Multi Byte strings) in PHP, but these are not handled with the native variable type and native string manipulation functions.

Strings in PHP can be up to 2Gb long on a 32-bit system. This requires PHP to be configured with enough memory to handle variables of this size. From PHP version 7 all integers provides true 64-bit support allowing the size of strings (and files) to be much larger than the previous 2Gb limit.

Strings are stored as a memory block and a length, which allows for binary safe strings. A binary safe string can contain one or more null bytes without causing any problems of losing a portion of the string.

Recipe 6-1. Creating Strings

Problem

Strings can be created in a number of different ways: assigning a value defined with single or double quotes or the return value from one of the many functions that return a string.

Solution

The str_repeat() and str_pad() are two of the functions that can be used to generate a string. The first one generates a string with a pattern of one or more characters repeated a number of times. The second adds a specific string to another string as padding either before or after in order to create a string of a specific length.

For a given string it's possible to change the order of the characters to generate a new string with the same characters but in random order. The function str_shuffle() acts like array_shuffle(); it takes all the elements and puts them in a random order.

How it Works

In the first example we have strings that contain times. Because the number of digits in the two times are different the overall length of the two strings are not the same. In order to print the two strings so the numbers align we would have to pad the two strings with spaces or zeros.

© Frank M. Kromann 2016

F.M. Kromann, *PHP and MySQL Recipes*, DOI 10.1007/978-1-4842-0605-8_6

```php
<?php
// 6_1.php
$t1 = "7:00 am";
$t2 = "11:00 am";

echo str_pad($t1, 8, '0', STR_PAD_LEFT) . "\n";
echo str_pad($t2, 8, '0', STR_PAD_LEFT) . "\n";
```

The two time values will be the same lengths:

07:00 am

11:00 am

If the strings were used as a response to a web request it could be simpler to set the CSS property for text-align to right in order to justify the strings to the right.

In the next example we create a string based on a pattern 'abc' repeated 15 times.

```php
<?php
// 6_2.php
$s = str_repeat('abc', 15);
echo $s . "\n";
```

This example generates the following output:

abcabcabcabcabcabcabcabcabcabcabcabcabcabcabc

A more practical example would be to create strings of a given length with a single character as shown in Recipe 6-2.

Recipe 6-2. Working with the Characters in a String

Problem

A string is, in essence, a long list of single characters. In many ways it looks like an array of characters, so is it possible to access or change characters at a given position of the string?

Solution

Using the square brackets after the variable name it's possible to access each character as if it's an element in an array. The characters start at index 0 and ends at index length -1. Getting the third character from a string $a="abcdef"; can be done by referencing $a[2].

How it Works

In the next example a string $s is declared with a static value and we use the array syntax to replace a single character based on the knowledge of where the character 7 is in the string.

```
<?php
// 6_3.php
$s = "The sun is up @ 7am";
$s[16] = '6';
echo $s . "\n";
```

This example shows how to replace a single character in an existing string. If you want to add characters or strings you can use the concatenate operator (. period) to build longer strings.

```
<?php
// 6_4.php
$s = "The sun is up @ 7am";
$s .= " and it sets again at 7pm";
echo $s . "\n";
```

Concatenation can either be done as $a = $b . $c; where a new variable is created to store the result or by using $a .= $b;. This is equivalent to $a = $a . $b; but it is slightly shorter.

Recipe 6-3. Replacing Characters

Problem

Knowing the exact position of one character is not always possible and replacing a single character with a different character is also limiting. Having the ability to replace a number of characters with zero or more characters gives more flexibility.

Solution

The function str_replace() is the simple way to replace all instances of a string with another string. The function takes three parameters. The first one is the string to replace, the second is the string to replace it with, and the third is the string to perform the replacement on.

The first two parameters can be arrays of strings. In that case the replace function will be performed for each string in the arrays. If the first argument is an array and the second is a string, the function will replace all elements defined in the first array with the string passed as the second parameter.

If the first array contains more values than the second array, any value in the first array without a matching value in the second will be replaces with the empty string.

If the first value is a string and the second is an array the string will be replaced with the word 'Array'.

There is a variant of str_replace() called str_ireplace(). This function is case insensitive on the search part of the function.

How it Works

Consider the HTML fragment '<h1>Document Title</h1>' stored in a string. If we decided to change the tag from <h1> to <h2> we could use the str_replace() function.

```
<?php
// 6_5.php
$s = "'<h1>Document Title</h1>";
echo str_replace("h1", "h2", $s) . "\n";
```

This only works if we know for sure that the string h1 only exists as a tag. If it was used as part of the string it would also be replaced there, but only if the case was exactly the same. To improve a little on this we could include the ending > and use the case-insensitive version of the function.

```php
<?php
// 6_6.php
$s = "'<H1>Document Title is h1</h1>";
echo str_ireplace("h1>", "h2>", $s) . "\n";
```

Now it's only the content of the tags that is replaced and even with the opening tag being H1 instead of h1 it still works.

For more advanced replacements that can account for attributes within the HTML tags we will have to use regular expressions. These are discussed in depth in chapter 9.

Recipe 6-4. Creating Long Strings with Heredoc and Newdoc

Problem

Building strings by concatenating string elements can take a lot of extra characters for line breaks, escaping characters, and quotation marks.

Solution

With the use of Heredoc and Newdoc it's possible to create long strings without the use of quotation marks in a way that will preserve line breaks. Heredoc works as a double quoted string where any PHP variable included will be resolved to its value where Newdoc acts as a single quoted string with no variable substitution. Both Heredoc and Newdoc strings are started with the operator <<< followed by a name. For Heredoc the name is simply a sequence of characters where Newdoc uses a name in single quotes. Both types will end the string declaration at the point where the name is repeated as the only thing on the line with no spaces before the name and a semicolon after the name to terminate the command.

How it Works

It is not necessary to use the identifiers HEREDOC or NEWDOC as long as the start and end of the block uses the same identifier.

```php
<?php
// 6_7.php
// defining a Heredoc block
$h = <<<HEREDOC
Some string
value
HEREDOC;
```

```php
<?php
// 6_8.php
// defining a Newedoc block
$n = <<<'NEWDOC'
A different
string value
NEWDOC;
```

These blocks can be used both as variable assignments and as inline structures in an array or function calls. In the example below we generate an array with two string elements.

```php
<?php
// 6_9.php
$a = [
  <<<HEREDOC
Some string
value
HEREDOC
,
  <<<HEREDOC
Second string
HEREDOC
,
];
```

This will produce the following output:

```
Array
(
    [0] => Some string
value
    [1] => Second string
)
```

Note how the line break is preserved in the string.

```php
<?php
// 6_10.php
printf("String = %s\n", <<<HEREDOC
This is a very long string
HEREDOC
);
```

Note that the final part of the string must be the only thing on the line, with the exception of a semicolon to terminate the statement. If the heredoc is used as part of an array declaration the closing name must be the only thing on the line. Commas to separate parameters or elements in the array must be on a separate line. Even whitespace after the closing name will cause parse errors.

Blocks of text defined as a heredoc block is very practical to define templates used to build sections of an HTML document. In the next example we use a database query to select two columns from a database, loop over them, and create a HTML fragment based on two templates.

```php
<?php
// 6_11.php
$con = mysqli_connect("127.0.0.1", "root", "secret", "book");
$rs = mysqli_query($con, "select * from person");
if ($rs) {
  $persons = array();
  while($row = mysqli_fetch_assoc($rs)) {
    $persons[] = $row;
  }
  mysqli_free_result($rs);
}
mysqli_close($con);

$person_tpl = <<<HEREDOC
<div>
  <span>%first_name%</span>
  <span>%last_name%</span>
  <span>%date_of_birth%</span>
</div>
HEREDOC;

$section_tpl = <<<HEREDOC
<div>%persons%</div>
HEREDOC;

$html = "";
$p = array();
foreach ($persons as $person) {
  $r = str_replace('%first_name%', $person['first_name'], $person_tpl);
  $r = str_replace('%last_name%', $person['last_name'], $r);
  $r = str_replace('%date_of_birth%',
      gmdate("M j Y", $person['date_of_birth']), $r);
  $p[] = $r;
}

echo str_replace('%persons%', implode('', $p), $section_tpl);
```

The inner template ($person_tpl) defines the layout used for each person and the outer template defines the section of HTML where all the records are injected.

Recipe 6-5. Escaping Strings

Problem

When strings are used as input to database queries where the single quote is used to start and end string values, it is necessary to indicate that single quotes in the string value are not the end of the string.

Without proper handling it would be very easy for a hacker to inject malicious code into the database. Escaping strings is the absolute minimum measure to prevent this. In general the programmer should never trust input from the user, and especially not use any input from the user (query string, form post, etc.) as direct injection into a database query.

Solution

Most databases use an escape string in the form of a backslash (\) or in some cases an extra single quote before the single quote in order to indicate that the quote should be part of the string. Using the function str_replace() to replace a single quote with two single quotes is one way to prepare strings to be used in update and insert statements. Many of the database extensions in PHP support a function to escape strings. The benefit of using a function provided by the database engine allows the database to handle the escape according to the selected character set.

There are two functions do add and remove slashes from a string. These are called addslashes() and removeslashes(). These functions are not to be used to escape strings for insertion into databases but rather to add slashes to code that is going to be evaluated or when outputting contents that is embedded in javascript code. The adslashes() function escapes the NULL character, a backslash, a single quote, and a double quote.

How it Works

In the next example we have a string variable that contains a name with an apostrophe. If we try to use this variable as is we will get an error from the SQL server, but if the string variable is properly escaped before inserting into the database it will succeed.

```php
<?php
// 6_12.php
$con = mysqli_connect("127.0.0.1", "root", "secret", "book");

// create table strings (
//    val  varchar(250);
// );

$name = "Mark O'Brian";
// This will fail
mysqli_query($con, "insert into strings (val) values ('{$name}');");

$name = mysqli_escape_string($con, $name);
// This will succeed
mysqli_query($con, "insert into strings (val) values ('{$name}');");
```

Remember that you should never trust the input of any kind. Always validate and escape any and all input to your code.

Consider the following code where the string $name could be the result of a user filling out a name value in an HTML form and submitting the form to the server.

```php
<?php
// 6_13.php
$con = mysqli_connect("127.0.0.1", "root", "secret", "book");

// create table strings (
//    val  varchar(250);
// );

$name = "My Name";
// This will fail
mysqli_query($con, "insert into strings (val) values ('{$name}');");
```

There is nothing in this code that prevents the user from entering SQL statements into the $name variable. Instead of entering My Name the user could enter My Name'; delete from strings; --.

This will cause the code to execute two statements. The first will fetch all matching rows from the strings table and the second will delete all rows from the same table.

Recipe 6-6. Reformatting Strings

Problem

Strings have many uses and often there is a need to work on parts of the string. This can be to reorder the parts, add or remove portions of the string, or add HTML tags to format the string.

Solution

Strings can be converted into arrays with the explode() function that takes two arguments. The first argument is the pattern to look for and perform the split on. This can be a space character, a newline, or any other string patterns. The second parameter is the string to convert into an array. The return value will be an array of strings.

The reverse functionality is handled with the implode() function that turns an array into a string, inserting the separator string (first argument) between each element in the array. The source array does not have to be an array of strings but each element will be converted into strings before concatenation. The function join() is an alias for implode().

Both of these functions do not alter the string or array in the argument so the system ends up with two variables that contain the data. If the string or array is large there might not be enough memory to hold both values. In that case it might be better to use the tokenizer function strtok(), which can split the string one token at the time and as such only keep the original string plus the current token in memory at any given time.

How it Works

There are many uses of explode() and implode(). Say you have a file that you want to read and process line by line; you can read the contents of the file and convert it into an array that can be used in a loop.

```php
<?php
// 6_14.php

$content = file_get_contents('file.txt');
$a = explode("\n", $content);

foreach ($a as $line) {
  // Do something
}
```

If you don't have a need for the contents as a string you can use the file() function. This function will read the file and return the lines as an array.

This is the same way we can take an array of integers and turn into a comma-separated string of integers that could be used in a SQL query.

```php
<?php
// 6_15.php

$a = [1, 5, 7, 9, 3, 4];

$s = implode(',', $a);

$sql = "select * form mytable where id in({$s})"
```

Recipe 6-7. Trimming Whitespace

Problem

When users enter string values in HTML forms they might add leading or trailing spaces by mistake. If those values are first and last name and you want to concatenate them into a full name you might end up with extra spaces. If the string is used as input to a search query and it contains leading or trailing spaces the search might not yield any results unless these characters are moved first.

Solution

Whitespace in the beginning, the end, or both can be removed with one of the functions ltrim(), rtim(), or trim(). Whitespace in the middle of the string is not removed by any of these functions. Whitespace characters include a space character, newline (\n), or carriage return (\r).

How it Works

If you are using input from a HTML form as a search parameter in a database query, you can use the trim() function to get rid of whitespace in the beginning and end of the string.

```php
<?php
// 6_16.php

$con = mysqli_connect('127.0.0.1', 'root', 'secret', 'book');

$q = mysqli_escape_string($con, trim($_POST['name']));

$sql = "select * form person where name like '%{$q}%'";
```

Recipe 6-8. Finding Strings in Strings

Problem

Checking to see if one string is included in another string, checking how many times a sting occurs in another string, or finding where in a string a specific string exists are common problems when working with strings.

Solution

In PHP there are functions to find the first or the last position of a string (needle) in another string (haystack). These functions are called strops() or strrpos() and will return an integer value for the position or NULL if the string is not found. The family of strops() functions are case sensitive and binary safe. The extra r in the function name indicates reverse or starting from the end instead of the beginning of the string. Many of the string functions have a version that starts from the beginning and a version that starts from the end of the string. All these have an extra r in the name. In the same way the name can have an extra i for case insensitive.

Both strpos() functions take an optional parameter to indicate where in the string the search should begin. This can be used to repeat the search to see if the string exists more than once. The functions are case sensitive but if you don't care about case you can use the case insensitive versions called stripos() and strripos().

In the same where there are functions to find the first and last occurrence of a character or a string in a string. These are called strchr(), strrchr(), strstr(), and strrstr(). Internally strchr() is an alias for strstr(). The return value is the first sting that starts from the first or last occurrence of the search string and the rest of the string. Even if you search for a single character these functions will return the rest of the string from the place where the character is found.

How it Works

In the next example we have a long string and we will be looking for the first and last occurrence of the string 'at'.

```php
<?php
// 6_17.php

$s = "Lorem ipsum dolor sit amet, has dicit eleifend no, legimus " .
     "voluptatibus ad mei. Ornatus sententiae vituperatoribus mel ea, " .
     "at veri maiorum quaerendum vel, vis at deleniti vulputate. An vis " .
     "quis percipitur reformidans. Eu agam tation vel, " .
     "pri nemore discere no.";

$p_first = strpos($s, 'at');
$p_last = strrpos($s, 'at');

echo "'at' is first found at positionn {$p_first}\n";
echo "'at' is last found at positionn {$p_last}\n";

$p = strchr($s, 'at');
echo "{$p}\n";

$p = strrchr($s, 'at');
echo "{$p}\n";
```

At first we use strops() and strrpos() to get the position of the first and last occurrence of 'at'. These functions return an integer for the 0-based index of the position in the string.

Next we use strchr() and strrchr() to get the string that starts at these positions. The output of the sample looks like this:

```
'at' is first found at positionn 65
'at' is last found at positionn 227
atibus ad mei. Ornatus sententiae vituperatoribus mel ea, at veri maiorum quaerendum vel,
vis at deleniti vulputate. An vis quis percipitur reformidans. Eu agam tation vel, pri
nemore discere no.
ation vel, pri nemore discere no.
```

Note that the functions are looking for an exact match to the string being searched for, even if that string is a part of a word.

Recipe 6-9. Dividing Strings into Substrings

Problem

Strings can be used to store different types of data and when the logic of the code calls for knowing a certain portion of the string we need functions that can cut the string into small elements.

Solution

This is handled with the substr() function. This function takes a string and one or two integers as parameters. The first integer is the starting position (0 offset numbers) and the optional second integer is the length. If the length parameter is omitted the function will return all characters from the start position.

The start parameter can be negative causing the function to start at the end of the string. Setting start to -3 will return the last three characters if the length is not given. If the start position is a number higher than the length of the string the substr() function will return null. If a negative value is given as the start and the length is a negative value that is less than or equal to the start value, the function will return an empty string.

How it Works

In the previous recipe we saw how we can find the position of characters and strings in another string. Now we are going to look at how this can be used to get a specific section of a string.

If we take the same long string and want to get the content of the string between the first and last occurrence of 'at' it would look something like this:

```php
<?php
// 6_18.php

$s = "Lorem ipsum dolor sit amet, has dicit eleifend no, legimus " .
    "voluptatibus ad mei. Ornatus sententiae vituperatoribus mel ea, " .
    "at veri maiorum quaerendum vel, vis at deleniti vulputate. An vis " .
    "quis percipitur reformidans. Eu agam tation vel, " .
    "pri nemore discere no.";

$p_first = strpos($s, 'at');
$p_last = strrpos($s, 'at');

echo substr($s, $p_first + 2, $p_last - $p_first - 2) . "\n";
```

135

Because we only want the content between the two positions we calculate the substring starting at the first position plus the length of the string and we count the number length of the substring as the difference between the two positions and here we subtract 2.

Getting the extension of a filename stored in a string in order to figure out what type of content the file might contain can be done in a similar way.

```php
<?php
// 6_19.php

$filename = "myfile.txt";
$ext = substr($filename, -3);

echo "Extension = {$ext}\n";
```

In this case the start of the substring is set to -3. That means 3 characters from the end of the string and there is no length provided so the function will return the rest of the string. This example only works for extensions that are 3 characters long. If we want to be able to get the extension of different file types we can use strrpos() to get the last occurrence of '.' and use that as a starting point for the substring. We will have to adjust the starting point by adding 1 as the period should not be part of the extension string.

```php
<?php
// 6_20.php

$filename = "myfile.txt";
$p = strrpos($filename, '.');
$ext = substr($filename, $p + 1);

echo "Extension = {$ext}\n";
```

This example calculates the starting point of the extension part of the filename, but not all filenames have an extension part. In that case strrpos() will return null. In order to compensate for that, we can turn this into a function that also checks if the position of '.' is valid.

```php
<?php
// 6_21.php

function GetExtension($filename) {
  $ext = null;
  $p = strrpos($filename, '.');
  if ($p !== false) {
    $ext = substr($filename, $p + 1);
  }
  return $ext;
}

$filename = "myfile.txt";
echo "Extension of {$filename} is " . GetExtension($filename) . "\n";

$filename = "myfile.info";
echo "Extension of {$filename} is " . GetExtension($filename) . "\n";
```

```php
$filename = "myfile";
echo "Extension of {$filename} is " . GetExtension($filename) . "\n";

$filename = ".cvsignore";
echo "Extension of {$filename} is " . GetExtension($filename) . "\n";
```

Note how the check for a valid position is done with $p !== false. This is because when the character that is searched for is found at the first position of the string, which is 0 and a simple compare will yield 0 == false but 0 !== false when we compare both type and value.

The output of the example looks like this:

```
Extension of myfile.txt is txt
Extension of myfile.info is info
Extension of myfile is
Extension of .cvsignore is cvsignore
```

Recipe 6-10. Displaying HTML Entities

Problem

When strings are used to store HTML code and you want to display the code instead of having the browser render the code, you will need to convert certain characters to HTML entities.

Solution

The simple way to handle this is to use str_replace() to replace < with < and > with >. That would require two function calls. Instead we can use htmlspecialchars(). This function will convert &, ', ", < and > to the corresponding HTML entities. The string might contain other substrings that have associated named entities. In order to convert all of these you must use the htmlentities() function.

Both functions take the string to convert as the first parameter followed by three optional parameters that define how the substitutions are made. Please see the PHP manual for details on these parameters at http://php.net/manual/en/function.htmlentities.php.

How it Works

Whenever your web site allows a user to input text values that are stored in a database and later presented back to the same or a different user, you might want to prevent the users from entering HTML that is then parsed by the browser and rendered as HTML instead of what the user actually entered. If you have a comments section on your blog page, a user might enter an image tag in the comment and if you don't do anything to the input the image will show up as part of the comment when it's shown to users as the image tag can reference any url on the server or any other server connected to the Internet.

You can call htmlentities() either before inserting the value into the database or before showing it to the user, but don't call it both times.

```php
<?php
// 6_22.php

$input = 'This is my comment <img src="https://example.com/image.jpg" />';

echo htmlentities($input);
```

The raw output of this script will show the following:

```
This is my comment &lt;img src=&quot;https://example.com/image.jpg&quot; /&gt;
```

When this is sent to a browser it will be shown as text and not be interpreted as an image tag. Converting the string back to a valid HTML string can be done with the html_entity_decode() function.

If you run this script on the command line the output will look like this:

```
This is my comment &lt;img src=&quot;https://example.com/image.jpg&quot; /&gt;
```

If you look at this output in the browser it will look exactly as the user typed it and the image will not be shown.

If no preventions are taken the user could insert script tags that could execute JavaScript or load script files from other sites. In this next example we use the strip_tags() function to remove all tags from the input.

```php
<?php
// 6_23.php

$input = <<<HEREDOC
Comment
<script src="https://example.com/script.js"></script>
<script>
MyFunction();
</script>
<img src="https://example.com/image.jpg" />
This is my opinion about that!
HEREDOC;

$i = strip_tags($input);

echo $i;
```

Although all tags are removed the function will preserve anything between the tags and the browser will be able to render the output as plain text. The output will look like this:

```
Comment

MyFunction();

This is my opinion about that!
```

Note that all the line breaks are preserved as it's only the tag portion of the string that is removed. You might still want to run htmlentities() on the string before sending it to the browser in order not to create an invalid HTML.

Recipe 6-11. Generating Hash Values for Files

Problem

When creating an asset management system where files of different types and sizes are stored on a file system and you want to make sure all the files are unique, you could use the file name as the key. That would however allow the user to just rename a file and store it again and you would end up saving the same file twice.

Solution

The solution is to generate a hash of the content of the file. There are a number of different functions to do this. The simplest (and probably oldest) is the md5() function that returns a string of 32 bytes based on the content of the string or file if you use md5_file(). A more comprehensive hashing algorithm is available through sha1() and sha1_file(). These functions produce a string of 40 bytes. As of version 5.1.2 of PHP includes the hash extension by default. This extension provides a long list of hashing algorithms from md2, md5, sha1, sha256, sha512, and many more.

How it Works

Before the hash extension was introduced PHP used discreet functions like md5() and sha1() to generate hashed, but with the hash() function it's possible to generate a number of different hash values with a single function. The hash() and hash_file() functions take two or three parameters. The first is the name of the hashing algorithm and the second is the string or file to create the hash from and the last optional parameter specifies if the function returns binary data or lowercase hexits to represent the data.

If you are creating a service to store images and other files you might end up with the same file being uploaded multiple times with the same or different names but by looking at the hash value of the content of the file it's possible to determine if the file is already on your system. In order to do that we will create a database table that contains an id, filename, and hash of each file. When a new file is added we check to see if the hash is already known, and if it is we return the existing hash; if it's not known we create a new record and store the file.

```php
<?php
// 6_24.php

// create table files (
//    id int auto_increment,
//    hash varchar(255),
//    filename varchar(255),
//    primary key(id)
// );
// create index ixHash on files(hash);

$con = mysqli_connect('127.0.0.1', 'root', 'secret', 'book');

function GetFile($hash) {
  global $con;
  $file = null;
```

```
  $sql = "select * from files where hash = '{$hash}'";
  $rs = mysqli_query($con, $sql);
  if ($rs) {
    $file = mysqli_fetch_row($rs);
    mysqli_free_result($rs);
  }
  return $file;
}

function SaveFile($filename) {
  global $con;
  $hash = hash_file('sha256', $filename);
  if (!GetFile($hash)) {
    mysqli_query($con, "insert into files (hash, filename) values ('{$hash}', '{$filename}')");
  }
}

SaveFile('6_1.php');
SaveFile('6_12.php');
SaveFile('6_1.php');

$rs = mysqli_query($con, "select * from files");
if ($rs) {
  while ($row = mysqli_fetch_row($rs)) {
    print_r($row);
  }
  mysqli_free_result($rs);
}
mysqli_close($con);
```

The function GetFile() will return the values stored in the database if the hash is already found and null if it's not already in the database. The function SaveFile() will call the GetFile() function before creating the new record to prevent duplicate records. This is shown at the end of the example where we insert three files. The first and the last is the same file so only two records get created and the output will look like this:

```
Array
(
    [0] => 1
    [1] => 866b1551930506766708fbb73cfdfc6fd5038cf812cb64983f43d771b8e0ff71
    [2] => 6_1.php
)

Array
(
    [0] => 2
    [1] => 125a71508e064ee34662498fcb040585fd1bf539cf4f09b203a79adffba8fc99
    [2] => 6_12.php
)
```

Recipe 6-12. Storing Passwords

Problem

Many web sites allow the users to register and create an account to get access to additional features or to view statuses on shopping orders. Many of these sites use an e-mail address as the user id and some form of password. Storing passwords as plain text values in a database is not very secure. If the site is hacked or the hard drive gets into the wrong hands, all the passwords might be exposed.

Solution

Instead of storing the plain text password we can store a hash value of the password. We can use the md5(), sha1(), or hash() function from the previous recipe or if you are using PHP 5.5 or newer, you can use the password_hash() function. It is recommended that the database schema allows for at least 60 characters (255 is better) for the password column as the hashing algorithm might change over time to improve security and create stronger hash values.

How it Works

If you have a table called users with the columns login and password you should use the password_hash() function before storing a password for a user and before checking if the login and password provided during the login is valid.

```php
<?php
// 6_25.php

 //create table myusers (
 //   id int auto_increment,
 //   login varchar(255),
 //   password varchar(255),
 //   primary key(id)
 //);
$con = mysqli_connect('127.0.0.1', 'root', 'secret', 'book');

function CreateUser($login, $password) {
  global $con;
  $login = mysqli_escape_string($con, $login);
  $password = mysqli_escape_string($con, password_hash($password, PASSWORD_BCRYPT));
  mysqli_query($con, "insert into myusers (login, password) values ('{$login}',
'{$password}')");
}

function CheckUser($login, $password) {
  global $con;
  $user = null;
  $login = mysqli_escape_string($con, $login);
  $rs = mysqli_query($con, "select * from myusers where login='{$login}'");
  if ($rs) {
        $user = mysqli_fetch_assoc($rs);
        if ($user && !password_verify($password, $user['password'])) {
```

```
            $user = null;
        }
        mysqli_free_result($rs);
    }
    return $user;
}

CreateUser('john@example.com', 'A secret Password');

if (CheckUser('john@example.com', 'A secret Password')) {
    echo "User exists and password is corect\n";
}
else {
    echo "User does not exist or password is incorrect\n";
}
```

Using the MySQL command-line tool to show the rows in the table will look something like this:

```
MariaDB [book]> select password from myusers;
+--------------------------------------------------------------+
| password                                                     |
+--------------------------------------------------------------+
| $2y$10$V4KWuQIzssFRmlQeZNLPeegsyQOMFpOvjUNl3FP9.7k5E4EiB5INi |
+--------------------------------------------------------------+
1 row in set (0.00 sec)
```

CHAPTER 7

■ ■ ■

Files and Directories

In this chapter we are going to discuss two basic ways that files are used with PHP. The first one is the script with the PHP code in the form of the main script file and includes any files that the script might use. The second one is in the form of more content or data that is read off the local or remote file system and processed by the script.

Recipe 7-1. Include and Require

Problem

When PHP is used to execute or interpret a script it always starts with a single file. This can be as an input parameter to the command-line version of PHP (php-cli) or indirectly from a web server request that is passed onto PHP.

Having a single file contain all the code needed for each request could lead to large script files and code duplication. In addition it makes sense to break the code into small units each serving a specific purpose. This is often done with a single class definition in each file.

Solution

This is where include and require come into play. Any time you have code that's shared between multiple scripts you can place it in a separate file and include the code everywhere it's needed. The basic differences between include and require is how these statements react if the requested file doesn't exist on the file system. Include will generate a warning and require will generate a fatal error and stop the script execution.

There are two different schools of thought on how to structure include files. The first is to place them in the same directory structure as the main script(s). Normally this forces the developer to use the same extension as the main scripts in order to avoid exposure of the content to the end user if they were to request the files directly. If the web server is configured to take files that have the .php extension and pass them through the PHP interpreter, files with other extensions like .inc might just be passed on as is and if the file includes database credentials and other secrets the end user might be able to access these. The simple fix to this is to make sure the web server is configured to hand all PHP files off to the interpreter. An include file that is used to configure database credentials will most likely not generate any output so the content the user will see will be an empty document.

The other school of thought is to place all include files outside the directory structure that is used to define the document root for the web site. In this case the files can have any extension, and they can't be exposed directly to the user because the web server does not know how to access these. This is the preferred method in my opinion.

© Frank M. Kromann 2016
F.M. Kromann, *PHP and MySQL Recipes*, DOI 10.1007/978-1-4842-0605-8_7

PHP uses a configuration option called include_path to locate include files. This works similarly to the operating systems environment variable PATH. On Mac and Linux the include path is a set of directories separated by a colon (:) and on Windows system the separator is a semicolon (;). When a file is included or required the interpreter will look for the file in any of the directories specified by the include_path. If the file exists in multiple directories, the first one found, when looking at the directories in the order they are defined, will be used.

Each directory in the include_path configuration can be specified as an absolute or relative path. If a relative path is specified it will start from the current working directory where the PHP except is executed from. This will in most cases be the document root or a directory under that. If you place all your php files in the document root and have configured include_path="../inc" you can place all your include files in a directory called inc that is located next to the document root.

Both include and require can have the files specified as absolute or relative paths. An absolute path starts with a / and the system will look for the include file in that location only. If a relative path is used the system will prepend the path with each section of the include_path configuration until it finds the file.

Depending on the content of the include file it might not be possible to include it more than one time. This is the case for include files that define functions or classes. Trying to declare the same function or class multiple times will lead to a compiler error.

Other files that contain variable definitions can be included multiple times. In most cases each file should only be included once but there are a couple of use cases where including files with the same name but from different directories makes sense.

There are special version of include and require called include_once and require_once. These will ensure that if the user tries to include the same file multiple times the system will not only load the files once and prevent errors coming from defining the same functions or classes multiple times.

Include and require can be used to load non-PHP files. This can be useful if you have a snippet of HTML code that should be read off the file system and served to the requesting browser as is. In that case the included file will not have the opening <?php tag and the content will be passed on as output. It will be injected to the output exactly where the file is included and the script can send other output to the browser before and after the included file.

Note: although Windows uses the backslash (\) as a directory separator PHP can use both slash (/) and backslash (\). This makes it possible to use PHP to write code that can work on Linux and Windows platforms without special considerations. It is recommended to always use the / as directory separator.

How it Works

If you have a class that's defined in one file and you want to access it from other files, you will have to include the file that defines the class.

```php
<?php
// 7_1.php

class Test {
  protected $a = null;
  function __construct($a) {
    $this->a = $a;
  }
}
```

```php
<?php
// 7_2.php

require "7_1.php";

class Test2 extends Test {
  function SetValue($a) {
    $this->a = $a;
  }

  function GetValue() {
    return $this->a;
  }
}

$t = new Test2(15);
echo $t->GetValue() . "\n";

$t->SetValue(30);
echo $t->GetValue() . "\n";
```

In the example above we define a class in one file and include the file in the next script where the calss Test() is extended to Test2(). Depending on how the include_path is defined in php.ini or if it's redefined with the ini_set() function you might have to add ./ in front of the name of the file if the file is located in the same directory as the main script.

If multiple files with the same name exists in any of the locations specified by the include_path definition the system will only include the first file based on the order of the directories listed in the include_path directive. You can specify an absolute path if you want to bypass the search for the file in all the directories included in the include_path. Doing so can cause problems if you intend to share the application with users who might install it in a different location.

Recipe 7-2. Reading Files

Problem

In the previous recipe we looked at including sections of code or other files that would either be executed or passed onto the client as output, but what if the file contains data that must be processed before it's sent to the client?

Solution

PHP comes with a bunch of functions to read from files. The most basic ones (fopen(), fclose(), fread(), etc.) mimics the low-level file handling functions of the operating system, and the more advanced ones (file_get_contents(), file() fgetcsv()) lets you read a file with a single command, read a file and turn it into an array, or read a file and parse its contents as comma separated values (CSV) file.

Other functions like readfile() and fpassthru() will simply read the contents of the file or file pointer and send it directly to the output.

How it Works

Using fopen() to create a file handle that can be used for read and/or write operations on the file works similar to how the same functions work in C/C++.

```php
<?php
// 7_3.php

$f = '';
$fp = fopen('myfile.txt', 'r');
if ($fp) {
  while ($s = fread($fp, 100)) {
    $f .= $s;
  }
  fclose($fp);
}
var_dump($f);
```

In this example the file 'myfile.txt' is opened for read operations as indicated by the second parameter to the fopen() function. The file can be specified as a relative or absolute path. In this case the file is expected to be in the same directory as the php script.

The fopen() function will return a file handle if the file was opened. It is good coding practice to check for errors before reading any content. If the file was missing or locked for writing by another process and the system was unable to open the file, it will return zero instead of a file handle. This makes the checks for errors very easy. Simply checking of the file handle has a value before continuing to the read step.

Reading from the file is done in a loop where a section of up to 100 bytes of the file is read. The internal file pointer is moved 100 bytes and the function is ready for the next iteration. This continues until the fread() function fails to read more data. The fread() function will return the actual number of bytes read. If the file is 233 bytes long the loop will get 3 iterations where the first two chunks will contain 100 bytes and the last one will contain the last 33 bytes. The fread() function is called a 4th time but as there is no more data to read the return value will be 0 and the loop will be exited. After that the file is closed with the fclose() function and the contents of the file are written to the standard output with the var_dump() function. The interpreter will automatically close any files not closed by the script, when the script terminates. This is convenient for scripts used in a web environment but if the script is used for a long running process it's always a good idea to close all files when they are no longer used.

Using fopen() and reading only a section of the file at any given time will help reduce the memory usage. The first argument to fopen() is the filename and path and the second is used to identify the mode used when the file is opened. This is done with one or more characters. The options are r for read, w for write, and a for append. These can be combined with + to add the opposite mode. In addition the use of x is allowed to open a file for writing. If the file exists the operation will fail. The mode c indicates that the file is opened for writing with the file pointer set at the beginning of the file but the file is not truncated as it is with the w mode.

If you are looking for a specific pattern in the file you can throw away each of the segments until you find the one you are looking for. Alternatively if you know a specific offset where you want to start the read from you can use the fseek() function to move the file pointer to that specific location before reading or writing. This will be faster than reading through the file one chunk at the time.

In the example above we end up reading and storing the entire file in a variable so we need to have enough memory to hold the entire file. Following is a simpler way to get the same result by using the file_get_contents() function.

```php
<?php
// 7_4.php

$f = file_get_contents('myfile.html');
echo $f;
```

This example reads the content of the file and sends the content back to the client. If the file contains the following content:

```
<!DOCTYPE html>
<html>
<head>
  <title>PHP and MySQL Recipes</title>
</head>
<body>
  <h1>Chapter 7</h1>
  <p>This chapter is about files and directpries</p>
</body>
</html>
```

The output in the browser will look like this:

Chapter 7

This chapter is about files and directpries

There is no need to open and close the file and no need to specify the read operation. That is all handled internally. A single command is used to open the file, read the contents, store it as a variable, and close the file.

Recipe 7-3. Writing Files

Problem

Not all output of PHP is intended to go to the browser or console (stdout). Logging functions that can be helpful when debugging problems in the code, writing cached content so it can be read by the web server without invoking PHP, or simply exchanging data with other systems all require some form of writing to files on the local file system.

Solution

Writing files follows the same sematics as described in the previous recipe for reading files. The basic functions (fopen(), fclose(), and fwrite()) are wrappers around the low-level functions, and functions like file_put_contents() and fputcsv() let you perform more advanced operations in a single command.

How it Works

In the following example a string is written to a file.

```php
<?php
// 7_5.php

$f = '';
$fp = fopen('myfile.txt', 'at');
if ($fp) {
  fwrite($fp, "The text that goes into this file\nAnd some on line 2");
  fclose($fp);
}
```

The file is opened with the options 'at'. That indicates that the text will be appended to the end of the file if it exists already. Using 'wt' will overwrite any existing content of the file. The t in the potion indicates that the content will be text. Using a b will indicate binary content.

Similarly it is possible to write to a file with a single function call. The function `file_put_contents()` takes two parameters where the first is the path to the file and the second is the content to write. If the file exists already it will be overwritten with the new content. It is possible to pass a third argument to the function call to force the content to be appended to the existing content. The third argument is a bitmapped flag where `FILE_APPEND` is the value that will make the function append the content. Adding the flag LOCK_EX to the third argument will ensure an exclusive lock on the file. No other process will be able to write to the file at the same time.

Writing a simple logging system could look something like this:

```php
<?php
// 7_6.php

$msg = date("Ymd H:i:s ") . "Script started\n";
file_put_contents('myfile.log', $msg, FILE_APPEND);
```

In the example the message to log is the date with a predefined format and then the actual message. Note the `date()` function is called with a single formatting parameter. This causes the function to use the current date/time when generating the string. The formatting string also contains a trailing space to create some separation to the actual message. The message ends with the \n character to force the next message to be logged on a new line. After running this script a few times the file will look something like this:

```
20160201 20:33:49 Script started
20160201 20:36:48 Script started
20160201 20:36:49 Script started()
```

Recipe 7-4. Copy, Rename, and Remove Files

Problem

Creating files and reading from then is handled by opening a file in a specified location, but what if you need to get rid of a file, copy it, or move it to a different location on the file system?

Solution

The functions copy() and rename() work on a source and destination file name. The first parameter is the source and the second is the destination. Each file name is a relative or an absolute path to the two files. The copy() function can only be used to copy files. If you want to copy a directory with all the files and subdirectories you will have to write a function that reads all of the directory and file names and makes a copy of each of them.

Moving files to a different location is the same as renaming the file. Using the same file name but a different path will move the file to the new location. The rename() function can be used on regular files, links, and directories.

Files can be removed or deleted with the unlink() function. This function works on both regular files and links but not on directories. To remove a directory you must first make sure all files and directories in it are deleted and then use the rmdir() function to remove the directory.

How it Works

To create a copy of a file to a new file in the same directory you can do something like this:

```php
<?php
// 7_7.php

copy('myfile.log', 'myfile.log.1');
```

This example uses the same log file we created in example 7_6. Both file names are relative to where the script is executed and in this case both files will be in the same directory.

If you want to copy a file from a different directory to the current directory you will simply change the source path to give an absolute or relative path to where the source file is located. This could be a file that comes from a set of distribution files in a config directory located next to the current directory.

```php
<?php
// 7_8.php

copy('../config/config.php.tmpl', 'config.php');
```

Running this script will copy the file config.php.tmpl located in ../config to the same directory as the script and it will rename the file to config.php. If you make changes to config.php and run the script again it will overwrite the file without warning so you are back to a copy of the original file.

If you didn't want to copy the file but simply move it from the config directory to the current directory simply replace the copy() function with the rename() function as shown in example 7_9.php.

```php
<?php
// 7_9.php

rename('../config/config.php.tmpl', 'config.php');
```

Both copy() and rename() will print out warnings if the source file is missing or if the target file/directory is missing the permission to write to the file for the user executing the script.

If you are creating a caching system and want to remove the cached file you can do that with the unlink() function. In example 7_10.php we show how to create function that checks if a file exists before attempting to remove the file. This will prevent warnings in the case that the file didn't exist.

```php
<?php
// 7_10.php

function DeleteCache($name) {
  if (file_exists($name)) {
    unlink($file);
  }
}

DeleteCache('cache.html');
```

This function will work on regular files and symbolic links to other files. If the file is a symlink only the link will be removed and the original file will still exist. See section 7-7 for more information on symbolic links.

Recipe 7-5. File Properties

Problem

Besides the name and content of a file there are other properties that could be useful to the developer and possibly the end user. Knowing the size of a file, when it was created or last changed could help determine if the file contains new information.

Solution

The functions `filesize()`, `filectime()`, `filemtime()`, and `fileatime()` provide information about size, create time, modify time, and access time. The `stat()` function can provide more detailed information about the file as it returns an array of values that includes device number, inode, file size, ctime, mtime, atime, and block size and number of blocks. In addition to these it's also possible to use `file_exists()`, `is_readable()`, `is_dir()`, `is_file()`, `is_link()` to determine if the file is a directory, plain file, or a symbolic link.

All the functions mentioned above take a single argument, which is the name of the file, including a relative or absolute path. These functions do not work on a file handle returned by the `fopen()` function. The `fstat()` function can be used to get the file information from a file handle. This function takes a file handle and not a file name as the parameter.

Many of the functions that provide information about files in the file system is cached in order to boost performance of these calls by not having to call the underlying system calls each time the function is called on the same file. In order to clear the cache you can call the `clearstatcache()` function. If the same file is checked multiple times during a single execution it is necessary to call the `clearstatcache()` function between each check.

How it Works

The functions `filesize()`, `filectime()`, `filemtime()`, and `fileatime()` all return integer values. The UNIX timestamps from the create, modify, and access times can be converted to human readable values with the `date()` function as shown in the next example. When using the `date()` function it's important to specify a time zone. This can be done in php.ini or with the user of the `date_default_timezone_set()` function. If no time zone is found the system will print a warning and use UTC.

```php
<?php
// 7_11.php

date_default_timezone_set("America/Los_Angeles");
clearstatcache();
$file = "7_11.php";

echo "File Size: " . filesize($file) . "\n";
echo "Created  : " . date("Y-m-d H:i:s", filectime($file)) . "\n";
echo "Modified : " . date("Y-m-d H:i:s", filemtime($file)) . "\n";
echo "Accessed : " . date("Y-m-d H:i:s", fileatime($file)) . "\n";
```

The output will look like this:

```
File Size: 354

Created  : 2016-04-10 11:30:46

Modified : 2016-04-10 11:30:46

Accessed : 2016-04-10 11:31:19
```

On some UNIX/Linux platforms it's possible to configure the system to ignore the updates of access time. This is usually done to increase performance. In this case the function fileatime() is of little use.

You can also use the stat() function to get similar data with a single function call.

```php
<?php
// 7_12.php

date_default_timezone_set("America/Los_Angeles");
clearstatcache();
$file = "7_11.php";

$stat = stat($file);
print_r($stat);
```

The output from this script will look like this:

```
Array
(
    [0] => 16777220
    [1] => 145615535
    [2] => 33188
    [3] => 1
    [4] => 502
    [5] => 20
    [6] => 0
    [7] => 356
    [8] => 1454365742
    [9] => 1454361413
    [10] => 1454361413
```

```
    [11] => 4096
    [12] => 8
    [dev] => 16777220
    [ino] => 145615535
    [mode] => 33188
    [nlink] => 1
    [uid] => 502
    [gid] => 20
    [rdev] => 0
    [size] => 356
    [atime] => 1454365742
    [mtime] => 1454361413
    [ctime] => 1454361413
    [blksize] => 4096
    [blocks] => 8
)
```

Note how the data is duplicated. The stat() function returns the values as a combined index with numerical and name values for the same data.

Recipe 7-6. Permissions

Problem

If the file system where PHP is used is shared with multiple users or files are shared among different processes for file exchange, it can be necessary to use file permissions to control what actions can be taken on a file.

Solution

PHP was born on a Linux platform and uses the POSIX system for file permissions. The POSIX system uses three bits to indicate execute (1) read (2) and write (4) access and access can be defined for the owner, the group and everyone else. It is customary to represent the access as an octal number with three digits. In PHP we add a 0 in front of the three digits to indicate that the number is octal and not decimal. The permission 0755 means execute, read, and write access for the owner and to execute and read permission for the group as well as everyone else.

The functions that are used to set access are chown() for setting the owner, chgrp() for setting the group, and chmod() for setting the permissions. These functions are similar to the command-line functions with the same names although the PHP functions do not have an option to set the permission recursively.

How it Works

When creating files with file_put_contents() or fopen()/fwrite() functions the default behavior is to set the owner and group to the same as the user who ran the script, and the default access mode is set to read/write for the owner and to read for the group and others. In order to change the mode so only the user can read and write you can do something like this:

```php
<?php
// 7_13.php

file_put_contents('private.txt', 'The content of this file is private');
chmod('private.txt, 0600);
```

And the result would be a file with permission like this:

```
-rw-------  1 kromannf  staff   35 Feb 1 14:16 private.txt
```

Similarly the chown() and chgrp() can be used to change the owner and the group for a file or directory. Note that only super users are allowed to change owner and group on files. These functions are most commonly used by shell scripts used by install processes or other long running processes.

In order to create files and directories the user running the PHP script must have write permissions to the folder where the file is created. On web installations the write access is often removed on files and directories to prevent the web site from making changes to its own code. If the web site contains a feature to upload images and other files the directory where these files are uploaded to must have the write permission set.

Recipe 7-7. Symbolic Links

Problem

Symbolic links are often used on Linux and Unix file systems to have the same file in multiple locations without using disk space for each file. If you open and read from a symbolic link, you will actually open the file that is linked to it in a different location. The same is the case for the write operation.

Solution

The function as_link() will return true if the filename passed as the parameter is in fact a link to a file or directory. You can use is_dir() and is_file() to test if the link points to a directory or a file. PHP can also create and remove symbolic links with the functions link() (hard link) and symlink() (soft link).

The difference between hard and soft links is in the way the links are created. For hard links the links is directly to the inode (the data portion of the file) and for soft links the link is to a different file name that internally links to an inode.

Soft links are used when the link is to a file on a different file system or when you want to link a directory. Hard links are used for files on the same file system and they have the advantage of being able to move the original file to a different location without breaking the links. Soft links can't do that as the link is to a file that could be (re)moved.

If you use the stat() function on a symbolic link you will get the information about the original file. To get information about the link you will have to use the lstat() function.

Links are removed with the unlink() function. If the path specified is a link or symbolic link, only the link will be removed. If the path is the last hard link that points to the data section or it's a real file, the file will be removed.

How it Works

Files that are stored outside the document root and its subdirectories are not accessible to the user through the browser and web server. If for some reason you want to make one of these files available for download you can create a symlink to the file and use that to generate a URL that can be downloaded. This only works only if the web server is configured to follow symlinks. For apache that looks like this:

```
<Directory path/to/documentroot">
        Options FollowSymLinks
        AllowOverride None
        Require all granted
</Directory>
```

153

The code to create a symlink and make it available for download would look something like this:

```php
<?php
// 7_14.php

// Perform some access control here
$token = sha1(random_bytes(50));
link('../data/bigfile.tgz', $token);
header("Location: $token");
```

This code generates a random string of bytes and then creates a sha1 hash of that string. This is done to make it difficult for other users to guess the actual string and still make it possible for the user to download file without reading it into memory in PHP. This method has a couple of flaws and should not be used in real life. First of all the symbolic links are never removed by the script. A cleanup script that runs periodically could solve this. But as long as the symbolic link exists it is possible for any user, who knows the URL, to download the file as there is no longer any validation or access control.

A better solution to this problem is to use a PHP script to read the file and send it directly to the client instead of redirecting to a symbolic link. This option does also have problems, especially with large files that exceed the memory limitation of the PHP configuration.

Using an extension to the Apache web server called mod_xsendfile solves this problem much better. The basic functionality allows Apache to download files in a predefined location outside of the document root, but only if a specific header is set before the download is set. Because the files are stored outside the web root they can't be accessed directly with a request from a browser or other client. The files are accessed through a PHP script that can validate if the user is allowed to download the file and if so tell Apache, through the header, that it is Ok to download the file. The Xsendfile extension must be configured with the directories where these downloads can take place from. The advantage of this extension is to allow the PHP script to terminate and release resources while Apache reads the file from disk and send the data to the client.

The Xsendfile extension can be downloaded from this website: https://tn123.org/mod_xsendfile/

With this extension installed and configured in Apache it's possible to download large files without affecting security or exceeding the memory limits of PHP.

```php
<?php
// 7_15.php

// Perform access control here
header("X-Sendfile: ../data/some_file.tgz");
```

If you are using NginX you can do the same thing without any special extensions.

```php
<?php
// 7_16.php

// Perform access control here
header("X-Accel-Redirect: ../data/some_file.tgz");
```

If you create an application that can be deployed on both Apache and NginX platforms you can create code that checks the type of server before selecting the right header.

```php
 <?php
// 7_17.php

// Perform access control here
if (stristr($_SERVER["SERVER_SOFTWARE"], 'nginx')) {
  header("X-Accel-Redirect: ../data/some_file.tgz");
else if (stristr($_SERVER["SERVER_SOFTWARE"], 'apache')) {
  header("X-Sendfile: ../data/some_file.tgz");
}
```

After setting the X- header the PHP code can end and the web server will take over and provide the selected file to the user. If the file is missing or the server is missing the configuration the web server will report a 404 – file not found status code.

Recipe 7-8. Directories

Problem

As we have seen already there is not much difference between a file and a directory on the file system. They are both identified with a relative or absolute path. Most of the functions used to get status or check for specific types all works on both files and directories but how can we create, move, and delete directories?

Solution

Creating a directory is done with mkdir() function. This function takes up to four parameters where the first is the relative or absolute path to the new directory and the second is the file permissions or mode in the same format as the chmod() function described earlier. The third parameter is a Boolean flag that indicates recursive functionality. This can be used to create nested directories. Instead of calling mkdir() multiple times you can supply a path and if the recursive flag is set the function will create all the directories not already exiting in the specified path. The forth parameter is the context and it's only used when the function is used with streams.

To remove a directory you will use the rmdir() function. Make sure the directory is empty before calling this function.

How it Works

In most cases web sites does not have a need to create new directories. It's designed to serve content already located on the server. If you are building a system that can be used to exchange files between users or allow users to upload images you might want to create a directory for each user. That way it's easy to keep track of where the files come from and you do not end up with one user overwriting other users' files. Your application could even allow the user to create directories to group files.

A simple script to create a directory could look like this:

```php
<?php
// 7_18.php

// Perform access control here
mkdir('MyFiolder', 0700);
```

Creating all the directories needed to complete a full path would look like this:

```php
<?php
// 7_19.php

// Perform access control here
mkdir('path/to/MyFiolder', 0700, true);
```

In this example the third parameter indicates that the system should create all the directories, if they are missing. This script will first create a directory called path next to the location of the script, after that a directory inside path called to, and finally the directory MyFolder inside the to directory. All three directories will have the permissions rwx for the owner and no permissions for group or other users.

Running the script twice will generate a warning the second time. This is because the final directory called 'MyFolder' already exists. Running the script when only the directories 'path' and 'path/to' exists will not generate any warnings.

Recipe 7-9. CSV Files

Problem

If you are working with large datasets it might be useful to export the data to a format that can be read by programs like Microsoft Excel or you might receive data from other systems using the comma separated values (CSV) format. There is a need to be able to create or parse CSV files with PHP based on parameters provided by the user to filter data, etc.

Solution

The functions fgetcsv() and fputcsv() are used to read or write CSV files. These functions work on file handles created by the fopen() function and require the file to be opened in the correct read or write mode before reading or writing.

How it Works

Creating a .csv file from an array of data, like a result set from a database query where each row contains the same number of columns could look something like this:

```php
<?php
// 7_20.php

$data = [
  ['orange', 10],
  ['blood orange', 10],
  ['apple', 25],
  ['pineapple', 1]
];
$fp = fopen('fruits.csv', 'wt');
if ($fp) {
  foreach($data as $fruit) {
    fputcsv($fp, $fruit);
```

```
    }
    fclose($fp);
}
```

This script will generate output that looks like this:

```
orange,10

"blood orange",10

apple,25

pineapple,1
```

Note how blood orange is enclosed in quotes. That's because there is a space in the string. The default enclosure character is a double quote.

Creating a tab separated file (.tsv) or any other separator, instead of comma separated file can be done by adding the third parameter for delimiter as shown in the next example.

```
<?php
// 7_21.php

$data = [
    ['orange', 10],
    ['blood orange', 10],
    ['apple', 25],
    ['pineapple', 1]
];
$fp = fopen('fruits.tsv', 'wt');
if ($fp) {
    foreach($data as $fruit) {
        fputcsv($fp, $fruit, "\t");
    }
    fclose($fp);
}
```

Which produces the following output:

```
orange              10

"blood orange"      10

apple               25

pineapple            1
```

As seen in the previous examples the fputcsv() function works on one line at the time. The fgetcsv() function works in a slightly different way. This has to do with the varying length of each line in the file. The fgetcsv() function takes the same number of parameters as the fputcsv() function. The second parameter is the length in bytes to read from the file. This number must be greater than the length of the longest line in the file. This is to allow the function to read up until the first line break. If the value is too small the system will only read part of the line and the returned array of data will be incomplete. The rest of the line will be read on the next iteration. As of PHP 5.1.0 it's possible to set the length parameter to 0. This will cause the reading to be slower as the function will read each byte separately until it reaches a line break or the end of the file.

The code to read the data from the fruits.csv file created in example 7_21 would look like this:

```php
<?php
// 7_22.php

$data = [];
$fp = fopen('fruits.csv', 'rt');
if ($fp) {
  while ($row = fgetcsv($fp, 25)) {
    $data[] = $row;
  }
  fclose($fp);
}
print_r($data);
```

And it will generate the following output:

```
Array
(
    [0] => Array
        (
            [0] => orange
            [1] => 10
        )

    [1] => Array
        (
            [0] => blood orange
            [1] => 10
        )

    [2] => Array
        (
            [0] => apple
            [1] => 25
        )

    [3] => Array
        (
            [0] => pineapple
            [1] => 1
        )

)
```

Recipe 7-10. Streams

Problem

Files might not always be located on the local file system, and there might be other types of data that could be consumed with the same set of basic functionality as provided for load files. This can be read, write, and seek functionality.

Solution

In PHP version 4.3 the concept of streams was introduced. Streams lets the developers read and write data from and to a number of different systems with the use of URL-style protocols. It is even possible to register your own stream wrappers so you can access your own data with `fopen()`, `fread()`, and `fwrite()` functions. Instead of reading files from the local hard drive you can use `file_get_contents()` to read data from a URL. The `file_get_contents()` function is the preferred method to read contents of a local or remote file into a string, as long as the contents of the file are small enough to fit in memory. This can be a normal when site that returns an HTML document or a web service that returns json or xml formatted data.

How it Works

Using the `file_get_contents()` function to download a file or document from a URL is as simple as reading it from a local disk drive. All you need to do is to provide a URL to the file instead of a path. So if you wanted to fetch the default html document from your favorite website you would do something like this:

```php
<?php
// 7_23.php

$html = file_get_contents("http://google.com");
echo $html;
```

HTML documents are designed to be rendered by a browser so unless you are building code to copy html documents to static files this example is not the most useful one, but web servers can also be used to host other types of content like XML files or json string. I will go in detail with these web services in a later chapter but the next example shows how PHP can be used to fetch a json string and turn it into a PHP object. Most web services or API's require authentication and other parameters to be passed to the server in order to retrieve data. There are a few API's available that can be used without authentication, like the one used here that will simply return the public IP address of your computer as seen by the web server.

```php
<?php
// 7_24.php

$data = json_decode(file_get_contents("http://jsonip.com"));
print_r($data);
```

The output from this example is the response from the API. In this case the response is an object with three properties.

```
stdClass Object
(
    [ip] => 180.190.203.15
    [about] => /about
    [Pro!] => http://getjsonip.com
)
```

Recipe 7-11. Stream Context

Problem

Working with streams of different types might require options and parameters that can't be passed in a generic way to the fopen() function. These options and parameters can be used to control how the stream reacts to various requests.

Solution

With the function stream_context_create() it's possible to create a context resuest that can be used as an optional parameter to most of the file handling functions. To create a stream context you must pass one or two associative arrays to the function. The first array will hold the options and the second optional array will be the parameters. The second params parameter is not widely used but can be used to set a notification callback function that can be used for things progress indication.

How it Works

By default when the function file_get_contents() is used to retrieve content with the http protocol the request will be created as a GET request where all the parameters are passed on as part of the URL. If you want to pass parameters as header values or you want to send a POST request you can use stream_contect_create() to generate these parameters in a form that can be passed to the third argument for file_get_contents(). The next example shows how to create a script that can generate a form post to a URL (the url in the example is fake but everything else works). The script starts with a function that generates the payload or body of the POST request. The function html_build_form() takes two parameters. The first is the string to use as a boundary between each of the variables in the post. and the second is an associative array of key and value pairs to submit to the server.

After the function the data is populated. This could be with input from a user or a query from a database. In the last section of the script the stream context is created from an array of options and the request is sent. Although the file_get_contents() is used it will actually start by sending all the data to the server and then retrieve the response for the request. The server might do a redirect after the post if that is the case it will be handled by the request. There is no need for additional code to handle that. If the response is a file not found (404), access denied (403), or any other status the script should handle that.

```php
<?php
// 7_25.php

function http_build_form($mime_boundary, $data) {
  $eol = "\r\n";
  $form_data = '';
  if (is_array($data)) {
    foreach ($data as $name => $value) {
      if (is_array($value)) {
        foreach($value as $val) {
          $form_data .= '--' . $mime_boundary . $eol .
          "Content-Disposition: form-data; name=\"{$name}[]\"" .
            $eol . $eol . $val . $eol;
        }
      }
      else {
        $form_data .= '--' . $mime_boundary . $eol .
        "Content-Disposition: form-data; name=\"{$name}\"" .
          $eol . $eol . $value . $eol;
      }
    }
  }
  $form_data .= "--" . $mime_boundary . "--" . $eol . $eol;
  return $form_data;
}

$data = [
  'name' => 'Donald Duck',
  'phone' => '555 555 1234'
];

$url = http://example.com/form;
$mime_boundary = md5(time());
$content = http_build_form($mime_boundary, $data);

$options = array('http' =>
  array(
    'method'  => 'POST',
    'header'  => 'Content-Type: multipart/form-data; boundary=' .
                  $mime_boundary,
    'content' => $content
  )
);
$context = stream_context_create($options);
$response = file_get_contents($url, FILE_TEXT, $context);
var_dump($response);
```

Recipe 7-12. File Iterators

Problem

When the same action is going to be performed on multiple files we need a way to figure out which files are stored in a directory and we need ways to traverse recursively through the directory structure.

Solution

The simple way to iterate over all the files in a directory is to use the glob() function to create an array of all the files that matches a specific file pattern and then use foreach() or one of the other looping methods to step through all the files. The glob() function looks in a single directory. In order to get files from subdirectories you must call the glob() function for each of them.

A second option is to use the opendir(), readdir(), and closedir() functions or the more object oriented approach with dir() that resturns an instance of the built-in class Directory. Since PHP 5.0 these funtions have supported the ftp:// URL wrapper.

Another option is to use one of the iterator classes that are included with the SPL extension. SPL stands for Standard PHP Library and it's an extension that is enabled by default. The iterator classes can be used directly with forech() and there is no need to read the contents of the file system into memory before iterating over the files.

How it Works

The next three examples show how to get the contents of a directory using the methods described above. The scripts will use the same directory as the script is located in and will print the name of each file and add a slash to the name if it's a directory.

```php
<?php
// 7_26.php

$pattern = "*";

$files = glob($pattern);
foreach ($files as $file) {
    echo $file;
    if (is_dir($file)) {
        echo "/";
    }
    echo "\n";
}
```

This method of getting the names of files in a directory works well for small number of files and for short paths. If you are looking at a directory with a long path or with many files it can consume too much memory.

```php
<?php
// 7_27.php

$dir = dir(".");
while (($file = $dir->read()) !== false) {
  echo $file;
  if (is_dir($file)) {
    echo "/";
  }
  echo "\n";
}
$dir->close();
```

In this example we only have one element of the directory in memory at any given time. Another difference is that his methods includes entries for './' and '../'. These are automatically excluded when the glob() function is used.

To do a similar thing with the SPL DirectoryIterators the could look like this:

```php
<?php
// 7_28.php

foreach (new DirectoryIterator('.') as $fileInfo) {
    if ($fileInfo->isDot()) continue;
    echo $fileInfo->getFilename();
    if ($fileInfo->isDir()) {
        echo "/";
    }
    echo "\n";
}
```

One advantage of using the SPL DirectoryIterator is it's very easy to make recursive although the behavior is slightly different.

```php
<?php
// 7_29.php

$iterator = new RecursiveDirectoryIterator('.',
  FilesystemIterator::CURRENT_AS_FILEINFO);
foreach (new RecursiveIteratorIterator($iterator) as $fileInfo) {
  if ($fileInfo->isDot()) continue;
  echo $fileInfo->getPathname();
  if ($fileInfo->isDir()) {
    echo "/";
  }
  echo "\n";
}
```

Recipe 7-13. Download Files

Problem

The standard output from a web server to a browser is some form of text file that contains HTML, JavaScript, CSS, or JSON content. The web server can also return other types of files that are supported by the browser for rendering (image and video files). But if the files are intended for other use than rendering in the browser, we need a way to download the content and save it to disk or have a different type of client consume it.

Solution

The standard web server configuration will know the mime type of a file based on its file extension. If the file is located in the directory structure available for the web server to serve files on you can in most cases simply link to the file directly and the browser will know that it don't know how to handle the file and it will save it to disk.

If the file is located outside of the available directory structure or the file has to be assembled based on input parameters you can use PHP to read or generate the file and use the header() function to specify Content-Type and Content-Disposition in order to help the browser handle the file as you intend. This is also useful if you want to download a file that contains HTML or an image and you want to prevent the browser from showing the file. This will cause the browser to show the save file dialog instead of just showing the content in the browser.

How it Works

If you have a link in your document that goes to an image you would create some html that looks like this:

```
<a href="myfile.gif"><img src="myfile.gif" /></a>
```

This will show an image and create a link to the same file so when the user click on the image the browser will simply show the image as the only content in the browser.

If you change the html to look like this:

```
<a href="myfile.php"><img src="myfile.gif" /></a>
```

You will need a PHP script to handle the rendering and also to set the headers. The script could look something like this:

```php
<?php
// 7_30.php

header("Content-Type: image/gif; Content-Disposition: attachment;");
readfile('myfile.gif');
```

This will tell the browser that the content of the response will be an image of type gif and it will also instruct the browser to open the save dialog rather than displaying the file. You can add more complicated logic to handle access control and generate the image on the fly or allow download of any file. Be sure to add a check to validate that the file can be downloaded. If not you might end up allowing users to download your php scripts or password files.

Recipe 7-14. Upload Files

Problem

The primary direction of content in a web environment is for a client (browser) to send a request to a server and retrieve the response in the form of a HTML document that then is rendered by the browser. The rendering process might send additional requests to the server or other servers to get additional content as identified by links in the original document. In this scenario the majority of the bites transferred are from the server to the client.

If you are building an application that requires the users to upload a picture or avatar, or you want to build a document library that holds files of many different kinds for other users to download you need a way to push files from the client to the server.

Using an FTP or SFTP server can solve this but they usually don't give you what you really need. These servers are simply a gateway to a preconfigured location on the file system where the user can create folders and upload files but the server does nothing to the files and there is usually no PHP integration. You could create a web-based API that would be called by the uploading application when the upload to the SFTP server is complete but that adds an extra layer of complexity and the user would not be able to perform the actions from a browser alsone.

Solution

Most modern browsers support multipart/form-data for the POST request and they allow you to include an input field of type file. This will instruct the browser to read one or more files off the local file system and send them to the server with the rest of the POST request. Only files selected by the user can be uploaded. If the target for the POST request is a PHP script the data will be available in the superglobals $_POST and $_FILES for processing by the script. The files will temporarily be stored in a folder specified by upload_dir in php.ini and they will be removed from that directory when the PHP request ends. It is up to the script to copy or move the file to its final destination.

The most modern browsers also supports a JavaScript based API for Form Data that will allow the user to use drag and drop of files from the local file system to a specific location in the browser window. This will trigger a JavaScript function that can read the file from the file system and create the post request. With this model it's possible to get accurate progress status without a separate process sending requests to the server every 500mS. The upload process does not have to be associated with a HTML form. This can be used to allow users easy access to upload a new profile image with a single drag and drop.

How it Works

The basic file upload has two components. The first is a HTML form with the attribute enctype set to multipart/form-data. The default is application/x-www-form-urlencoded and will cause the data to be encoded the same way as URL or query string parameters. The HTML form needs at least one input field of type file and could look something like this:

```
<html>
<body>
<form method="POST" enctype="multipart/form-data" action="/upload.php">
  <input type="file" name="file" />
  <button type="submit">Upload</button>
</form>
</body>
</html>
```

This will create a form that will allow the user to select a file from the local file system and click the submit button to send the file to the server. On the server there should be a PHP script to receive the file. In this case called upload.php. In the example below the PHP script simply displays the content of the $_FILES variable after the upload.

```php
<?php
// upload.php
header("Content-Type: text/plain");
print_r($_FILES);
```

And the output of this script shows information that looks like this:

```
Array (
    [file] => Array
        (
            [name] => myfile.gz
            [type] => application/x-gzip
            [tmp_name] => /tmp/php1zqVJF
            [error] => 0
            [size] => 23435
        )
)
```

This array provides meta data and a location for the temporary file that can be used for further processing. The file located in /tmp/php1zqVJF will be deleted automatically when the script ends and it can be copied/moved to the desired location is the function move_uploaded_file(). This function takes to parameters. The first is the path to the temporary file and the second is the path to the new location. It is also a good idea to call is_uploaded_file() before mofing the file.

Recipe 7-15. Zipped Files

Problem

Although the upload system can be used to select and upload multiple files to a web server it's only possible to download one file per request. If a user want's to download all the images in a gallery it can be a slow process to click on the links for each image and select where to save the file. It would be great if there were a way for the server to receive a single file for upload or to create a single file that contains multiple files for download.

Solution

The ZipArchive() class can be used to assemble or disassemble zip files on the server.

How it Works

A simple function to take all files in a directory on the server, zip them to a sinkle file and send the content as a response could look like this:

```php
<?php
// 7_31.php

ini_set("zlib.output_compression", "Off");

$files = glob('.');
if (!empty($files)) {
  $zip = new ZipArchive();
  $tmp_name = tempnam("/tmp", "zipfile");
  $res = $zip->open($tmp_name . ".zip", ZipArchive::CREATE);
  if ($res === true) {
    foreach($files as $file) {
      if (is_file($file) || is_link($file)) {
        $zip->addFile($file);
      }
    }
    $zip->close();
    if (file_exists($tmp_name . ".zip")) {
      $file_name = 'archive.zip';
      $file_size = filesize($tmp_name . ".zip");
      header('Content-Type: application/octet-stream; Content-Disposition: attachment');
      readfile($tmp_name . ".zip");
      unlink($tmp_name . ".zip");
      unlink($tmp_name);
    }
  }
}
```

First the output compression is turned off. Having this on can cause problems with the downloaded file and it's a zip file so it's already compressed.

Then we generate a list of files from the current directory. If there are files in the array the temporary archive is created in the /tmp folder. The zip file can easily be too large to handle in memory so it will be created on disk. If the creation is successful the files are added one by one, and finally if the zip file still exists we set the headers for downloading the file and send the file to the client. Any temporary files are removed at the end of the script.

Instead of uploading many individual files it might be faster, and fewer clicks in the browser, to zip the files locally, upload a single file, and unzip the files on the server so individual files can be accessed. The script to perform the unzip function could look something like the next example. The script should be called from a form POST request with at least one input field of type file, with the name file.

```php
<?php
// 7_32.php

// This script es expecting a a POST request from a form with at
// least one input
// <input type="file" name="file" />
```

```php
// This will generate the followng values in the $_FILES superglobal
// $_FILES['file']['error']
// $_FILES['file']['name']
// $_FILES['file']['tmp_name']
// $_FILES['file']['type']
// $_FILES['file']['size']

// Get the file extension from a file name
function GetExtension($file_name) {
        $arrParts = explode(".", $file_name);
        if (sizeof($arrParts) > 1) {
                return strtolower(end($arrParts));
        }
        else {
                return null;
        }
}

$res = false;
$ext = GetExtension($_FILES['file']['name']);
if ($ext == "zip") {
        $zip = new ZipArchive();
        $res = $zip->open($_FILES['file']['tmp_name']);
}
if ($res === true) {
        $zip->extractTo('folder');
        $zip->close();
}
```

■ ■ ■

## CHAPTER 8

Dynamic Imaging

Images uploaded to a web site might not always be usable as is. Images that come directly from a smart phone or high-resolution digital camera might have resolution/size that is too high to use on a web site. If the image is to be used as a profile image or thumbnail it might be a good idea to scale it down or crop a section out in order to get rid of irrelevant areas of the image. Scaling and cropping can be done with CSS, but that still requires the full image to be downloaded to the client and that would be a waste of bandwidth.

Using the GD extension in PHP makes it possible to perform these and many other image manipulation tasks on the server. This chapter will demonstrate how to perform these and many other tasks. The function names used in the examples are written in so-called camel case where the first letter of each word is capitalized. This is done for readability. All internal functions in PHP are case insensitive and can be written in any way you like, as long as all the letters are in the right order.

Recipe 8-1. Creating Images

Problem

Browsers can render a number of different image formats. These are all binary encodings of pixels and colors with or without compression. The most common are GIF, JPEG, and PNG. Although it would be possible to build images as a string of bytes according to the specifications of each file format, that is not practical and would most likely lead to performance problems.

Solution

The GD extension for PHP is a wrapper around a library called libgd as well as a number of other libraries to handle and create various image formats and compression. The libgd is bundled with PHP source code so it is relatively easy to enable the extension. The GD extension is also available in most distributions of Linux and it comes as a standard dll with the Windows version of PHP.

There are a couple of functions in the GD extensions to create images. This can be done by copying an image that exists in the file system with the functions ImageCreateFromJpeg(), ImageCreateFromGif(), ImageCreateFromPng(). PHP also supports the formats GD and GD2. These are not supported in browsers but can be used as the base format for creating images of other types.

The ImageCreateFrom*() functions all takes a single parameter that can be the path to a file from the local file system or a URL. In most case it is faster to load the image from the local file system but if images are shared among multiple servers it might be practical to use an URL to fetch the image before manipulation. If no manipulation is needed it will be faster to instruct the client to load the image directly from the URL or by using a simple HTTP redirect.

© Frank M. Kromann 2016
F.M. Kromann, *PHP and MySQL Recipes*, DOI 10.1007/978-1-4842-0605-8_8

Additionally the image can be created from a string with the function ImageCreateFromString(). This is useful if the image is stored in a database or other storage or the image is retrieved from an API call. The function will emit an error if the string passed in doesn't represent a valid image.

Finally it's possible to create a new blank image of a specified size. This is done with the functions ImageCreate() and ImageCreateTrueColor(). Both functions take two parameters: the width and height of the new image. It is recommended to use ImageCreateTrueColor() as it provides the highest quality of the image. Using ImageCreate() will create a palette based image where each pixel is represented by an index in the color palette. When using ImageCreateTrueColor() each pixel will be represented by the actual color.

Although PHP provides an automated cleanup when the script ends it is always a good idea to manually get rid of the image resources when they are no longer needed by the script. This is done by calling the function ImageDestroy().

How it Works

The simplest image is one where all the pixels have the same color. When you create a new blank image with ImageCreateTrueColor() that is what you will get. Depending on what format you want to send to the browser you can choose the output function that corresponds to it. In this example we create a small image of 50x50 pixels and use a query parameter f to select the format. If the parameter f is missing, empty, or an unsupported format the default format will be GIF.

```php
<?php
// 8_1.php

$img = ImageCreateTrueColor(50, 50);
$f = $_GET['f'] ?: 'gif';
switch (strtolower($f)) {
  case 'jpg' :
  case 'jpeg' :
    header('Content-Type: image/jpeg');
    ImageJPEG($img);
    break;
  case 'png' :
    header('Content-Type: image/png');
    ImagePNG($img);
    break;
  default :
    header('Content-Type: image/gif');
    ImageGIF($img);
    break;
}
ImageDestroy($img);
```

The standard value for the Content-Type from a PHP script is text/html. When the browser returns a stream of binary data, it's a good idea to help the browser understand what type of data it's getting. Modern browsers are able to look at the content of the data and determine what it is. This is especially the case with image data where the formats are well known. In this case we set the Content-Type to image/jpeg, image/png, or image/gif depending on the type of file requested.

If this script is executed form the command line it will produce a binary output starting with the letters GIF87a22?,223?????. If it's placed on a web server and requested from a browser it will provide a small black image.

Images with a single color are not that useful. In fact the same effect can be done with HTML and CSS without any impact to the server, but the example demonstrates the basic functionality of image generation. So let's move on to some more useful examples.

Recipe 8-2. Image Resize

Problem

On your web site you have a section that allows registered users to upload an image they can use as an avatar when they add comments to your blog. The user takes a selfie with the latest smart phone and uploads the image to your site. This will be a high-resolution image that takes up space and bandwidth each time a new visitor look at pages on your site. It is possible to scale the image in the browser, but that will still cause the high-resolution image to be transferred from the server to the browser at least once per visitor.

Solution

Building on the previous example we can create a script that loads an image from a file. And then it will calculate a smaller version of the same image. In order not to skew the image we will have to maintain the same aspect ratio as the original image. To get the size of the we can either use the functions ImagesX() and ImagesY() on the image resource or we can use GetImageSize(), which also returns additional information like the type of the image. When you know the width and height of the original image you can calculate the new width and height in order to stay within the borders of a fixed size. In the example the size of the scaled image is set to be within 160x120 pixels.

From PHP 5.6.3 you can provide -1 as the height and the scaling will be done so the aspect ratio is retained.

How it Works

The base image used in the example is named IMG_0099.JPG. It is 2048x1536 pixels wide and tall. First we look at the values returned by GetImageSize().

```php
<?php
// 8_2.php

$orig = GetImageSize('IMG_0099.JPG');
print_r($orig);
```

This will produce the following output:

```
Array
(
    [0] => 2048
    [1] => 1536
    [2] => 2
    [3] => width="2048" height="1536"
    [bits] => 8
    [channels] => 3
    [mime] => image/jpeg
)
```

The first two values contain the width and height. The third value is the image type. You can use the constants IMG_GIF, IMG_JPG, IMG_JPEG (same as IMG_JPG), IMG_PNG, IMG_WBPM, and IMG_XPM to compare the value to determine the type, or you can use the mime string directly. The third value is a string representation of the width and height and the values for bits and channels indicates the number of bits and channels. In this example the image has 8 bits and 3 channels allowing for 24 bits per pixel.

```php
<?php
// 8_3.php

$size = [160, 120];
$orig = GetImageSize('IMG_0099.JPG');

$a1 = $size[0] / $size[1];
$a2 = $orig[0] / $orig[1];

if ($a1 > $a2) {
  $d = ceil($orig[0] / $size[0]);
}
else {
  $d = ceil($orig[1] / $size[1]);
}
$w = $orig[0] / $d;
$h = $orig[1] / $d;
$img = ImageCreateFromJpeg('IMG_0099.JPG');
$thumb = ImageScale($img, $w, $h);
header('Content-Type: ' . $orig['mime']);
switch ($orig[2]) {
  case IMG_JPG :
  case IMG_JPEG :
    ImageJPEG($thumb);
    break;
  case IMG_PNG :
    ImagePNG($thumb);
    break;
  case IMG_GIF :
    ImageGIF($thumb);
    break;
}
ImageDestroy($thumb);
ImageDestroy($img);
```

First we calculate the aspect ratio of the new image ($a1) and the aspect ratio of the original. This is then used to determine the scaling factor based on the size ratio on either the width or height. This will ensure that both sizes are scaled with the same factor and that the whole image will fit in the smaller box.

This code assumes the original image is larger than the desired thumbnail. If it's smaller no scaling is needed and the original could be used as is.

At the end there are two calls to the ImageDestroy() function. This is because the ImageScale() creates a copy of the original resource and we need to get rid of both the original and the copy. ImageDestroy() only removes the image from memory. Use unlink() to delete the image file from disk.

The resulting image looks like this:

Recipe 8-3. Image Crop

Problem

In the previous example we made an effort to keep the same aspect ratio as the original image had. What if we want to create a square image from the uploaded image? In other words, scale the image based on the smallest side and cut off any part of the other dimension that won't fit within the square.

Solution

Instead of using the ImageScale() function we can use ImageCrop(). This is a relatively new function (PHP 5.5.0 and PHP 7.0.0). If you are using an older version of PHP you can use ImageCopyResampled() to achieve the same result. This function is used to copy a rectangular section of one image to a rectangular section of another image (or the same image) and it will resample the pixels to make the copy as smooth as possible. The ImageCrop() function takes two parameters. The first is an image resource for the original image and the second is an array with four values for x, y, width, and height of the section to return. The coordinates x, y is from the upper-left corner of the image.

How it Works

If we use the same image as before but want to crop and scale it to fit in a box of 150x150 pixels we first need to calculate which side to crop, and then calculate the x, y, width, and height to copy of the original image. When we have a square image it can be scaled to the size required. It is assumed that both width and height of the original image are larger than 150 px. There are no checks for this in the example but that could easily be added. There is no need to crop an image that already fits within the box.

```php
<?php
// 8_4.php

$size = [150, 150];
$orig = GetImageSize('IMG_0099.JPG');

$a1 = $orig[0] / $size[0];
$a2 = $orig[1] / $size[1];

if ($a1 < $a2) {
  $width = $size[0] * $a1;
  $height = $size[1] * $a1;
  $x = 0;
  $y = ($orig[1] - $height) / 2;
}
else {
  $width = $size[0] * $a2;
  $height = $size[1] * $a2;
  $x = ($orig[0] - $width) / 2;
  $y = 0;
}
$area = ['x' => $x, 'y' => $y, 'width' => $width, 'height' => $height];
$img = ImageCreateFromJpeg('IMG_0099.JPG');
$crop = ImageCrop($img, $area);
$thumb = ImageScale($crop, $size[0], $size[1]);
header('Content-Type: ' . $orig['mime']);
switch ($orig[2]) {
  case IMG_JPG :
  case IMG_JPEG :
    ImageJPEG($thumb);
    break;
  case IMG_PNG :
    ImagePNG($thumb);
    break;
  case IMG_GIF :
    ImageGIF($thumb);
    break;
}
ImageDestroy($thumb);
ImageDestroy($crop);
ImageDestroy($img);
```

In this example we end up with three image resources to free at the end of the script. The image created from this code is now a square with the center of the image.

If you are using an older version of PHP or just want to work with one less image resource you can use the ImageCopyResampled() function to achieve the same result.

```php
<?php
// 8_5.php

$size = [150, 150];
$orig = GetImageSize('IMG_0099.JPG');

$a1 = $orig[0] / $size[0];
$a2 = $orig[1] / $size[1];

if ($a1 < $a2) {
  $width = $size[0] * $a1;
  $height = $size[1] * $a1;
  $x = 0;
  $y = ($orig[1] - $height) / 2;
}
else {
  $width = $size[0] * $a2;
  $height = $size[1] * $a2;
  $x = ($orig[0] - $width) / 2;
  $y = 0;
}
$img = ImageCreateFromJpeg('IMG_0099.JPG');
$thumb = ImageCreateTrueColor($size[0], $size[1]);
ImageCopyResampled($thumb, $img, 0, 0, $x, $y, $size[0], $size[1], $width, $height);
header('Content-Type: ' . $orig['mime']);
switch ($orig[2]) {
  case IMG_JPG :
```

```
  case IMG_JPEG :
    ImageJPEG($thumb);
    break;
  case IMG_PNG :
    ImagePNG($thumb);
    break;
  case IMG_GIF :
    ImageGIF($thumb);
    break;
}
ImageDestroy($thumb);
ImageDestroy($img);
```

In this example we create a new blank image and we copy a resized section of the original image onto this image. There are 10 parameters to keep track of to the ImageCopyResampled() function. This include destination and source image and x, y, width, and height of both images.

Recipe 8-4. Image Rotate

Problem

Images that come from cell phones are either portrait or landscape (or something in between). Sometimes they even show up upside down depending on how the cell phone was held when the picture was taken. Cell phone software and some image viewing programs can use metadata in the image to correct this when showing the image. Typically browsers do not support that. When users upload images from phones they might want to rotate the image before sizing or cropping it.

Solution

Images can be rotated any number of degrees with the user of the ImageRotate() function. The rotation is measured anticlockwise. If you want to rotate an image 90 degrees clockwise either use -90 or 270 degrees as the rotation angle. As most of the image functions this one also takes an image resource as the first parameter. After that the angle of rotation followed by the color to use in any areas that's no longer covered by the image and finally an optional parameter to ignore transparent values.

The center of the rotation is the center of the original image. The rotated image might have other image dimensions compared to the original. If you rotate a square image 45 degrees you will end up with an image that is 1.41 times larger in both directions. If you rotate an image 180 degrees you will end up with an image with the exact same directions.

How it Works

The following example shows how to rotate an image 30 degrees. The background color of the new areas of the image is set to black.

```php
<?php
// 8_6.php

$orig = GetImageSize('IMG_0099.JPG');

$img = ImageCreateFromJpeg('IMG_0099.JPG');
$thumb = ImageRotate($img, 30, 0);
header('Content-Type: ' . $orig['mime']);
switch ($orig[2]) {
  case IMG_JPG :
  case IMG_JPEG :
    ImageJPEG($thumb);
    break;
  case IMG_PNG :
    ImagePNG($thumb);
    break;
  case IMG_GIF :
    ImageGIF($thumb);
    break;
}
ImageDestroy($thumb);
ImageDestroy($img);
```

Recipe 8-5. Image Flip

Problem

In the previous recipe we discussed how to rotate an image to correct for different camera orientation. What if you need to create a copy of the image that is the mirror image horizontally or vertically?

Solution

This can be handled with the ImageFlip() function.

■ **Note**   this function is only available if the GD extension is compiled with the bundled version of libgd.

The ImageFlip() function can flip the image horizontally, vertically or both, although flipping in both directions would be the same as a 180 degree rotation.

How it Works

ImageFlip() takes two parameters. The first is an image resource and the second is the flip direction. This can be one of the predefined constants: IMG_FLIP_HORIZONTAL, IMG_FLIP_VERTICAL or IMG_FLIP_BOTH.

```php
<?php
// 8_7.php

$orig = GetImageSize('IMG_0099.JPG');

$img = ImageCreateFromJpeg('IMG_0099.JPG');
ImageFlip($img, IMG_FLIP_HORIZONTAL);
header('Content-Type: ' . $orig['mime']);
switch ($orig[2]) {
  case IMG_JPG :
  case IMG_JPEG :
    ImageJPEG($img);
    break;
  case IMG_PNG :
    ImagePNG($img);
    break;
  case IMG_GIF :
    ImageGIF($img);
    break;
}
ImageDestroy($img);
```

The ImageFlip() function works slightly different compared to the copy and rotate functions. This function does not create a copy of the image but it simply flips the image in place (In memory. The file is not changed). No need to destroy extra copies at the end of the script.

Recipe 8-6. Adding a Watermark

Problem

If you are a photographer and want to show high-resolution images on your web site you might want to protect the images by adding a watermark. The same technology can be used if you are selling images for use on other web sites and you want to prevent the buyer from using images from your catalog pages without paying. In either case it's always a good idea to keep the original image and create a new copy when the files are uploaded and add the watermark to that image.

Solution

Watermarks can be as simple as adding a string of text somewhere on top of the image, but is can also be an image that is overlayed on top of the image. Add text will be covered in Recipe 8-10. This recipe will cover the merging of two images into one.

In recipe 8-3 we discussed image cropping and the use of the function ImageCopyResampled() was used to copy and resize a section of one image onto another image. We can use the same function to copy a small image onto a larger image.

How it Works

If all your images are the same size it's relatively straightforward to add a watermark to them, but if they are different sizes you might have to resize the watermark to fit on the image. I suggest creating a watermark file that is the same width as the widest image you are working with and then scale it down so it will fit on top of smaller images. If the size difference between the smallest and largest image are too big you can also create multiple watermarks and choose the one that fits best.

```php
<?php
// 8_8.php

$orig = GetImageSize('IMG_0099.JPG');
$wm = GetImageSize('watermark.png');

$img = ImageCreateFromJpeg('IMG_0099.JPG');
$watermark = ImageCreateFromPng('watermark.png');

if ($orig[0] > $wm[0]) {
  $width = $wm[0];
  $height = $wm[1];
  $x = ($orig[0] - $wm[0]) / 2;
  $y = ($orig[1] - $wm[1]) / 2;
}
else {
  $d = $orig[0] / $wm[0];
  $width = $orig[0];
  $height = $wm[1] * $d;
  $x = 0;
  $y = ($orig[1] - $height) / 2;
}

ImageCopyResampled($img, $watermark, $x, $y, 0, 0, $width, $height, $wm[0], $wm[1]);
header('Content-Type: ' . $orig['mime']);
switch ($orig[2]) {
  case IMG_JPG :
  case IMG_JPEG :
    ImageJPEG($img);
    break;
  case IMG_PNG :
    ImagePNG($img);
    break;
  case IMG_GIF :
    ImageGIF($img);
    break;
}
ImageDestroy($watermark);
ImageDestroy($img);
```

The calculation in the beginning compares the width of the original image to the width of the watermark. If the original image is wider than the watermark the watermark will be centered on the original image. If the watermark is wider the watermark will be scaled down to fit in the width. It will still be centered vertically.

If the original image is taller than it is wide or if you want a watermark that is narrow and tall you will need to modify the calculations of x, y, width, and height, but the same logic for adding the watermark can be used.

Recipe 8-7. Changing Colors

Problem

When working with images, creating them from scratch or adding to existing images, there is a need to define the colors used for the objects that are added to the image.

Solution

Bitmapped images are generally represented by pixels where each pixel is provided a color and perhaps some transparency/opacity. Depending on the image format and image compression the way these are handled varies. The gd extension uses an internal GD/GD2 format to represent the image and when the final image is generated for output the format is converted to the target format.

In the GD format each color is placed in a palette where an index points to a specific color. When you add color to a pixel in the image you simply tell the system to use a specific index. If you later want to change all the pixels of a given color you can just change the color for that index and all pixels with that index will change color.

This concept then requires the allocation of colors in the palette before the color can be used. If you are using an existing image the palette will be initialized with all the different colors already used in the image, but if you are starting from scratch the palette will be empty. There are three functions used to allocate and deallocate colors in the image; these are called ImageColorAllocate(), ImageColorAlocateAlpha(), and ImageColorDeallocate(). The first color allocated will define the background color of the image. As shown in recipe 8-1, when a blank image is created using ImageCreate(), the background color will be black, unless you define it with a call to one of the allocate functions. The allocation functions use three integer values between 0 and 255 for each of the color components (red, green, and blue). If you are allocating a color with alpha transparency you need a fourth value to indicate the amount of transparency. This is a value between 0 and 127 where 0 indicates opaque and 127 is total transparency.

How it Works

If we take the code from example 8_1.php, change the ImageCreateTrueColor() to ImageCreate() and add a line to allocate a yellow color, the image generated will no longer be black.

```php
<?php
// 8_9.php

$img = ImageCreate(50, 50);
ImageColorAllocate($img, 0xe3, 0xda, 0x2b);
$f = $_GET['f'] ?: 'gif';
```

```php
switch (strtolower($f)) {
  case 'jpg' :
  case 'jpeg' :
    header('Content-Type: image/jpeg');
    ImageJPEG($img);
    break;
  case 'png' :
    header('Content-Type: image/png');
    ImagePNG($img);
    break;
  default :
    header('Content-Type: image/gif');
    ImageGIF($img);
    break;
}
ImageDestroy($img);
```

You can also do the same with `ImageCreateTrueColor()` but then you would have to set the color of all the pixels. This can be done with the `ImageFill()` function. This performs a flood fill function that takes four parameters. The first is a valid image resource, the second and third parameters are the X and Y coordinates of where the fill should start and the last argument is the color of the fill. On a blank image it's common to start the fill at the upper-left corner (0,0).

```php
<?php
// 8_10.php

$img = ImageCreateTrueColor(50, 50);
$col = ImageColorAllocate($img, 0xe3, 0xda, 0x2b);
ImageFill($img, 0, 0, $col);
$f = $_GET['f'] ?: 'gif';
switch (strtolower($f)) {
  case 'jpg' :
  case 'jpeg' :
    header('Content-Type: image/jpeg');
    ImageJPEG($img);
    break;
  case 'png' :
    header('Content-Type: image/png');
    ImagePNG($img);
    break;
  default :
    header('Content-Type: image/gif');
    ImageGIF($img);
    break;
}
ImageDestroy($img);
```

When working with truecolor images it is not necessary to allocate the color before using it. The index and the RGB value of the color are going to be the same.

```php
<?php
// 8_11.php

$img = ImageCreateTrueColor(50, 50);
ImageFill($img, 0, 0, 0xe3da2b);
$f = $_GET['f'] ?: 'gif';
switch (strtolower($f)) {
  case 'jpg' :
  case 'jpeg' :
    header('Content-Type: image/jpeg');
    ImageJPEG($img);
    break;
  case 'png' :
    header('Content-Type: image/png');
    ImagePNG($img);
    break;
  default :
    header('Content-Type: image/gif');
    ImageGIF($img);
    break;
}
ImageDestroy($img);
```

Recipe 8-8. Draw on Images

Problem

We have seen how to scale, crop, and even merge images but what about adding things to an image? Is there a way to draw pixels, lines, and other shapes on a blank image or even an existing image?

Solution

The gd extension provides a long list of functions to manipulate the content of an image ranging from setting the color of a single pixel to drawing of lines, squares, arches, and ellipses, etc. All the drawing functions work on an image resource, a color one, or more coordinate sets and other parameters used to define the shape.

How it Works

The simplest drawing function is the one that sets the color of a single pixel. We can use that to create an image with a white background and 10 randomly placed black dots.

```php
<?php
// 8_12.php

$img = ImageCreateTrueColor(50, 50);
ImageFill($img, 0, 0, 0xffffff);
for ($i = 0; $i < 10; $i++) {
  $x = mt_rand(0, 49);
  $y = mt_rand(0, 49);
  ImageSetPixel($img, $x, $y, 0);
}
$f = $_GET['f'] ?: 'gif';
switch (strtolower($f)) {
  case 'jpg' :
  case 'jpeg' :
    header('Content-Type: image/jpeg');
    ImageJPEG($img);
    break;
  case 'png' :
    header('Content-Type: image/png');
    ImagePNG($img);
    break;
  default :
    header('Content-Type: image/gif');
    ImageGIF($img);
    break;
}
ImageDestroy($img);
```

This will generate an image that looks like this:

Note that the coordinates are 0 based. The image is 50x50 pixels in size but the coordinates of each pixel goes from 0, 0 to 49, 49.

Now we can move on to more advanced shapes. The function to draw a line takes two sets of coordinates indicating the starting and ending point of the line. The next example will draw three lines starting and ending at random locations but all connected as one line.

```php
<?php
// 8_13.php

$img = ImageCreateTrueColor(50, 50);
ImageFill($img, 0, 0, 0xffffff);
$sx = mt_rand(0, 49);
$sy = mt_rand(0, 49);

for ($i = 0; $i < 3; $i++) {
  $x = mt_rand(0, 49);
  $y = mt_rand(0, 49);
  ImageLine($img, $sx, $sy, $x, $y, 0);
  $sx = $x;
  $sy = $y;
}
$f = $_GET['f'] ?: 'gif';
switch (strtolower($f)) {
  case 'jpg' :
  case 'jpeg' :
    header('Content-Type: image/jpeg');
    ImageJPEG($img);
    break;
  case 'png' :
    header('Content-Type: image/png');
    ImagePNG($img);
    break;
  default :
    header('Content-Type: image/gif');
    ImageGIF($img);
    break;
}
ImageDestroy($img);
```

The resulting image could look like this:

As you can see the lines are created with a width of a single pixel so they will not look quite as straight lines unless they are vertical or horizontal.

To get lines that look better (a bit more smooth) you can turn on the initializing mode. This will cause the drawing functions to blend the line color with the background color. This only works for true color images and there is no support for alpha components (transparency). The next example shows the difference between two lines drawn without and with the antialias turned on.

```php
<?php
// 8_14.php

$img = ImageCreateTrueColor(100, 50);
ImageFill($img, 0, 0, 0xffffff);
ImageLine($img, 0, 49, 49, 0, 0);
ImageAntialias($img, true);
ImageLine($img, 49, 49, 99, 0, 0);

$f = $_GET['f'] ?: 'gif';
switch (strtolower($f)) {
  case 'jpg' :
  case 'jpeg' :
    header('Content-Type: image/jpeg');
    ImageJPEG($img);
    break;
  case 'png' :
    header('Content-Type: image/png');
    ImagePNG($img);
    break;
  default :
    header('Content-Type: image/gif');
    ImageGIF($img);
    break;
}
ImageDestroy($img);
```

Note how the second line has some gray pixels on either side to make it look smoother. The gray is chosen automatically because the background is white and the line is black. Other color combinations will give different colors.

There are two functions to draw rectangles: one that draws an outline and one that fills the rectangle. These are called ImageRectabgle() and ImageFilledRectangle(). Both functions work with two sets of coordinates. This limits the shape to have all sides parallel to the edges of the image. If you need a rectangle placed at different angles you can either create a small image, rotate it, and merge it on to the large image or you can use the ImagePolygon() function.

The next example draws a red square at a random location on the image:

```php
<?php
// 8_15.php

$img = ImageCreateTrueColor(50, 50);
ImageFill($img, 0, 0, 0xffffff);
$x1 = mt_rand(0, 49);
$y1 = mt_rand(0, 49);
$x2 = mt_rand(0, 49);
```

```php
$y2 = mt_rand(0, 49);
ImageRectangle($img, $x1, $y1, $x2, $y2, OxFF0000);
$f = $_GET['f'] ?: 'gif';
switch (strtolower($f)) {
  case 'jpg' :
  case 'jpeg' :
    header('Content-Type: image/jpeg');
    ImageJPEG($img);
    break;
  case 'png' :
    header('Content-Type: image/png');
    ImagePNG($img);
    break;
  default :
    header('Content-Type: image/gif');
    ImageGIF($img);
    break;
}
ImageDestroy($img);
```

This can easily be modified to draw a filled square by changing the function call to ImageFilledRectangle() with the same parameters. This function is commonly used to draw patterns using a loop to iterate over a set of data points. If you have two rectangles that are overlapping each other you can use the ImageFillToBorder() function to fill only the area that's overlapping as shown in the next example where two red rectangles are drawn and the overlapping area is colored in a different color.

```php
<?php
// 8_16.php

$img = ImageCreateTrueColor(50, 50);
ImageFill($img, 0, 0, Oxffffff);
$x1 = 1; $y1 = 1; $x2 = 35;$y2 = 35;
ImageRectangle($img, $x1, $y1, $x2, $y2, OxFF0000);
$x1 = 15; $y1 = 15; $x2 = 48;$y2 = 48;
ImageRectangle($img, $x1, $y1, $x2, $y2, OxFF0000);
ImageFillToBorder($img, 16, 16, OxFF0000, Ox00FFFF);
$f = $_GET['f'] ?: 'gif';
switch (strtolower($f)) {
  case 'jpg' :
  case 'jpeg' :
    header('Content-Type: image/jpeg');
    ImageJPEG($img);
```

```php
    break;
  case 'png' :
    header('Content-Type: image/png');
    ImagePNG($img);
    break;
  default :
    header('Content-Type: image/gif');
    ImageGIF($img);
    break;
}
ImageDestroy($img);
```

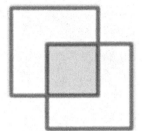

A circle is a special form of an ellipse where the width and height are the same value. The ImageEllipse() function is used to draw these shapes. The width of the ellipse is always parallel to the X axis and the height is parallel to the Y axis of the image.

```php
<?php
// 8_17.php

$img = ImageCreateTrueColor(50, 50);
ImageFill($img, 0, 0, 0xffffff);
ImageFilledEllipse($img, 20, 20, 20, 10, 0xFF0000);
$f = $_GET['f'] ?: 'gif';
switch (strtolower($f)) {
  case 'jpg' :
  case 'jpeg' :
    header('Content-Type: image/jpeg');
    ImageJPEG($img);
    break;
  case 'png' :
    header('Content-Type: image/png');
    ImagePNG($img);
    break;
  default :
    header('Content-Type: image/gif');
    ImageGIF($img);
    break;
}
ImageDestroy($img);
```

The final drawing functions in this recipe are `ImageArc()` and `ImagePolygon()`, and as the name indicates these functions will draw an arch and a polygon. The center coordinates – width, height, and start and stop angles as well as a color describe the arc. Drawing an arch with 360 degrees between a start and stop angle will draw an ellipse.

```php
<?php
// 8_18.php

$img = ImageCreateTrueColor(50, 50);
ImageFill($img, 0, 0, 0xffffff);
ImageFilledArc($img, 5, 25, 70, 70, -45, 45, 0xFF0000, IMG_ARC_PIE);
$f = $_GET['f'] ?: 'gif';
switch (strtolower($f)) {
  case 'jpg' :
  case 'jpeg' :
    header('Content-Type: image/jpeg');
    ImageJPEG($img);
    break;
  case 'png' :
    header('Content-Type: image/png');
    ImagePNG($img);
    break;
  default :
    header('Content-Type: image/gif');
    ImageGIF($img);
    break;
}
ImageDestroy($img);
```

Note how the width and height is wider than the width and height of the image. The width and height represent the size of the ellipse if it was drawn from 0 to 360 degrees.

The last parameter called style determines how the object is drawn. This is a bitmapped value with four different options. `IMG_ARC_PIE` will draw a rounded arch and `IMG_ARC_CHORD` will connect the two points from the start to end angle with a straight line. These two values are mutually exclusive. The last two options are `IMG_ARC_NOFILL` (make it an outline) and `IMG_ARC_EDGED` (connect the point at the starting and ending angle to the center).

The ImageFilledArc() and ImageFilledPolygon() take the same parameters but will fill the object entirely with the drawing color.

So far we have seen how to draw objects described with a number of integer or float values. The ImagePolygon() function is a bit different because it works on an arbitrary number of points or coordinates. The coordinates are passed to the function as an array of integer values. Two integer values are needed for each point. The function needs at least three points to create a polygon. The last side of the polygon, the one that connects the last point to the first is handled automatically. No need to add the starting point as the last point of the array.

```php
<?php
// 8_19.php

$img = ImageCreateTrueColor(50, 50);
ImageFill($img, 0, 0, 0xffffff);
$points = [
  10, 10,
   45, 5,
   25, 25,
   45, 45,
   10, 40
];
ImagePolygon($img, $points, sizeof($points) / 2,  0xFF0000);
$f = $_GET['f'] ?: 'gif';
switch (strtolower($f)) {
  case 'jpg' :
  case 'jpeg' :
    header('Content-Type: image/jpeg');
    ImageJPEG($img);
    break;
  case 'png' :
    header('Content-Type: image/png');
    ImagePNG($img);
    break;
  default :
    header('Content-Type: image/gif');
    ImageGIF($img);
    break;
}
ImageDestroy($img);
```

Recipe 8-9. Transparency

Problem

Images are represented with a square box of a given width and height. If you draw objects on the image you might not use the entire canvas down to every last pixel. Placing an image on top of a web page will show all the pixels of the image, unless there is a way to make them transparent so that the background behind the image is visible through part of the image.

Solution

Some image formats (GIF and PNG) supports transparent pixels. Transparency is not supported with the JPEG format.

Images created with the GD extension can have one of the colors defined as the transparent color or it's possible to set partial transparency on specific colors to allow the background to be partially visible. This is called alpha blending. To create a color with transparency use the function ImageColorAllocateAlpha().

How it Works

The simple way to set transparency is to use a specific color, that's not otherwise used in the image and convert that color to transparent. This can be done like this:

```php
<?php
// 8_20.php

$img = ImageCreateTrueColor(50, 50);
ImageFill($img, 0, 0, 0xffffff);
ImageColorTransparent($img, 0);
ImageLine($img, 10, 10, 40, 10, 0xFF0000);
ImageLine($img, 10, 30, 40, 30, 0);
$f = $_GET['f'] ?: 'gif';
switch (strtolower($f)) {
  case 'jpg' :
  case 'jpeg' :
    header('Content-Type: image/jpeg');
    ImageJPEG($img);
    break;
  case 'png' :
    header('Content-Type: image/png');
    ImagePNG($img);
    break;
  default :
    header('Content-Type: image/gif');
    ImageGIF($img);
    break;
}
ImageDestroy($img);
```

First the image is created with the size 50x50 pixels. Then the background is filled with the color white. The transparent color is selected to black. This can happen at any time before the image is rendered. The two lines that are drawn with the red and black colors will behave differently when the image is used. As shown in the next image where the image is covering a colored background, the red line shows up as red but the black is the same color as the background.

Recipe 8-10. Adding Text

Problem

In the past few recipes we have seen how to draw on images and merge one image onto another image, but what if you want to add text? Can you use fonts or can it only be done with a system-defined font?

Solution

Depending on how PHP and the GD extension is compiled there are a few options to add text. The basic functionality is provided with the function ImageString(). This function will insert a string using one of five built-in fonts or you can use ImageLoadFont() to load a GD font. These font files must be generated on the same CPU architecture as they are being used on. This function can only draw horizontal text.

In addition to this PHP can be compiled with FreeType support. When this is enabled you can use and TrueType font (.ttf) from your computer to render text on your images. The function ImageTTFText() is used to draw text with a TrueType font. The fonts used must be located on the server but there is no need to have them installed on the client computer.

Using TrueType fonts makes it difficult to know the size (in pixels) of the resulting string. The size will depend on the font, font size and the characters written. The function ImageTTFBox() can be used to calculate the size of the surrounding box for a given text. This is useful if you want to check if a given string fits on the image or you want to center the text.

How it Works

The first example shows how to use the ImageString() function to add a text to an image.

```php
<?php
// 8_21.php

$img = ImageCreateTrueColor(250, 50);
ImageFill($img, 0, 0, 0xffffff);
ImageString($img, 4, 10, 10, "PHP Recipes", 0);
$f = $_GET['f'] ?: 'gif';
switch (strtolower($f)) {
  case 'jpg' :
  case 'jpeg' :
    header('Content-Type: image/jpeg');
    ImageJPEG($img);
    break;
  case 'png' :
    header('Content-Type: image/png');
    ImagePNG($img);
    break;
  default :
    header('Content-Type: image/gif');
    ImageGIF($img);
    break;
}
ImageDestroy($img);
```

This will generate an image like the one shown below:

PHP Recipes

There is a similar function called ImageChar(). In general it takes the same parameters as ImageString but it will only draw the first character of the string value passed.

To create a similar image using TrueType fonts you need a version of PHP where TrueType/FreeType is compiled into the GD extension. This is not standard on Mac OSX but it's available on most Linux distributions. The code would look something like this:

```php
<?php
// 8_22.php

$img = ImageCreateTrueColor(250, 50);
ImageFill($img, 0, 0, 0xffffff);
ImageTTFText($img, 12, -10, 10, 10, 0, "Verdana.ttf", "PHP Recipes");
$f = $_GET['f'] ?: 'gif';
switch (strtolower($f)) {
  case 'jpg' :
  case 'jpeg' :
    header('Content-Type: image/jpeg');
    ImageJPEG($img);
    break;
  case 'png' :
```

```
    header('Content-Type: image/png');
    ImagePNG($img);
    break;
  default :
    header('Content-Type: image/gif');
    ImageGIF($img);
    break;
}
ImageDestroy($img);
```

And the resulting output would be an image with the text:

Besides the fact the text is slanted on a 10 degree angle there is another difference between the two ways of drawing text. This has to do with the positioning of the text. `ImageString()` takes the upper-left corner of the text and places it at the coordinates specified in the function call. The function `ImageTTFText()` takes the lower-left corner and positions it at the coordinates provided.

Recipe 8-11. Caching Images

Problem

Although images can be created, scaled, and rotated, etc., it is not optimal to do so on every request. These image manipulations take many CPU cycles and, to some extent, memory. Holding onto these resources for a long time will reduce the number of requests the server is capable of handling within a given time frame.

Solution

Images that can be generated once and stored on the disk to be shared with other users will provide a much better performance. The very first user who is accessing an image could experience load time if the image generation is handled as part of the request. If this becomes a problem the image generation can be linked to the upload process or an offline process that detects new images and generates the needed files.

How it Works

This example is an extension to Recipe 8-6 for adding a watermark to an image. If your web site is hosting images that you want to protect from being copied and used elsewhere you might create lower resolution versions and add a watermark with your logo. Instead of doing this on every request a caching system can be implemented that checks if the requested image exists on the desk and use that instead.

In the next example a script takes three parameters (file name and maximum width) to show how we can look for a previously generated image and use that if it exists; otherwise create a new image based on the parameters, save it to disk for the next request, and return it to the user.

```php
<?php
// 8_23.php

$file = $_REQUEST['file'] ?: 'IMG_0099.JPG';
$max_width = $_REQUEST['w'] ?: 600;

if (file_exists($file)) {
  $orig = GetImageSize($file);
  header('Content-Type: ' . $orig['mime']);
  header('Content-Disposition: inline;  filename="'. $file . '"');

  if (!file_exists("_" . $file)) {
    if ($orig[0] > $max_width) {
      $src = ImageCreateFromJpeg($file);
      $img = ImageScale($src, $max_width);
      ImageDestroy($src);
      $orig[0] = ImageSX($img);
      $orig[1] = ImageSY($img);
    }
    else {
      $img = ImageCreateFromJpeg($file);
    }
    $wm = GetImageSize('watermark.png');
    $watermark = ImageCreateFromPng('watermark.png');
    if ($orig[0] > $wm[0]) {
      $width = $wm[0];
      $height = $wm[1];
      $x = ($orig[0] - $wm[0]) / 2;
      $y = ($orig[1] - $wm[1]) / 2;
    }
    else {
      $d = $orig[0] / $wm[0];
      $width = $orig[0];
      $height = $wm[1] * $d;
      $x = 0;
      $y = ($orig[1] - $height) / 2;
    }
    ImageCopyResampled($img, $watermark, $x, $y, 0, 0,
                       $width, $height, $wm[0], $wm[1]);
    switch ($orig[2]) {
      case IMG_JPG :
      case IMG_JPEG :
        ImageJPEG($img, '_' . $file);
        break;
      case IMG_PNG :
        ImagePNG($img, '_' . $file);
        break;
      case IMG_GIF :
        ImageGIF($img, '_' . $file);
        break;
    }
```

```
        ImageDestroy($watermark);
        ImageDestroy($img);
    }
    readfile("_" . $file);
}
```

The first step is to get two parameters for file name and max width. Then there is a check for a cached version of the file. In this case an underscore is used in front of the filename to indicate that the file is cached. We could also include the width of this image. This will allow us to have multiple versions of the same image cached. This could be one for thumbnail and one for a preview, for example. If the cached file is missing the script will scale the image to the max size if needed and then add the watermark. In this case the three Image...() functions use an extra parameter that will cause the image to be saved to disk instead of returned to the client. The last step is to read the image file from disk and send it to the client.

CHAPTER 9

■ ■ ■

Regular Expressions

PHP is often described as a templating language where HTML sections and script are mixed to generate HTML documents for rendering in a browser. As the web technology is advancing PHP is used to generate other types of content (JSON, see chapter 14; and images see chapter 8, etc.) and the PHP scripts contain less embedded HTML sections. Instead the script will read a template from disk or a database and perform string replacements on the content before sending it to the client.

Simple string replacements can be done with the str_replace() function, but this function will replace a fixed string of characters with a different string of characters and unless the str_ireplace() version of the function is used the replacement is case sensitive. It is possible to create other types of logic with the use of the str_pos() and substr() functions, but that often ends up creating complex logic that can be difficult to maintain, and because it's written in PHP it might not be the most efficient use of resources.

With the Regular Expression functions it is possible to do advanced search and/or replace functionality with very few lines of code. The syntax for regular expressions is very powerful but can sometimes be hard to understand.

In the early days of PHP the regular expressions were made up of a few system functions: ereg(), erigi(), ereg_replace(), and eregi_replace(). These functions were deprecated in PHP 5.3 and removed completely in PHP 7.0. The functions are replaced with a more powerful library called Perl Compatible Regular Expressions (PCRE). The PCRE library is bundled with the PHP source and is enabled standardly by most PHP distributions on Linux, OSX, and Windows.

The heart of regular expressions is a pattern or sequence of characters that describes the expression. The expression is made of a number of components called metacharacters, character classes, subpatterns, qualifiers, and branches.

A metacharacter is a regular character with a special meaning for the expression. This can be an escape character that can change the meaning of the character following the escape. The backslash '\' character is used as the escape character and it will turn the character 'n' into a new line by adding the backslash in front '\n'. It can also be used to turn a metacharacter into a regular character like '\ (' or '\)' etc. Table 9-1 shows a full list of supported metacharacters.

Table 9-1. *Meta characters*

\	Escape character
^	Matches the beginning of the string or line
$	Matches the end of string or line
[	Start of character class
]	End of character class
(	Start of subpattern
)	End of subpattern
.	Match any character
*	Qualifier to repeat 0 or more times
+	Qualifier to repeat 1 or more times
{	Start qualifier range
}	End qualifier range
?	Allows the pattern to be there or not

A character class is defined with square brackets []. This can define a list or range of characters. [abc] will match any of the characters a, b, or c and [a-z] will match any character between a and z. A character call will match a single character in the subject string, but they can be used with repetitions to match any number of characters all being defined by the character class.

Subexpressions or subpatterns are created with regular parentheses () and are used for both grouping and to extract specific portions of a pattern for further use.

Finally the qualifiers are used to indicate that something is repeated. The asterisk * indicates 0 or more repetitions, the plus + indicates 1 or more repetitions, and with the use of curly brackets {} you can specify either a fixed number of repetitions or a range like {3,7}, which will take the pattern before the qualifier and allow repetition between 3 and 7 times. The asterisk and plus are short for {0,} and {1,} indicating 0 or more and 1 or more. The same way the question mark could be written as {0,1} meaning 0 or 1 of the preceding element.

The repetition qualifiers can be used after a single character as a{1,3} indicates a string with 1, 2, or 3 a's. When used after a character class [^"]* it means that the class defines any character but the double quotes and is repeated 0 or more times. And if used with a subpattern ([a-z0-9]+\.){2,4}, it indicates that the pattern must match a string of 2 to 4 sections where each section contains 1 or more characters from a-z or the numbers 0-9, and each section is ended with a period.

There are three metacharacters, as listed in Table 9-2, that can be used inside a character class. Besides the general escape character it's the ^ for negation and the – for ranges.

Table 9-2. *Metacharacters in a character class*

\	General escape character
^	Negate. When used as the first character in a character class the class will match any character but the one listed in the class
-	Range separator

There are a number of characters that gives a special meaning when they are preceded by the escape character. Some of these are listed in Table 9-3. Please see the PHP documentation for a full list: http://php.net/manual/en/regexp.reference.escape.php.

Table 9-3. *Special characters*

\b	A word boundary. This can be a space, a period, or other characters.
\d	A decimal digit
\D	Any character that is not a decimal digit
\n	New line
\r	Carriage return
\t	Tab
\s	A whitespace character (space, newline, tab, etc.)
\S	A character that is not a whitespace character

This concludes the brief description of the building blocks of a regular expression. In practice there is a bit more to it. The expression is typically placed between two slashes and when used in PHP you also need to place the entire expression in quotes to create a string. In JavaScript it's not necessary to create the expression as a string as the language natively supports the regular expression. A regular expression that matches any instance of the word 'new' is written like this: /new/.

Although the / is commonly used as the delimiter it is also valid to use a hash sign (#), plus (+), and percentage (%). /new/, #new#, +new+ and %new% are all the same regular expression.

One benefit of using different delimiters is it eliminates the need to use the escape character. If you want to create a regular expression that matches a specific protocol like http:// it would be written as this when the / delimiter is used:

`/http:\/\/(.*)/`

And by using the # delimiter it would look like this:

`#http://(.*)#`

This is perhaps a bit more readable but both provide the exact same result.

In addition to the building blocks of regular expressions there are a couple of modifiers. These are identified by characters placed after the closing delimiter (/). In PHP there are a number of modifiers that can be used to change how the expression works. Table 9-4 lists some of these. A full list can be found here: http://php.net/manual/en/reference.pcre.pattern.modifiers.php.

Table 9-4. *Modifiers*

i	Make the pattern case insensitive.
m	Treat the subject as a multiline subject. Without this modifier the pattern will be treated as a single line string where ^ and $ will match the beginning and ending of the string, even if the string contains new line characters. If the m modifier is used ^ and $ will match the beginning and end of each line in the string.
s	Changes how the dot (.) metacharacter works. Without this modifier the dot will not match newline characters.
u	This modifier will cause the pattern and subject strings to be treated as UTF-8 encoded strings.

With the expression from before /new/ we can add a modifier that will match all possible upper- and lowercase versions of the word new by assigning the I modifier /new/i.

Recipe 9-1. Format Validation

Problem

Regular expressions can be used in both PHP and Javascript to validate the input from a user. Validating the input in the browser with Javascript can be used to prevent the submission of a form with invalid data, but the data should still be validated on the server side as there is no guarantee that the client validated the content before submitting the request. The post could come from a non-browser-based client.

How can we use regular expressions to validate things like e-mail addresses or phone numbers?

Solution

Any content validation starts with a definition of the pattern to validate. An e-mail address will always contain some letters and/or numbers followed by the @ character, followed by more letters and numbers then a dot and some more letters. A simple validation pattern can be created with a character class, the @ character, another character class, a dot, and a final character class.

```
/[a-zA-Z0-9]+@[a-zA-Z0-9]+\.[a-zA-Z0-9]+/
```

This can be made a bit shorter by using the case insensitive modifier.

```
/[a-z0-9]+@[a-z0-9]+\.[a-z0-9]+/i
```

In this example we allow characters from a-z and A-Z as well as numbers in all three character classes and the + sign after each indicates that we need at least one character from the character class in each of these locations.

Not too long ago the top-level domain (the characters after the last dot) was two or three characters but lately top-level domains with more letters such as f.eks. .info, .software, and other longer names require that more characters are allowed.

A phone number also follows some patterns. Depending of the country those patterns might vary a bit. A U.S. phone number is usually described with the country code 1 followed by 10 digits. These digits are often separated with spaces, dashes, parentheses, etc., to increase readability.

The pattern to validate a U.S. phone number could look something like this:

1?\d{7}|\d{10} this will allow an optional leading 1 for the country code and 7 or 10 digits. This format will not allow the user to enter spaces or other characters and we could allow for that by extending the expression to 1?\d{7}|\d{10}|(\d{3} \d{3} \d{4}), or written as the full regular expression:

```
/1?\d{7}|\d{10}|(\d{3} \d{3} \d{4})/
```

This pattern will allow a string that starts with an optional one followed by one of 3 options; 7 digits, 10 digits or 10 digits with 3 spaces in the format ### ### ####.

How it Works

In this first example we take the input from a post request that contains a value with the name e-mail. Only if the field contains a valid e-mail address will it be added to the database.

```php
<?php
// 9_1.php

function AddEmail($email) {
  // do the database query.
  echo "$email was added to the database\n";
}

if ($_POST['email']) {
  if (preg_match("/[a-z0-9]+@[a-z0-9]+\.[a-z0-9]+/i", $_POST['email'])) {
    AddEmail($_POST['email']);
  }
}
```

It is assumed that the function AddEmail() will take an e-mail address and add a row to a database table.

The function of interest in this example is the preg_match() function. This function takes at least two parameters where the first is the pattern and the second is the subject. If the subject matches the pattern it will return true; otherwise it will return false.

With the expression used above it would be possible for the user to enter more than the valid e-mail address and get that full string inserted into the database. This can be prevented by using the third parameter, called $matches. This is used to return the actual values that match the pattern. $matches will return an array of all the strings that match. So instead of calling the AddEmail() function with the input provided by the user we take the value that is returned from the preg_match() function.

```php
<?php
// 9_2.php

function AddEmail($email) {
  // do the database query.
  echo "$email was added to the database\n";
}

if ($_POST['email']) {
  if (preg_match("/[a-z0-9]+@[a-z0-9]+\.[a-z0-9]+/i",
                 $_POST['email'],
                 $matches)) {
    AddEmail($matches);
  }
}
```

With this code the user can write "email@example.com," "My Name email@example.com," or "My Name <email@example.com>" and the regular expression will pick out the e-mail address portion and add just that to the database.

In the next example we will look closer at the phone number example from before. With the pattern /1?\d{7,10}|(\d{3} \d{3} \d{4})/ there is no need to use the I modifier as only digital digits are of interest, but it might be useful to get rid of anything that is not a digit before inserting the number into the database. This can be done with the preg_replace() function. This function works a bit like str_replace() but instead of matching one or more predefined strings it uses a regular expression to find the sections of the string to replace. If we assume the user can enter numbers, spaces, dots, dashes, and parentheses in the phone number field we could get rid of those with the use of the str_replace() function by doing something like this:

```php
<?php
// 9_3.php

$phone = str_replace([' ','.','-','(',')'],
                     ['','','','',''],
                     $_POST['phone']);
```

To do the same operation with a regular expression, we use a character class that defines anything that is not a digit [^\d] and replace that with the empty string. The regular expression will get rid of anything that is not a digit. In the example above it's only the special characters listed in the first array that will be removed.

```php
<?php
// 9_4.php

$phone = preg_replace("/[^\d]/", "", $_POST['phone']);
```

With all the non-digits removed it's easy to perform the validation to check if the user entered enough digits for the number to be a valid U.S. phone number. That would require 10 or 11 digits with the first digit being a 1. Checking the length of the string alone will not work but the check could be done without regular expressions:

```php
<?php
// 9_5.php

$phone = preg_replace("/[^\d]/", "", $_POST['phone']);
if (strlen($phone) == 10 || (strlen($phone) == 11 && $phone[0] == '1')) {
  echo "$phone is a valid US number\n";
}
```

To do the same check with a regular expression would be a bit shorter:

```php
<?php
// 9_6.php

$phone = preg_replace("/[^\d]/", "", $_POST['phone']);
if (preg_match("/^1?\d{10}$/", $phone)) {
  echo "$phone is a valid US number\n";
}
```

Note that the metacharacters ^, ?, and $ are used in the pattern. The ^ makes a thematic start at the beginning of the line, and then look for an optional 1 and then finally 10 digits at the end of the line. Without the ^ in the beginning and $ at the end, the pattern could match other numbers that have more than 10 or 11 digits. This would be the case for the string of numbers 00**1321555444**99 that would be matched by the pattern /1?\d{10}/ as indicated with the bold digits.

Recipe 9-2. SubPatterns

Problem

In the previous example the branching (|) was used to define multiple options of content, but how can the parser know when the last option ends?

Solution

The solution is subpatterns. These are defined surrounding the patterns with parentheses. To look for multiple phrases: new car, new house, or just the word new by itself we could create a pattern that looks like this:

```
/new|new car|new house/
```

This can be written more efficiently by using subpatters. The word new is used in the beginning of all three branches so that can be pulled outside of a subbranch like this:

```
/new( car| house|)/
```

Note that there is nothing between the last pipe and the closing parentheses. This allows an empty branch in the subpattern. Putting the empty string at the beginning of the subpattern will not work.

How it Works

The next example shows how a regular expression can be used to scan a text and find all the instances of the phrases new, new car, and new house. The approach here is to start with the preg_match() function used in the previous examples.

```php
<?php
// 9_7.php

$txt = "I got a new car and I'm now looking for a new house";
if (preg_match("/new(( car| house)|)/", $txt, $matches) {
  print_r($matches);
}
```

The output of this is an array of three elements. The first element with index 0 corresponds to the string found by the entire pattern. The following two elements correspond to the matching string for each of the subpatterns.

```
Array
(
    [0] => new car
    [1] =>  car
    [2] =>  car
)
```

This shows that the `preg_match()` function only returns the first instance found. It is possible to pass a parameter with a character count used as an offset for where the search should start.

To get all the strings that match the pattern in the subject string we can use the function `preg_match_all()` instead. This function will return an array of arrays, where the first array contains all the strings found matching the full pattern and then an array for each of the subpatterns.

```php
<?php
// 9_8.php

$txt = "I got a new car and I'm now looking for a new house";
if (preg_match_all("/new(( car| house)|)/", $txt, $matches)) {
  print_r($matches);
}
```

The output looks like this:

```
Array
(
    [0] => Array
        (
            [0] => new car
            [1] => new house
        )

    [1] => Array
        (
            [0] =>  car
            [1] =>  house
        )

    [2] => Array
        (
            [0] =>  car
            [1] =>  house
        )

)
```

Having the matches for each of the subpatterns as well as the full pattern, is useful as it's not necessary to call the `preg_match()` function multiple times to get this information. In the next example a list of e-mail addresses with varying amounts of information is used to generate two lists. The first is a list of names and the second is a list of e-mail addresses. Starting with a regular expression that will match any of the lines could look like this: /^"?[a-z0-9,]*"? ?<[a-z0-9]+@[a-z0-9]+.[a-z0-9]+>$/mi. This pattern does not contain any subpatterns so the returned array will be a list of the matches to the full pattern. Adding a couple of subpatterns makes it possible to separate out the name and e-mail portions. /^"?([a-z0-9,]*)"? ?<([a-z0-9]+@[a-z0-9]+.[a-z0-9]+)>$/mi. The subpattern for the name portion uses the * meta character that specifies 0 or more repetitions of the character class and the two quotation marks and the space between name and e-mail address are made optional with the question marks.

```php
<?php
// 9_9.php

$emails = <<<HEREDOC
Joe Smith <smithj@example.com>
"Scott, Colin" <scottc@example.com>
<new@example.com>
some other content
HEREDOC;

if (preg_match_all(
    '/^"?([a-z0-9, ]*)"? ?<([a-z0-9]+@[a-z0-9]+.[a-z0-9]+)>$/mi',
    $emails, $matches)) {
  echo "names: " . implode(", ", $matches[1]) . "\n";
  echo "emails: " . implode(", ", $matches[2]) . "\n";
}
```

The output is just two lines of comma-separated lists.

```
names: Joe Smith , Scott, Colin,
emails: smithj@example.com, scottc@example.com, new@example.com
```

One of the e-mail addresses in the list does not have a name. That's why the output for the names has a trailing comma. All the arrays in the $matches variable will have the same number of elements.

Note that the first name 'Joe Smith' is listed with a trailing space. That happens because there is no clear way to determine if the space belongs to the name or is the optional space between the name and the e-mail address. E-mail addresses, and especially RFC822 addresses, are very complex and to take all the possible options into account in one single regular expression would create a very long pattern. It is most likely more efficient and readable to make a regular expression that matches only a subset of the allowed combinations. A good reference to documentation and to test patterns in a dynamic environment can be found at http://regexr.com/.

Recipe 9-3. String Replacement

Problem

In Recipe 9-1 it was shown how to use preg_replace() to find a string from a pattern and replace all instances of that string with a new static string. How can this be used if part of the matching substring should be retained? In other words, how can the replace function use some of the content found when creating new values in the string?

Solution

The solution is to use subpatterns and special placeholders that will be used to substitute the values. Subpatterns are numbered based on the order they show up in the pattern. The first parenthesis will indicate the start of the first subpattern and it will be referenced with the index 1. This is inline with the numbering within the arrays returned from preg_match() and preg_match_all() functions. Subpatterns can be contained within other subpatterns and the numbering follows the order in which the opening parenthesis for the pattern is located in the pattern.

A specific subpattern is referenced with the escape character followed by the index of the subpattern, when replacing strings. If the replacement string is provided as a double quoted string the backslash must be escaped. Otherwise the string will try to use an escaped version of the index.

The PCRE replace function is called `preg_replace()` and it takes three parameters. The first is the regular expression pattern that is used to match sections of the subject string, the second parameter is the replacement string, and finally the third parameter is the subject string where the replacements are performed. This is similar to the `str_replace()` function.

How it Works

HTML documents contain images and other resources that are often referenced with a src attribute and a relative URL. This works well when the HTML document is sent as a response to a request to the web server, but if the same HTML document is embedded in an e-mail, fully qualified URL's are needed for the e-mail client to be able to render the images.

If all the relative URL's are known it's easy to replace them using the `str_replace()` function but in most cases the exact URL's are unknown. The only thing that is known is the pattern src="/some/path/image." This can be turned into a regular expression /src="[^"]*"/. This expression does not contain any subpatterns so in order to be able to identify the URL portion a subpattern is introduced by adding () around [^"]*. The final pattern becomes /src="([^"]*)"/. The character class in the subpattern will match any character except the double quote that is expected to end the src attribute.

```php
<?php
// 9_10.php
$html = <<<HEREDOC
<img src="/images/logo.png" />
<img alt="Photo" src="/images/photo.jpg" />
HEREDOC;
$body = preg_replace('/src="([^"]*)"/mi',
                     'src="http://mydomain.com\1"', $html);
echo $body;
```

In this case the pattern and replacement string is created as single quoted strings. If double quoted strings were used the patterns would look slightly different as both the double quotes and the escape characters would have to be escaped.

```php
$body = preg_replace("/src=\"([^\"]*)\"/mi",
                     "src=\http://mydomain.com\\1\", $html);
```

This script will output the reformatted html that looks like this:

```
<img src="http://mydomain.com/images/logo.png" />
<img alt="Photo" src="http://mydomain.com/images/photo.jpg" />
```

In this example it's assumed all URL's are absolute with regards to the document root (starts with a slash) and no URL's are fully qualified. To handle the various ways URL's can be written we can use the `preg_match_all()` function to identify all the places that potentially needs replacement and loop over all the matches and replace them one at the time.

```php
<?php
// 9_11.php
$html = <<<HEREDOC
<img src="/images/logo.png" />
<img src="background.png" />
<img alt="Photo" src="/images/photo.jpg" />
<img src="http://example.com/images/photo.jpg" />
HEREDOC;
if (preg_match_all('/src="([^"]*)"/mi', $html, $matches)) {
  foreach ($matches[0] as $i => $str) {
    if ($matches[1][$i][0] == "/") {
      $html = str_replace($str,
                          "src=\"http\"//mydomain.com{$matches[1][$i]}\"",
                          $html);
    }
    else if (substr($matches[1][$i], 0, 7) == "http://" ||
             substr($matches[1][$i], 0, 8) == "https://") {
      // Do nothing the URL is complete.
    }
    else {
      $dir = dirname($_SERVER['REQUEST_URI']);
      $html = str_replace($str,
                  "src=\"http\"//mydomain.com/{$dir }/{$matches[1][$i]}\"",
                  $html);
    }
  }
}
echo $html;
```

The $matches array will have two elements (arrays). The first will contain the matches to the full pattern and the second (index 1) will contain the matches to the first subpattern. There will be the same number of elements in both arrays. The loop iterates over the first array and the index ($i) is used to reference corresponding elements in the second array.

In the example above the HTML contains four images with URL's written in different ways. The first URL is absolute from the document root. Only the domain name should be added to this one. The second URL is relative to where the current script is executed from. In this case the domain and the path to the file are added. The third URL is also absolute to the document root and the fourth and last URL is an absolute URL to a different web site so no need to do anything with this one.

When the script is executed from a directory called folder the output will look like this:

```
<img src="http"//mydomain.com/images/logo.png" />
<img src="http"//mydomain.com/folder/background.png" />
<img alt="Photo" src="http"//mydomain.com/images/photo.jpg" />
<img src="http://example.com/images/photo.jpg" />
```

CHAPTER 10

■ ■ ■

Variables

Variables are used to store data temporarily in memory. Variables only exist as long as the PHP script is running. They are identified with a dollar sign followed by a name. The name of a variable can begin with a letter (a-z or A-Z) or an underscore. Any of the following characters can be a number, a letter, or any ASCII character from 127 to 255 (0x7f – 0xff). There is no restriction on the number of characters in the name. Variable names are case sensitive so $var, $Var, and $VAR will be three different variables.

PHP is a loosely typed language where variables can change type depending on the result of a calculation or operation. If an integer value is increased above the maximum size it will be converted to a floating point value. If an integer is used as part of a string operation it will be converted to a string.

The use of the dollar sign to designate variables makes it possible to use the same name for variables and functions like in the case with the built-in function date() and the variable $date. The statement $date = date('c'); will generate a string with the current date formatted according to the ISO 8601 standard.

PHP has a set of predefined variables that will be available based on the version of PHP, the type of web server, the configuration, the type of HTTP request, and other factors. A full list of these predefined variables can be found in the online PHP manual: http://php.net/manual/en/reserved.variables.php. These variables typically contain information about the environment, parameters passed to the script, etc.

It is not necessary to perform any special declaration of variables before using them; simply define it by writing the dollar sign followed by the name when it's needed. Variables can be used in an assign statement or it can be part of a statement or calculation. If no value has been assigned to the variable when it's used in a statement the system might produce a notice. This depends on the configuration of error_reporting in php.ini. This does not happen when assigning a value to a new variable but if a value is used without getting a value assigned the notice will be issued and a default value will be used. This can be an empty string or an integer with the value 0 depending on the context the variable is used in.

Recipe 10-1. Converting Variable Type

Problem

In a loosely typed language like PHP there is no way to define a variable to be of a specific type. The result of the calculation determines the actual type used.

Solution

Overwriting the variable with a new value or casting the values to a different type can help the programmer control the specific type a variable has.

© Frank M. Kromann 2016
F.M. Kromann, *PHP and MySQL Recipes*, DOI 10.1007/978-1-4842-0605-8_10

How it Works

A variable does not have a strict type and the type of any variable can be changed at any time during execution simply by assigning it a value of a different type or by casting to a new type. In the following example the variable $a is assigned an integer value of 5 and then a string value. The reference to the integer value is lost when a new value is assigned and the memory used by the integer is released. The variable $b is also assigned an integer value of 5 and then it's converted to a string and assigned back to itself.

```php
<?php
// 10_1.php
$a = 5;
$a = "Some string";
$b = 5;
$b = (string)$b;
```

PHP will try to convert any variable value to best match the context the variable is used in. If the variable is a string and it's used in a math operation it will be converted to a numeric value before the math operation is applied. This might lead to the value of 0 if the sting can't be converted to a numeric value. The conversion of the variable type is only temporary and it does not affect the variable itself. It is necessary to allow the comparison or calculation to become meaningful.

In the following example two variables (integer and string) are compared. This will be done by converting the string "10" to the integer value 10 before the two are compared.

```php
<?php
// 10_2.php
$a = 5;
$b = "10";
if ($b > $a) {
   echo '$b is greater than $a';
}
```

Recipe 10-2. Allocating Memory

Problem

When variables are defined and assigned values the system will handle all memory allocation needed based on the type and size of data. It will also allocate memory as needed when the variable changes size. The limit on available memory is handled by the configuration option `memory_limit` in `php.ini`. If the memory exceeds the maximum allowed size a fatal error will be thrown and the execution will stop. For performance reasons it's recommended to keep this configuration to a low value but large enough to be able to handle the memory needed for any requests to the web site.

Using many variables or storing large sets of data in arrays or strings might cause memory overflow. In these cases it is convenient to get rid of unused variables and release the memory used by them.

Solution

In most cases it's not necessary to get rid of variables or free memory. All references to them are removed automatically when the script ends and all memory used will be released back to the system. With PHP's primary usage being to generate responses to HTTP requests the script should not be running for more than a few seconds or even a few hundred milliseconds. If the script works on large datasets it can help on memory consumption to remove references to variables that are no longer needed for the execution of the script before assigning values to new variables. This will help the memory usage to stay under the configured limit.

How it Works

If the script is used to serve dynamic content to the web browser the script usually terminates fast and in most cases it's not necessary to perform cleanup even for large datasets. In some cases the memory limit will not make it possible to keep large amounts of data in memory and it might be necessary to process the data in batches. If the script is executed from the command line or as a cron job it might run for a long time and process large amounts of data. In those cases it's always good to be conservative and free up unused resources. Releasing memory is done by assigning a null value to the variable or by using the unset() function.

```php
<?php
// 10_3.php
$a = array("abc", "def", "ghi");
$a = null;

$a = array("abc", "def", "ghi");
unset($a);
```

Both methods will get rid of the data and free the memory and if isset(), empty(), or is_null() is used to check the variable they will all give the same result and that would be false, true, and true. The next example shows the use of the three functions on a variable that's assigned a null value or unset with the unset() function.

```php
<?php
// 10_4.php
$a = 5;
$a = null;
var_dump(isset($a));
var_dump(empty($a));
var_dump(is_null($a));
unset($a);
var_dump(isset($a));
var_dump(empty($a));
var_dump(is_null($a));
```

will produce the following output:

```
bool(false)
bool(true)
bool(true)
bool(false)
bool(true)
bool(true)
```

The result is shown with line breaks as when the code is executed with the CLI version of PHP. Adding the header for Content-Type and setting it to text/plain will give the same result in a browser.

Recipe 10-3. Determining Memory Use

Problem

Working on large sets of data or when debugging the use of system resources, it's advantages to know how much memory the script is using.

Solution

PHP has a couple of built-in functions to check the actual memory use of the current script. These are called memory_get_usage() and memory_get_peak_usage(). The functions return the values in bytes used. To get kb, Mb, and Gb, etc., these results must be divided with a multiple of 1024 (2 to the power of 10). The first function returns the current memory usage and the second one returns the maximum usage during execution. Both functions will return the memory usage in bytes.

How it Works

The following example shows how an array grows from empty to holding 100 elements and how memory usage is increased and decreased when elements are added and removed.

```php
<?php
// 10_5.php
$a = array();
for ($i = 0; $i < 100; $i++) {
  $a[] = "This is a short string";
  echo "Memory usage for $i elements = " . memory_get_usage() . "\n";
}
while (($i = sizeof($a))) {
  echo "Memory usage for $i elements = " . memory_get_usage() . "\n";
  unset($a[$i - 1]);
}
echo "Maximim memory usage = " . memory_get_peak_usage() . "\n";
```

This script produces a fairly long amount of output. Below is a listing of the first few lines.

```
Memory usage for 0 elements = 352736
Memory usage for 1 elements = 352768
Memory usage for 2 elements = 352768
Memory usage for 3 elements = 352768
Memory usage for 4 elements = 352768
Memory usage for 5 elements = 352768
Memory usage for 6 elements = 352768
Memory usage for 7 elements = 352768
Memory usage for 8 elements = 353088
Memory usage for 9 elements = 353088
Memory usage for 10 elements = 353088
Memory usage for 11 elements = 353088
Memory usage for 12 elements = 353088
Memory usage for 13 elements = 353088
Memory usage for 14 elements = 353088
Memory usage for 15 elements = 353088
Memory usage for 16 elements = 353728
```

The first loop adds the same string to the array 100 times and each time the memory usage is printed out. The second loop runs as many times as the array has elements and each time the current memory usage is printed and the last element of the array is removed.

Recipe 10-4. Taking Advantage of Variable Scope

Problem

The same variable can be used in different places of the code and hold different values. Thus the same name can be used to designate different variables. This is often the case with temporary variables or variables used in loops ($i, $j, $k).

Solution

Variables are valid within the scope they are defined. The most basic scope in PHP is the global scope. In addition to the global scope PHP has a class scope and a function/method scope. Variables defined in the global scope are only valid and available in the global scope. If the same variable name is used for variables in different scopes they are considered to be two different variables unless special measures are used to reference the same variable.

It is always recommended to use unique variable names to avoid confusion.

How it Works

In the following example the variable $a is defined in the global scope and assigned the value of 5. $a is also defined as a variable in the MyTest() function and here it is assigned the value of 7. At runtime the function is called and the local version of $a is assigned but the function ends before it does anything else and the local version of $a is discarded. The global variable $a is not affected by the function.

```php
<?php
// 10_6.php
$a = 5;
function MyTest() {
   $a = 7;
}
MyTest();
echo $a;
```

It is possible to access variables from the global scope from within a function or class method. By using the keyword global in front of the variable before the first usage of the variable will make the local variable a reference to the global variable and any updates to the local variable will also affect the global variable. If the variable is undefined in the global scope it will be defined in the global scope and any value assigned to it will be preserved after the function ends.

In the following example the internal variable $a is assigned a value of 7. Later in the same function $a is changed to be a reference to the global version of $a and then assigned a new value. So after executing this script the value of the global version of $a becomes 6. When the variable is changed from a local variable to a reference to the global variable, the local value is lost.

```php
<?php
// 10_7.php
$a = 5;
function MyTest() {
  $a = 7;
  global $a;
  $a = 6;
}
MyTest();
echo $a;
```

Recipe 10-5. Avoiding Global Variable Problems with Super Globals

Problem

Accessing global variables with the use of the global keyword can cause issues if you forget to use it. In that case the variable becomes a local variable and the code will behave differently than expected.

Solution

An alternative to using the global keyword is to use what's called a **super global** to reference variables from the global scope. Super globals are predefined variables that are accessible in the global scope as well as any function or method scope without the use of the global keyword. These are populated with get ($_GET), post ($_POST), cookie ($_COCKIES), environment ($_ENV), server ($_SERVER), and a special version for global variables ($GLOBALS).

The availability of the super globals is controlled by a configuration option in php.ini called variables_order. This configuration is a string of any of the letters E, G, P, C, and S, which is short for Environment, Get, Post, Cookie, and Server. If the configuration is set to the empty string, none of these super globals will be populated.

How it Works

The super globals are all associated arrays (key value pairs) and the variable names all start with $_ with the exception of $GLOBALS. That's for historical reasons as it was named like this before any of the other super globals were introduced to the language. The next example shows how to use the $GLOBALS variable to change the value of a global variable.

```php
<?php
// 10_8.php
$a = 5;
function MyTest() {
  $GLOBALS['a'] += 7;
}
MyTest();
echo $a;
```

When a script uses a combination of GET (query string) and POST (request body) requests it is possible to access the contents in a single super global called $_REQUEST. This can simplify the code so only one variable is checked for the existence of specific values instead of checking both $_GET and $_POST. The elements of this array are populated in the order specified by the configuration option request_order and if that's not defined the system will use the same order as used in configuration variables_order.

If the request_order is set to "GP" the system will take all variables corresponding to the $_GET array first and then apply all values from $_POST. If the same index exists in both arrays the $_REQUEST variable will only contain the value from $_POST. Changing the configuration to "PG" will change the order and if it's set tp "P" or "G" the $_REQUEST variable will only contain get or post values.

Recipe 10-6. Determining Variable Type

Problem

Variables in PHP can change type based on assignments and results of calculations, etc. How can we know the actual type of a given variable?

■ **Note**   Recipe 10-1 covers how to change the type of a PHP variable.

Solution

The basic variable types in PHP are integer, float, string, array, object, and resource and each of these have a corresponding function that will check the data type and return true or false depending on the actual type of the variable: is_integer(), is_float(), is_string(), is_array(), is_object(), and is_resource(). In addition to these there are a couple of other is_* functions that can be used to check the content of a variable; is_numeric(), is_nan() (not a number), is_finite(), is_infinite(), is_null(), empty() and isset(). The names empty() and isset() are kept this way for historical reasons to preserve compatibility with older versions of PHP.

How it Works

When integers are assigned values greater than PHP_INT_MAX constant the variable will automatically change to a float. The actual value of PHP_INT_MAX depends on the platform and version of PPHP. For 32-bit versions the value is 2 to the power of 31 and for 64-bit values the value is 2 to the power of 63. The last bit is used for the sign as all integer values in PHP are signed.

Instead of checking a variable for a specific type the gettype() function can be used to get a string representation of the type. The possible return values for gettype() are one of the strings "Boolean," "integer," "double," "string," "array," "object," "resource," "NULL," and "unknown type." This is demonstrated in the next example where a variable is assigned the value of PHP_INT_MAX and then incremented.

```php
<?php
// 10_9.php
$i = PHP_INT_MAX;
echo $i . "\n";
echo gettype($i) . "\n";
$i++;
echo $i . "\n";
echo gettype($i) . "\n";
```

The first call to gettype() will return 'integer' and the second will return 'double'. The string double is used instead of float for historical reasons.

On a 64-bit system the output will look like this:

```
9223372036854775807
integer
9.2233720368548E+18
double
```

It is not possible to create a variable of type resource without calling a function that returns a resource. This can either be a built-in function or a function from one of the many extensions. The resource type is used for things like file handles, database connections, and results sets, etc. These are usually returned by a function that opens the file or connects to a database and they are passed back to other functions when actions are performed against that specific resource like sending a query to a database or writing content to a file.

The functions is_finite() and is_infinite() might yield different results on 32-bit and 64-bit platforms as they use the limits of the float type to determine if the number will fit.

Recipe 10-7. Reducing Memory Use with References

Problem

In certain cases it is useful to have multiple variables that point to the same value in memory. This will reduce the need for additional memory.

Solution

In general variables are assigned by value and PHP does not support pointers as known from C and other languages. Assigning by value will cause each value to have its own memory segment and even if a variable is assigned to another variable they will each reference a unique memory segment.

How it Works

The following example shows how one variable is assigned the value of another variable and when any of two variables are updated the other will not be affected.

```php
<?php
// 10_10.php
$a = 5;
$b = $a;
$a++;
echo "\$a = $a\n";
echo "\$b = $b\n";
```

```
$a = 6
$b = 5
```

In some cases it might be necessary to have multiple variables referencing the same value or internal memory segment. Using the global keyword to make an internal variable access the value of a global variable is one way to do this. It can also be done for variables in the same scope by adding & in front of the variable name of the variable on the right side of the assign operator, and finally it can be done when passing variables to functions. If the function is defined with an ampersand (&) in front of any of the parameters, these will be passed as a reference to, instead of a copy of the original value.

Passing variables by reference means that the variables that are references to the same memory object all will have access to read and write to that object. Updating one of the variables will affect all the variables that are a reference to that memory object. This is also the case across the scope so if a variable is passed by reference to a function from the global scope or a different function, both will still reference the same memory object.

PHP also use the concept of copy-on-write, which means variables are passed by reference, even if it's not intended to be, and only if the internal function changes the content of a variable it will be copied before the change is made. This saves a great deal of time when passing large strings or arrays to functions as the data will only be copied if the function makes changes to the variable. If the pass by reference is set explicitly the copy operation will never be performed. In the next example the variable $a is assigned a value of 5 and the variable $b is created as a reference to $a. When the variable $a is changed it will affect both variables.

```php
<?php
// 10_11.php
$a = 5;
$b = &$a;
$a++;
echo "\$a = $a\n";
echo "\$b = $b\n";
```

```
$a = 6
$b = 6
```

In this case the two variables $a and $b will reference the same value (memory) and when one is changed the other will also change. Internally PHP will keep a reference count to each value and it will not release the memory until the reference count is 0; in other words no variables are referencing the value.

Working with references can also be handy when working with arrays and iteration. Consider the code that loops over an array and performs an action on each element:

```php
<?php
// 10_12.php
$a = array(1,2,3,4,5,6,7,8,9);
foreach($a as $e) {
  if ($e % 2 == 0) {
    $e *= 2;
  }
}
print_r($a);
```

The output of this code when executed with PHP CLI is this:

```
Array
(
    [0] => 1
    [1] => 2
    [2] => 3
    [3] => 4
    [4] => 5
    [5] => 6
    [6] => 7
    [7] => 8
    [8] => 9
)
```

This code does some work by iterating over the array, checking to see if the elements are even, and calculating a new value, but it does not make any changes to the original array, $a. All updates to the variable $e is done on a copy of each element and the updates are thrown away after each iteration when $e is assigned a copy of the next element. Changing the loop to also include the index of each element in the array makes it possible to make changes to the original array.

```php
<?php
// 10_13.php
$a = array(1,2,3,4,5,6,7,8,9);
foreach($a as $i => $e) {
  if ($e % 2 == 0) {
    $a[$i] = $e * 2;
  }
}
print_r($a);
```

The output of this code is this:

```
Array
(
    [0] => 1
    [1] => 4
    [2] => 3
    [3] => 8
    [4] => 5
    [5] => 12
    [6] => 7
    [7] => 16
    [8] => 9
)
```

This is a bit clumsy and it requires the use of the extra index variable. By making the variable $e a reference to each element of the array the script becomes a bit cleaner:

```php
<?php
// 10_14.php
$a = array(1,2,3,4,5,6,7,8,9);
foreach($a as &$e) {
  if ($e % 2 == 0) {
    $e *= 2;
  }
}
print_r($a);
```

This is about as simple as the first example but with the benefit that the values of the original array $a are changed when the references to the elements $e are updated.

Recipe 10-8. Using Constants

Problem

Some values like configuration options or special values used to control flow should never change throughout the program. We could use variables to store these values but that would allow the code to change the values and thereby perhaps the functionality of the program.

Solution

It is possible to define values that can be accessed globally without the use of super globals or the use of the global keyword. This is done with the definition of constants. Constants follow the same naming convention as variables but they do not have the leading dollar sign before the variable name and they can only be defined with the help of the define() function, or they can be defined by internal PHP functions or extensions. It is common practice that constants are written in all caps, but this is not required.

How it Works

The next example defines MY_CONSTANT in the global scope and it's used to perform simple multiplication inside the function MyFunc().

```php
<?php
// 10_15.php
define('MY_CONSTANT', 12);
function MyFunc($v) {
  return $v * MY_CONSTANT;
}
echo MyFunc(2);
```

Constants can be defined in the global scope or inside a function or as a member method of a class. No matter where they are defined they will be available globally.

To avoid warnings it can be necessary to check if a constant is defined before trying to use it. That is done with the defined() function. This function takes the constant name as a string as a parameter and returns true or false. The function is used like this: if (defined('MY_CONSTANT')) { ... }. Using the constant instead of the string value of the name will still result in a runtime warning unless the constant holds a string value. In that case the function might return false because the value of the constant does not match a constant that is defined.

Constants can also be removed if the script no longer needs them or if they need to be changed to different values. That's done with the undefine() function that also takes a string with the name of the constant as a parameter.

PHP comes with a number of predefined constants: the most common ones are probably the Boolean values for TRUE and FALSE but also constants to identify the version of php (PHP_VERSION) and the number pi (M_PI) are defined. In addition constants might be defined by the extensions loaded at any given time. These constants are usually prefixed with the extension name and they are used as flags or parameters for various functions within the extension. Examples of such extension specific constants are MYSQL_ASSOC, MYSQL_NUM and MYSQL_BOTH. These are used to tell the extensions mysql_fetch_row() function how to return arrays. Constants are useful to make the code more readable. A list of predefined constants can be found here: http://php.net/manual/en/reserved.constants.php.

Recipe 10-9. Variable Variables

Problem

It can be useful to programmatically use the value of one variable to find the content of a different variable.

Solution

PHP has a concept of variable variables that allows defining and using variables based on the content of other variables that contain a string value. This works as long as the content of the variable follows the rules for naming of variables.

How it Works

A variable variable is defined by adding an extra dollar sign in front of a regular variable.

```php
<?php
// 10_16.php
$var = "abc";
$$var = 6;
echo $var . "\n";
echo $abc . "\n";
```

In this example a variable $abc is created based on the content of the variable $var. The two dollar signs in front of var takes the value of $var ("abc") and turns it into $abc. The value 6 will be assigned to $abc and not to $var as shown in the following output:

```
abc
6
```

This pattern can be repeated as long as the variable naming convention is followed.

```php
<?php
// 10_17.php
$var = "abc";
$$var = "def";
$$$var = "ghi";
$$$$var = 6;

echo $ghi;
```

A more useful example of variable variables is to use logic to calculate the name of a variable to use for a certain operation.

```php
<?php
// 10_18.php
$us = "m/d/Y";
$eu = "d-m-Y";
$format = "us";
echo date($$format);
```

Defining an array with the possible values and then calculating the index to use can achieve a similar result.

```php
<?php
// 10_19.php
$format = array(
    'us' => 'm/d/Y',
    'eu' => 'd-m-Y',
);
echo date($format['us']);
```

Super globals cannot be used as variable variables.

Recipe 10-10. Comparing Variables

Problem

With the loosely typed nature of PHP, comparing two variables can yield unexpected results.

Solution

Comparing variables can be done with a number of operators as listed in Table 10-1 below. The loosely typed nature of PHP provides a way to compare variables by value or by value and type.

Table 10-1. *Comparison operators*

Operator	Meaning	Description
==	Equal	True if both values are the same
!=	Not equal	True if both values are different
<>	Not equal	True if both values are different
===	Identical	True if type and values are the same
!==	Not identical	True if type or value are different
>	Greater than	True if left side is greater than the right side
<	Less than	True if the left side is less than the right side
>=	Greater than or equal	True if left side is greater than or equal to the right side
<=	Less than or equal	True if the left side is less than or equal to the right side
<=>	"Spaceship"	Returns -1, 0, or 1 if the left side is greater, the two values are equal, or the right side is greater. This is new in PHP 7.

How it Works

Comparing the integer 7 to the string "7" will give two different results depending on the method of comparison selected. Using the loose compare method, 7 == "7" will give a true and the strict compare 7 === "7" will give false. This is because the loose compare will first convert one of the two sides to the same type as the other side. The rules for how one side is converted depend on the types of the variables on either side. If one side is NULL and the other is a string the NULL value will be converted to the empty string "" before the two values are compared. If one side is a Boolean the other side will be converted to Boolean before comparing. If one side is a number and the other is a string or resource, the string and resources are converted to numbers before comparison. In the case of strings with numerical values the strings will also be converted to numbers before comparing the values.

Arrays are basically compared on the number of elements in each object or if all the keys of the two objects are the same, the arrays are compared value by value.

Objects that are instances of different classes are always different but objects instantiated from the same classes can be equal, when compared with the loose operator (==), if they have the same attributes and values. If they are compared with the strict operator (===) they must refer to the same instance to be equal.

A full list of the rules can be found in the PHP manual here: http://php.net/manual/en/language.operators.comparison.php

The next example shows a few examples of how the compare operations work when comparing values of different or same values.

```php
<?php
// 10_20.php
$i = 100;
$f = 12.2;
$s = "abc";
$s2 = "100";

var_dump($i == $s2);
var_dump($i === $s2);
var_dump($i != $s2);
var_dump($i !== $s2);
```

```
var_dump($i >= $f);
var_dump($s <=> $s2);
var_dump($s2 <=> $s);
var_dump($s <=> $s);
```

The output will be a series of true and false values with the exception of the last three.

```
bool(true)
bool(false)
bool(false)
bool(true)
bool(true)
int(1)
int(-1)
int(0)
```

Recipe 10-11. Working with Strings

Problem

The most common use of PHP is to generate HTML documents (or other dynamic documents). The documents are often created by concatenating strings or inserting variable content into other strings in the form of templates.

Solution

PHP supports both single (') and double (") quotes when defining strings. There is no difference in the resulting string but the way PHP handles the content of the string is slightly different. When single quotes are used the dollar sign ($) will be accepted as a character without the need to escape it with a backslash (\) and there is no variable substitution. Variable substitution makes it possible to embed variables into a string without using concatenation. Simple variables can be embedded directly into a string (the double quoted version). More complex variables like arrays and objects will have to be wrapped in curly brackets {} to be embedded in a string.

How it Works

```php
<?php
// 10_21.php
$a = 5;
$s1 = '$a = 5';
$s2 = "$a = 5";
```

Strings can also be generated by concatenating multiple variables using the . (period) operator. It is possible to mix strings with single and double quotes and any variable. Variables will be converted to strings before the concatenation.

```php
<?php
// 10_22.php
$a = 5;
$s = 'This string is '.
    'created by concatination of '.
    'strings and the variable $a '.
    "with the value $a\n";
```

Comparing strings can be done with the normal compare operators but that might not always give the desired results.

Recipe 10-12. Handling Floating Point Numbers

Problem

Working with floating point numbers can cause some confusion. Numbers that have an exact representation in base 10 do not always translate to an exact representation in the binary base 2. This is causing rounding errors when math operations are performed on these values. Even simple math and comparison options that look obvious can yield results that seem wrong.

Solution

You should never rely on comparing two floating point values and expect to make exact comparisons. A better way is to look at the difference between the two values and determine if the difference is greater or less than a certain threshold.

How it Works

The operation 8 – 7.7 should give the result 0.3 but performing the math and then comparing to the value 0.3 will show a different result.

```php
<?php
// 10_23.php
$v = 8 - 7.7;
$u = 0.3;
echo "$v\n";
if ($v == $u) {
  echo "\$v == \$u\n";
}
else {
  echo "\$v != $u\n";
}
```

Instead of comparing if the two variables are identical it would be better to look at the difference between the two and compare that to a number representing the precision required. This number is often referred to as epsilon.

```php
<?php
// 10_24.php
$epsilon = 0.00001;
$v = 8 - 7.7;
$u = 0.3;
echo "$v\n";
if (abs($v - $u) < $epsilon) {
  echo "\$v == \$u\n";
}
else {
  echo "\$v != $u\n";
}
```

The output of this script looks like this:

```
0.3
$v == $u
```

Recipe 10-13. Special Language Constructs

PHP has a large number of functions built in and a few language constructs that look like functions but act slightly different.

Problem

Arrays are indexed lists of variables where the index can be a numerical key or a string value. If no keys are defined PHP will auto-assign values each time a new element is added. In order to work with arrays it is necessary to use special language constructs to create arrays or to extract values, etc.

Solution

There are a few special language constructs in PHP that makes working with arrays simple. The first is array(). Although it looks like a function it is actually a language construct used to define array variables. If nothing is written between the parentheses the variable will become an empty array.

How it Works

Below is a common way to initialize an array variable.

```php
<?php
// 10_25.php
$a = array();
```

Other languages treat arrays as objects and they must be instantiated with the new operator. That's not needed in PHP as an array is its own native type. If values are listed as a comma separated list these will become elements of the array. Array elements can be of any supported type, including arrays, and they can even be mixed.

```php
<?php
// 10_26.php
$a = array(1, 2, "3", array(4, 5, 6));
```

Because PHP and JavaScript are often used together a new shorter syntax for creating arrays was introduced in PHP version 5.4. This new syntax looks more like a JSON encoded string:

```php
<?php
// 10_27.php
$a = [1, 2, "3", [4, 5, 6]];
```

In the examples above all the values are added without providing a key. This will cause PHP to generate index values for each element starting at the value 0. It is not necessary to start at 0 and it is allowed to have "holes" in the index.

```php
<?php
// 10_28.php
$a = [7 => 1, 2, "3", 100 => [4, 5, 6]];
```

This will cause the first values to be set at key 7 and all subsequent values will have the indexes 8, 9, and the last one 100.

In addition to numeric values, strings are also allowed as keys. This is a very common way of working with key value pairs.

```php
<?php
// 10_29.php
$a = [
  'host' => 'localhost',
  'user' => 'root'
];
```

Checking of a specific key exists in an array can be done with the isset() function or by use of array_key_exists(). It takes two parameters where the first represents the key and the second the array. Depending on the values of the array elements the two functions might yield different results as seen in this next example:

```php
<?php
// 10_30.php
$a = [
  0 => '123',
  1 => null,
  'a' => 'abc',
  'b' => null
];

var_dump(isset($a[0]));
var_dump(isset($a[1]));
var_dump(isset($a['a']));
var_dump(isset($a['b']));
```

```
var_dump(array_key_exists(0, $a));
var_dump(array_key_exists(1, $a));
var_dump(array_key_exists('a', $a));
var_dump(array_key_exists('b', $a));
```

This script will produce the following output:

```
bool(true)
bool(false)
bool(true)
bool(false)
bool(true)
bool(true)
bool(true)
bool(true)
```

The same way arrays can be created with the array() construct it's also possible to use the list() construct to decompose arrays. The list() construct belongs on the left side of the assignment and it is used to take the elements of an array and assign them to individual variables as shown in this next example.

```php
<?php
// 10_31.php
$a = [1, 2, 3];

list($v1) = $a;
echo "$v1\n";
list($v1, $v2) = $a;
echo "$v1, $v2\n";
list($v1, $v2, $v3) = $a;
echo "$v1, $v2, $v3\n";
list($v1, $v2, $v3, $v4) = $a;
echo "$v1, $v2, $v3, $v4\n";

$b = ['a' => 7, 'b' => 8];
list($x1, $x2) = $b;
echo "$x1, $x2\n";
```

This example will not assign any values to $x1 and $x2 because the list() construct only works on numerical indexes starting with 0. The output from this script looks like this:

```
1
1, 2
1, 2, 3
1, 2, 3,
,
```

With the use of extract() it is possible to work on associative arrays and convert them to variables in the scope of where the construct is used.

```php
<?php
// 10_32.php
$a = [
  'host' => 'localhost',
  'database' => 'mydb',
  'user' => 'user'
];
foreach($a as $key => $value) {
  if (isset($$key)) {
        $key = "prefix_" . $key;
  }
  $$key = $value;
}

echo "$host, $database, $user\n";
```

This can be simplified with the use of the extract() construct.

```php
<?php
// 10_33.php
$a = [
  'host' => 'localhost',
  'database' => 'mydb',
  'user' => 'user'
];
extract($a, EXTR_PREFIX_SAME, 'prefix');

echo "$host, $database, $user\n";
```

The output looks like this:

```
localhost, mydb, user
```

Recipe 10-14. Iterating Over Array Values

Problem

Working with arrays often requires the program to perform the same action for each row in the array. Fetching a result set from a database query and turning it into a HTML structure for presentation is an example of this.

Solution

There are a number of ways to access elements in an array. If the elements are indexed with integers and the starting value is known a for(;;) or while() loop could be used. If there are holes in the index or string values are used as the keys it's possible to use each() or foreach() language constructs to iterate over the array.

How it Works

The each() construct takes an array as the parameter and returns the element at the current internal index pointer. It will also increment the internal index pointer to the next element. This is useful when iterating over the elements of an array.

```php
<?php
// 10_34.php
$a = [10, 15, 20, 25];
while ($b = each($a)) {
  echo $b . "\n";
}
```

This can be written a bit cleaner with the use of the foreach() construct:

```php
<?php
// 10_35.php
$a = [10, 15, 20, 25];
foreach($a as $b) {
  echo $b . "\n";
}
```

It is not necessary to call the reset() function on the array if the same array is used in multiple foreach() statements. With each() it is necessary to use reset() between multiple iterations.

There are a couple of other language constructs to be aware of. These do not have anything to do with variables but they are important for the program flow.

The construct include() will include the contents of the file specified if the file exists; otherwise a warning message will be printed. The require() statement works like include() but it will throw a fatal error and stop execution if the file is missing. Both of these are useful when the code base is growing and it is necessary to use the same code in multiple scripts. A variant of these constructs called include_once() and require_once() will not throw errors if the same file is included more than once; it will simply be skipped as the file is already loaded. In general it is recommended to write code that includes files only once and only includes files that are actually used. This will give the best performance.

Recipe 10-15. Generating Output

Problem

Generating output is a key functionality of PHP as it is most commonly used to generate HTML (or other web-related documents) dynamically based on database queries and other resources.

Solution

PHP implements a couple of language constructs: echo(), print(), and die(). The first two have to do with output alone and the last function will print the content of the parameter passed and then stop script execution.

Although the language constructs all look like functions they can be used both with and without the parentheses.

How it Works

Writing echo "a"; and echo("a"); will give the same result. In addition echo can handle any number of parameters separated by commas, without concatenating them to a single string first.

```php
<?php
// 2_36.php
$a = 'value 1';
$b = 'value 2';
//This will output $a and $b
echo $a, $b, "\n";
// This will concatenate $a and $b and output the result
print $a . $b . "\n";
```

CHAPTER 11

■ ■ ■

Functions

Functions are a way to structure code that is used several times into a convenient structure. This is a great way to reduce code duplication and increase reusability. There are more than 1000 built-in functions in PHP and user-defined functions can be declared in the main script or in an include file, and it is up to the script developer to make sure the correct files are included before a function is called.

Recipe 11-1. Calling Functions

Problem

In chapter 2 we discussed the use of classes to build objects of data (member variables) and functionality (methods). Using a class to instantiate an object and then call one of the methods might be too complicated when here is a way to simply wrap the logic into a single function that works more or less like any of the functions that are built into the language.

One major difference between classes and functions is the ability to declare members as public, protected, or private. This does not exist for functions, with the exception of functions in functions as described later in this chapter.

Functions can define variables that are only available within the function, almost like private member variables as described in the recipe about function scope.

Solution

The simplest form of a function is defined with the keyword function followed by a function name and a set of parentheses and a set of curly brackets for the function definition.

```
function DeleteRows() {}
```

Function names are case insensitive. A function that is declared as MyFunc() can be called as myfunc(); or MYFUNC(); but it is recommended to use the same case as used in the function definition. To make this function do something we need to write the logic between the curly brackets. The code in a function follows the exact same structure as any PHP script. Any function that is callable outside of the function is also available inside the function. This is true for both built-in functions and user-defined functions.

Functions can be called as a statement or as the right side of a calculation, assuming the function has a return value.

There are a few examples of language constructs that look like functions. The most basic is the array() construct that is used to define a variable of the array type. This is used as the right side of an assignment. The list() construct is used to take an array and split its elements into individual variables. The list() construct is used on the left side of an assignment.

F.M. Kromann, *PHP and MySQL Recipes*, DOI 10.1007/978-1-4842-0605-8_11

How it Works

In this example we have a function that can delete all rows in a specific table. The function does not have any parameters as input and it does not return any values.

```php
<?php
// 11_1.php

function DeleteRows() {
  $con = mysqli_connect('host', 'user', 'secret');
  if ($con) {
    mysqli_select_db($con, 'mydb');
    mysqli_query($con, "delete from mytable;");
    mysqli_close($con);
  }
  else {
    echo "No database connection";
  }
}

// Call the function
DeleteRows();
```

If overall the script doesn't have to do anything else it's not really needed to wrap the delete operation in a function, but if the delete function is being used in multiple scripts or there is logic to check if the condition is right it will increase readability of the code to have the logic for the delete operation in a separate function. In that case it's important to use meaningful function names.

Recipe 11-2. Variable Scope

Problem

In the previous example the DeleteRows() function created a connect to the database before deleting the rows and the connection was closed at the end of the function. If the script performs many operations on the database there would be an impact on performance as the connect operation is relatively expensive. If it's possible to connect at the beginning of the script and use the same connection in all database operations the connect operation would only be performed once for the entire request.

It's always a good idea to minimize the number of database operations the script is performing in order to get the best possible performance of the script.

Solution

Variables defined outside of a function are not directly accessible inside the function. This is called scope. In PHP there is the global scope that includes all variables defined outside of any function. These can be accessed directly by any code that is executed outside of any function.

Variables defined inside a function are only available to code defined as part of the function.

There are two ways to access variables from the global scope from within a function. The first way is to use the super global variable $GLOBALS. The built-in variable $GLOBALS does not have the leading _ as the other super globals because it was introduced in the language a long time before the concept of the super globals. All super globals can be accessed in all scopes. The $GLOBALS variable is an array of all the variables defined in the global scope. The second option is to use the keyword global in front of one or more variable names separated by commas. This will create and reference the variable in the global scope.

How it Works

With this knowledge we can now rewrite the code from example 11_1.php to use either of the two methods of accessing global variables.

```php
<?php
// 11_2.php

$con = mysqli_connect('host', 'user', 'secret');
if ($con) {
  mysqli_select_db($con, 'mydb');
}

function DeleteRows() {
  if ($_GLOBALS['con']) {
    mysqli_query($_GLOBALS['con'], "delete from mytable;");
  }
  else {
    echo "No database connection";
  }
}

// Call the function
DeleteRows();

mysqli_close($con);
```

Using the $_GLOBALS array makes the code a bit unreadable but it's clear what's happening. The same code using the global keyword looks like this:

```php
<?php
// 11_3.php

$con = mysqli_connect('host', 'user', 'secret');
if ($con) {
  mysqli_select_db($con, 'mydb');
}

function DeleteRows() {
  global $con;
  if ($con) {
    mysqli_query($con, "delete from mytable;");
  }
  else {
    echo "No database connection";
  }
}

// Call the function
DeleteRows();

mysqli_close($con);
```

In this case the script is a bit more readable but it's also common to forget to add the global statement causing the script to show the error message even though the script might have a database connection.

233

Recipe 11-3. Passing Parameters

Problem

Deleting all the rows in a specific table is not a practical function. It does a single thing and it can only be used for that. How can we create a more generic function that can delete specific rows from any table?

Solution

The solution is to extend the function definition with one or more parameters. Function parameters act as variables defined inside the function but allow the passing of information to or from the function. The order of the variables is important. If the function defines three variables $a, $b, and $c in that order then that first value passed in will be assigned to $a, the second to $b, etc.

All supported variable types can be used as parameters. Names are not directly supported but can be implemented by passing an array where each element is a key value pair. That way the order of the parameters is no longer important.

As with any input it's the best practice to validate the type and content of variables before using them. This can prevent errors.

How it Works

Expanding the DeleteRows() function with two parameters where the first is a string with the name of the table to delete from and the second is an array of id's to delete. This assumes that all the tables include an id column as the primary key.

```php
<?php
// 11_4.php

$con = mysqli_connect('host', 'user', 'secret');
if ($con) {
  mysqli_select_db($con, 'mydb');
}

function DeleteRows($table, $ids) {
  global $con;
  if ($con) {
    $where = "";
    if (is_array($ids) && sizeof($ids)) {
      $strids = implode(", ", $ids);
      $where = " where id in ({$strids})";
    }
    mysqli_query($con, "delete from {$table}{$where};");
  }
  else {
    echo "No database connection";
  }
}

// Call the function
DeleteRows("mytable", [1, 3, 5]);

mysqli_close($con);
```

234

Passing an empty array as the second parameter will cause the where clause to be empty and the function will delete all rows from the table.

There is no validation of the $table variable. This will allow the user to pass any type of variable that could cause a SQL error. If an array is passed to the $table parameter the string replacement will cause the SQL statement to be "delete from Array."

In addition the function will allow the user to delete records from any table in the database. It could be a good idea to validate that the table exists and the user is allowed to perform the delete operation.

The same example could be implemented with a single array parameter where the parameters are named.

```php
<?php
// 11_5.php

$con = mysqli_connect('host', 'user', 'secret');
if ($con) {
  mysqli_select_db($con, 'mydb');
}

function DeleteRows($options) {
  global $con;
  if ($con) {
    if (is_array($options) && $options['table']) {
      $where = "";
      if (is_array($options['ids']) && sizeof($options['ids'])) {
        $strids = implode(", ", $options['ids']);
        $where = " where id in ({$strids})";
      }
      mysqli_query($con, "delete from {$options['table']}{$where};");
    }
    else {
      echo '$options must be an array';
    }
  }
  else {
    echo "No database connection";
  }
}

// Call the function
$params = [
  'ids' => [1, 3, 5],
  'table' => 'mytable'
];
DeleteRows($params);

mysqli_close($con);
```

Now the function takes a single parameter called $options. It must be an array and the key called 'table' must be defined, otherwise the function will print an error message. The order the parameters are created in the array does not matter.

Using arrays as parameters makes it possible to change how a function works without breaking existing code that uses the function. That is only the case if new parameters are added. Renaming or removing parameters might still require changes to existing code that is calling the function.

Recipe 11-4. Optional Parameters

Problem

In the previous examples the parameter for the ids to delete could be an empty array causing the function to delete all rows in the table. In the example where the parameters was passed as an array it would be possible to leave out the ids key and the function would still work, but in the example where table and ids were passed as two separate variables the ids would have to be passed, even if it was an empty array. It would be nice to be able to only pass the parameters that make sense in the context of calling the function.

Solution

Optional parameters are a way to tell the function to use a specific value for a parameter if the caller provides none. Optional parameters are defined from right to left in the parameter list. The first optional parameter that can be defined is the last parameter in the list and when that is optional the one before that can be defined optional. This can continue until all parameters are defined as optional.

Optional parameters are defined by assigning a value to the variable in the parameter list. If the $ids parameter should have a default value of an empty array it's written as $ids = [] or $ids = array() if you prefer the classic syntax.

How It Works

By changing the last parameter to have a default value of an empty array it's possible to call the DeleteRows() function with a single parameter. In that case the function will delete all rows from the specified table.

```php
<?php
// 11_6.php

$con = mysqli_connect('host', 'user', 'secret');
if ($con) {
  mysqli_select_db($con, 'mydb');
}

function DeleteRows($table, $ids = []) {
  global $con;
  if ($con) {
    $where = "";
    if (is_array($ids) && sizeof($ids)) {
      $strids = implode(", ", $ids);
      $where = " where id in ({$strids})";
    }
    mysqli_query($con, "delete from {$table}{$where};");
  }
  else {
    echo "No database connection";
  }
}

// Call the function
DeleteRows("mytable");

mysqli_close($con);
```

Variables with an optional value will either be assigned the optional value, when nothing is passed to the parameter, or the value passed by the caller. In the case where the options are passed as an array, that might cause an unwanted overwrite effects. Consider the function declaration:

```php
function DeleteRows($options = ['table' => 'mytable']) {}
```

If this function is called with `DeleteRows(['ids' => [1, 3, 5]);` the table name is lost and the function will not delete anything. To get around this we can define the default values inside the function and merge the options that are passed in onto the internal variable. This can be done with the `array_merge()` function.

```php
<?php
// 11_7.php

$con = mysqli_connect('host', 'user', 'secret');
if ($con) {
  mysqli_select_db($con, 'mydb');
}

function DeleteRows($opt = []) {
  global $con;
  $options = array_merge(['table' => 'mytable'], $opt);
  if ($con) {
    if (is_array($options) && $options['table']) {
      $where = "";
      if (is_array($options['ids']) && sizeof($options['ids'])) {
        $strids = implode(", ", $options['ids']);
        $where = " where id in ({$strids})";
      }
      mysqli_query($con, "delete from {$options['table']}{$where};");
    }
    else {
      echo '$options must be an array';
    }
  }
  else {
    echo "No database connection";
  }
}

// Call the function
$params = [
  'ids' => [1, 3, 5]
];
DeleteRows($params);

mysqli_close($con);
```

The $opt parameter is not optional and the internal variable $options is defined as the merge between a static array defining the table parameter and the values from $opt, if any. The `array_merge()` function will overwrite keys from the first array with values from the second array or add keys that are missing in the first array and exist in the second array.

Calling the DeleteRows() function without any parameters will delete all the rows in the mytable table. Adding only a parameter for ids will delete the matching rows in mytable. If deletion is required for a different table the caller can simply provide an option for table with an optional list of ids.

Again this function does not provide any checks if the table exists or if the user is allowed to delete the data (access control).

Recipe 11-5. Type Declarations

Problem

In a strict typed language like C the compiler will check that all parameters passed to functions are the correct type and the compilation will fail before the code can be executed. In a loosely typed language like PHP (see chapter 10) it's possible for variables to accept any type of data and they can change type during runtime. Is it possible to enable features that can help the developer passing the correct types of data to functions and class methods?

Solution

Type Declarations was introduced in PHP version 5.0. Back then the concept was called type hinting. In this version it was only possible to use class/interface or self as a type declaration. PHP version 5.1 added support for array, PHP version 5.4 added support for callable, and PHP 7.0 added support for scalar types (bool, int, float, and string).

Type declaration works by adding a type string in front of the variable. The type string can be a name of a class or interface, the word 'self' to indicate an object of the same class as the method is defined on or one of the keywords array, callable, bool, int, float, or string.

When a type declaration is used the parameter will not accept a null value. A null value does not have any type. It is however possible to allow the parameter to accept null values by making the parameter optional and defining the default value as null.

How it Works

In the next example the function definition is changed to have a string and array as the parameters.

```php
<?php
// 11_8.php

$con = mysqli_connect('host', 'user', 'secret');
if ($con) {
  mysqli_select_db($con, 'mydb');
}

function DeleteRows(string $table, array $ids = []) {
  global $con;
  if ($con) {
    $where = "";
    if (is_array($ids) && sizeof($ids)) {
      $strids = implode(", ", $ids);
      $where = " where id in ({$strids})";
    }
```

```
    mysqli_query($con, "delete from {$table}{$where};");
  }
  else {
    echo "No database connection";
  }
}

// Call the function
DeleteRows("mytable");

mysqli_close($con);
```

If this function is called with other types of parameters than a string and an array, PHP will cause a catchable fatal error (PHP 5) or throw an exception of TypeError (PHP 7).

```
Catchable fatal error: Argument 1 passed to DeleteRows() must be an instance of string, integer given
```

Recipe 11-6. Return Values

Problem

So far we have looked at calling functions and passing parameters but what about getting the result of a database calculation or a database query?

Solution

There are two ways of getting values from a function call. The first option is to define a return value. This is done with the use of the keyword return. The return keyword can be used alone and will cause the function to stop executing at that point, without returning any value.

If the return keyword is followed by a value or expression the function will return the value. This can be a scalar or a more complex value like an array or object.

The other way to return data from a function is to use parameters passed by reference. This is done by adding an & in front of the parameter name in the function declaration. Older versions of PHP would allow this at call time but this has been deprecated. It can only be done at the declaration.

A function can return a value with the use of the return statement and at the same time return one or more values by parameters passed as reference. It is common to use the return value as a status code that's easy to check and then use the returned parameters as the actual data returned.

How it Works

The DeleteRows() function used as an example throughout this chapter can be extended to return the number of rows actually deleted.

```
<?php
// 11_9.php

$con = mysqli_connect('host', 'user', 'secret');
if ($con) {
  mysqli_select_db($con, 'mydb');
}
```

```php
function DeleteRows(string $table, array $ids = []) {
  global $con;
  if ($con) {
    $where = "";
    if (is_array($ids) && sizeof($ids)) {
      $strids = implode(", ", $ids);
      $where = " where id in ({$strids})";
    }
    mysqli_query($con, "delete from {$table}{$where};");
    return mysqli_affected_rows($con);
  }
  else {
    echo "No database connection";
    return -1;
  }
}

// Call the function
DeleteRows("mytable");

mysqli_close($con);
```

The function contains two return statements that each will terminate execution at that point. The second return statement is used in the case of an error condition where no connection to the database exists. The possible return values for a successful deletion are 0 or higher so to indicate an error a return value outside of this range is chosen.

It is good programming practice to have as few places a function can return as possible. That makes the code easier to understand. In the example above we could assign the number of affected rows to a variable and do the same with the -1 value and simply have a single return statement at the end of the function.

To show how a function can return data in parameters passed by reference we can create a function that selects rows from a table.

```php
<?php
// 11_10.php

$con = mysqli_connect('host', 'user', 'secret');
if ($con) {
  mysqli_select_db($con, 'mydb');
}

function SelectRows(string $table, &$data) {
  global $con;
  $data = [];
  if ($con) {
    $where = "";
    $rs = mysqli_query($con, "select * from {$table};");
    if ($rs) {
      while($row = mysqli_fetch_assoc($rs)) {
        $data[] = $row;
      }
      mysqli_free_result($rs);
    }
```

```
  }
  else {
    echo "No database connection";
  }
  return sizeof($data);
}

// Call the function
if (SelectRows("mytable", $mytable)) {
  // Do Something
}

mysqli_close($con);
```

In this example the function SelectRows() takes two parameters. The first is a string that indicates the name of the table to use. The second parameter does not have any type declaration, as the function will overwrite any data already in it as the return value.

This function will always return a value of 0 or higher, even if there is an error.

Recipe 11-7. Check if Function Exists

Problem

Calling a function that is undefined will cause a fatal error. Most of the time this happens due to spelling errors but there can be cases where the programmer wants to check if a function is defined and then act accordingly.

Solution

There are a number of built-in functions that can help the programmer determine if a function exists. The first one is get_defined_functions(). This function does not take any parameters and it will return a multidimensional array with two keys, 'internal' and 'user'. There are over 1500 internal functions, depending on the number of extensions installed. This makes this method less practical to check for a single function.

The next function is called function_exists(). This function takes a single parameter describing a specific function to look for. This can either be a string value or a variable with a string value. The value is not case sensitive as it is the case with any function name in PHP.

Finally there is a function called is_callable(). This function will check if the content of the variable passed in is a callable function or a method on a class. The variable can either be a string value that points to a function or an array with two values where the first is an object and the second is a string with the name of a method on that object.

How it Works

A simple use of the function function_exists() could be to determine if a specific include file is loaded.

```
<?php
// 11_11.php

if (!function_exists('MyFunction')) {
  include "myfunc.inc";
}
```

241

Recipe 11-8. Calculated Function Names

Problem

If your script contains a number of functions that do similar things, and you need to call the right function based on the value of a variable you might end up writing a set of nested if statements or a switch/case statement. If there are a few functions that might not be a big problem but if the number of functions is growing it can create long and complicated logic.

Solution

The solution is to use PHP's ability to use a variable as a function. Just like it's possible to have variable variables (multiple $ signs in front of the name) it's also possible to start a function call with a $. In that case PHP will take the contents of the variable and use that as the function name. If the variable contains a non-string value or the value is a string that can't be matched to a function name the system will throw a fatal error.

How it Works

Let's first look at the example using a traditional switch/case statement to call the desired function.

```php
<?php
// 11_12.php

$v = 1.25;

function FormatInteger($i) {
}
function FormatFloat($f) {
}
function FormatBool($b) {
}
function FormatString($s) {
}

switch (gettype($v)) {
  case 'integer' :
    FormatInteger($v);
    break;
  case 'double' :
    FormatFloat($v);
    break;
  case 'boolean' :
    FormatBool($v);
    break;
  case 'string' :
    FormatString($v);
    break;
}
```

The same functionality can be obtained by calculating the name of the function. First we need to make sure the functions are named correctly, so the name matches an actual name of a valid type.

```php
<?php
// 11_13.php

$v = 1.25;

function FormatInteger($i) {
}
function FormatDouble($f) {
}
function FormatBoolean($b) {
}
function FormatString($s) {
}

$f = "Format" . gettype($v);
if (is_callable($f)) {
  $f($v);
}
```

Then we can create a variable that contains the prefix of all the functions (Format) and then add the name of the variable type. The name of the variable type will be all lowercase, but because function names are case insensitive this will still resolve to the correct option. We use the function is_callable() to check if $f points to a function. In this little example there are no functions defined for arrays, objects, or resources so the code would fail if $v had a value of any of these types.

Recipe 11-9. Anonymous Functions

Problem

In the previous section we saw how function names can be calculated, assigned to a variable, and then executed. Is it also possible to "store" complete functions in variables?

Solution

The answer is yes and these are called anonymous functions or closures. These have been available since PHP 5.3 and are useful in a couple of ways.

The most basic use is as a callback function. This is used as a parameter to another function that will execute the callback one or more times. By using an anonymous function this function will only be available within the scope of the function that is called.

Another use are functions that can exist for a short amount of time and be redefined as needed. This is done by creating a variable and assigning it a function value $a = function($b) {};

How it Works

Let's first look at the use as a callback function. PHP has a number of building functions that takes a callback as a parameter. The function usort() is one of these. This function is designed to take a user-defined function and use it to sort an array.

Before closures were introduced the usort function would be used like this:

```php
<?php
// 11_14.php

function compare($a, $b) {
  if ($a == $b) {
    return 0;
  }
  return ($a < $b) ? -1 : 1;
}
$arr = [1, 9, 3, 1, 5, 7, 4];
usort($arr, 'compare');
print_r($arr);
```

With the introduction of the 'spaceship' operator (<=>) in PHP 7.0 and the use of closures it's possible to write this same code a bit simpler.

```php
<?php
// 11_15.php

$arr = [1, 9, 3, 1, 5, 7, 4];
usort($arr, function($a, $b) { return $a <=> $b; });
print_r($arr);
```

The spaceship operator will compare the two values on each side and return -1 if the left side is smaller than the right side, 0 if the two sides have the same value, and 1 if the right side is smaller than the left.

The anonymous function will only exist in memory as long as the usort() function is running and it is not callable when the function ends.

The combination of anonymous functions and variable functions can be used to modify functions based on logic or other criteria during execution. In the next example we create an anonymous function to calculate the profit on sales. It is decided to give the customers who shop on Wednesdays a small discount. Instead of checking the day of the week for all transactions we can make the check once and define the function to do the calculation.

```php
<?php
// 11_16.php

if (date('w') == 3) {
  $profit = function($p) {
    return $p * 1.25;
  };
}
else {
  $profit = function($p) {
    return $p * 1.30;
  };
}
// read all transactions from the database
foreach($transaction as $t) {
  $p = $profit($t);
}
```

This example could have been implemented with regular function definitions. Only one of the functions would be defined, based on the logic. But if you want to redefine a function during execution you would have to use closures.

```php
<?php
// 11_17.php

$profit = function($p) {
  return $p * 1.30;
};

echo $p = $profit(100) . "\n";

// Do some stuff

$profit = function($p) {
  return $p * 1.25;
};

echo $p = $profit(100) . "\n";
```

In this case the first profit function is used once and after that isn't thrown away when a new function is assigned to the variable $profit. This is done without compiler or runtime errors.

As a side effect of how the PHP parser works it's possible to define nested functions. Although this is possible it is not recommended. The inner function will only be defined if the outer function is executed and if the outer function is called more than once the inner function will be redefined causing a fatal error as shown in the next example.

```php
<?php
// 11_18.php
function A() {
  function B($i) {
    echo "B called with $i\n";
  }
  for ($i = 1; $i < 3; $i++) {
    B($i);
  }
  echo "A called\n";
}
A();
B(0);
```

In this case A() is called first causing the function B() to be defined so when B() is called after A() it will still work. If B() was called first or A() was called more than once a fatal error would be raised.

Closures can be used to get around this and create "private" functions within functions

```php
<?php
// 11_19.php
function A() {
  $f = function ($i) {
    echo "B called with $i\n";
  };
```

```
  for ($i = 1; $i < 3; $i++) {
    $f($i);
  }
  echo "A called\n";
}
A();
A();
```

Now we can call the A() function as often as needed and the function defined by the variable $f can only be called from within the function A().

Recipe 11-10. Variable Parameter List

Problem

Is it possible to define a function that takes a variable number of arguments?

Solution

A function can be called with more parameters than it was declared to have. In that case there are a couple of special functions that can be used to get information about the parameters. The function func_num_args() returns the number of arguments passed to the function. The functions func_get_arg() and func_get_args() can be used to fetch a single argument (by ordinal number) or all the arguments passed to the function.

A warning will be issued if any of these functions are called from the global scope. They should only be called from within a function or method.

How it Works

In the next example a function is declared with no required parameters and then it's called with a string, an integer, and an array as the parameters. The function will show that three parameters were passed to the function.

```php
<?php
// 11_20.php

function MyFunc() {
  echo func_num_args() . "\n";
}

MyFunc("A", 1, [1,2,3]);
```

If the function has some required and optional parameters it's still possible to pass and process additional parameters.

```php
<?php
// 11_21.php

function MyFunc(string $s, int $i = 0) {
  echo func_num_args() . "\n";
  print_r(func_get_args());
}

MyFunc("Abc", 1, [1,2,3]);
```

Although the parameters $s and $i are defined, they will be assigned the first two parameters that are passed in the function func_num_args() and func_get_args() will count and return the total number of parameters passed. The output will look like this when executed with PHP 7:

```
3
Array
(
    [0] => Abc
    [1] => 1
    [2] => Array
        (
            [0] => 1
            [1] => 2
            [2] => 3
        )

)
```

CHAPTER 12

■ ■ ■

Web Fundamentals

The primary purpose of PHP is to process web or http requests from a browser through a web server and to generate valid responses to such requests. The nature of a web request is that it's usually short lived and it does not have any knowledge about previous or future requests. The principle makes it possible for even a modest hardware configuration to serve a large number of requests in a short amount of time. This is often measured in the average response time or the number of requests per second or per hour.

In the beginning PHP was a way to inject values or sections of content into existing HTML documents but from PHP version 3 it has been possible to dynamically create complete HTML documents from the scripting language and any resource available to PHP at runtime. The structure of the PHP file can include static HTML sections with sections of PHP code that will resolve to dynamic content or it can contain no static blocks and just be a single script where the output of the script is returned to the requesting client.

Recipe 12-1. Headers

Problem

The Hyper Text Transport Protocol (HTTP) is very simple. When a TCP/IP socket connection is created between a browser and a web server the browser will send a request that has two basic sections. The first are the headers and the second is the body of the message. When the server returns the response it will also consist of headers and a body. The separation between headers and body is \r\n\r\n (two sets of carriage return and line feed).

For most simple requests the developer can ignore the header values in both the request and the response. The default configuration of PHP will automatically set the valid headers, assuming the response is a HTML document, but in other cases it might be necessary to overwrite these headers or add additional information. For the request it might be necessary to validate a header in order to proceed.

Solution

The default header (for Content-Type) that is sent with a PHP response is configured in php.ini, with the setting called default_mimetype, and is set to text/html. In addition there is also a setting called default_characterset and it defaults to UTF-8. Older versions of PHP used ISO-8889-1 as the default character set. If you want to add or overwrite any of the headers you use the header() function. Each header is a key value pair with a name of the header followed by a colon (:) and then the value. Setting the Content-Type header looks like this:

```
header("Content-Type: text/html");
```

© Frank M. Kromann 2016
F.M. Kromann, *PHP and MySQL Recipes*, DOI 10.1007/978-1-4842-0605-8_12

There are a couple of ways to get the request headers. With a standard configuration the headers end up in the super global called $_SERVER and the keys are prefixed with HTTP_. In addition to the request headers the $_SERVER variable also contains environment variables and other data.

A commonly used request header is the user agent ($_SERVER['HTTP_USER_AGENT']) variable. This can be used to detect the type of client requesting the content and, based on that, format the response specifically to the client.

All header values can easily be spoofed and any header value should be handled as any other user input.

How it Works

In this next example we use the header() function to set the Content-Type to text/plain and then send some plain content to the client. All calls to the header() function should be done before any other output is sent to the client.

```php
<?php
// 12_1.php
header("Content-Type: text/plain");
?>
This software is licensed under the MIT license
Plese see https://opensource.org/licenses/MIT for details
```

If you want to redirect users of mobile devices to a special version of a website you can do that by checking the user agent string and a regular expression that checks for certain keywords and if one of them is found use the header function to redirect the request.

```php
<?php
// 12_2.php
$mobile = '/(ios|ipod|mobile|pad|phone|tablet|' .
          'symbian|android|blackberry|webos)/i';
if (is_set($_SERVER['HTTP_USER_AGENT']) &&
    preg_match($mobile_agents, $_SERVER['HTTP_USER_AGENT'])) {
    header("Location: http://m.mysite.com");
}
```

The first part of the if statement where we check if the variable is set is to avoid warnings when the script is requested from a client that doesn't set a value for the user agent. This could be a PHP script that's using the open wrappers to request content from a remote server. This could be a simple call to file_get_contents(), This is the preferred way to read the content of a file or stream into a variable. Unless a stream context is provided no headers will be set.

Please note that all header values must be set before any other output is generated. If headers are set after output is generated, PHP will generate a warning.

Recipe 12-2. $_GET and $_POST

Problem

GET and POST are two HTTP request methods support by browsers. The GET method is used when a user clicks a link in a document or types a URL in the address bar. The POST method is associated with submitting the HTML form from a web page.

How can the data from a GET or POST request be access in a PHP script?

Solution

The solution is again the super globals. Depending on the configuration value `variables_order` in php.ini the super globals will be populated with values from the request. The valid configuration options are zero or more of the letters G, P, C, E, and S. Each of these represents Get, Post, Cookie, Environment, and Server. Environment variables are not commonly used by PHP scripts so a common configuration is `variables_order = "GPCS"`. In addition to `variables_order` you can also configure `request_order` to define which of the request data is populated into the `$_REQUEST` array.

The `$_REQUEST` super global is a combination of data from other the requests and there can be overlap, so the order of whose data is populated matter. If you are posting a form with a field named 'phone' and the post URL is http://mydomain.com?phone=123 you will end up with an index called phone in both the `$_GET` and the `$_POST` super global. When the data is populated into the `$_REQUST` array it's the value from the array defined last in the `request_order` configuration. If the request_order is set to "GP" the value from the `$_POST` array will win. Setting it to "PG" will give you the value from the `$_GET` array.

How it Works

When a get request is performed without any parameters the `$_GET` array will be an empty array. When parameters are added to the URL each of the parameters will end up in the `$_GET` array as a key. The URL `http://mydomain.com?p1=test&p2=123` will produce the following values in the `$_GET` variable:

```
Array (
  [p1] => test
  [p2] => 123
)
```

It is possible to use the same variable name multiple times, but only the last one is registered, as keys must be unique. The URL `http://mydomain.com?p1=test&p2=123&p1=abc`, where the parameter p1 is included twice with two different values will give these values in the `$_GET` array.

```
Array (
  [p1] => abc
  [p2] => 123
)
```

Just like PHP can add elements to an array with the syntax $a[] = 'abc'; it's possible to generate elements in the `$_GET` array that contains an array of values. The URL `http://mydomain.com?p1[]=test&p2=123&p1[]=abc` will do just that.

```
Array (
  [p1] => Array (
    [0] => test
    [1] => abc
  )
  [p2] => 123
)
```

If you want to specify the keys in the array you can do that too. The URL `http://mydomain.com?p1[a]=t` `est&p2=123&p1[b]=abc` will generate the keys a and b on the p1 element in the $_GET array.

```
Array (
  [p1] => Array (
    [a] => test
    [b] => abc
  )
  [p2] => 123
)
```

Getting data into the $_POST array is a bit more complicated. Although it follows the exact same rules as the $_GET array it requires the user to submit a HTML form from a browser (or other client that can generate a POST request). This is one reason why POST requests are used or even preferred for API requests. Requiring a POST request will prevent a user from sending requests from a browser or the wget command-line tool. It can also make testing a bit more complicated. There is no real security in requiring a POST request but it makes it more difficult.

Creating a post request in a browser starts with a HTML form and a button to submit the form. The form has two HTML components. The first is the form tag that wraps one or more input tags. The form tag has attributes to define the method (GET or POST) and an action. The action is the target URL that will receive the post. This can be an absolute or relative URL to the URL where the HTML document that included the form was loaded from, or it can be a URL on a completely different web site. A HTML form that can populate the $_POST array with similar values as in the previous examples could look like this:

```
<form method="POST" action="/">
  <input name="p1[a]" type="text" />
  <input name="p1[b]" type="text" />
  <input name="p2" type="text" />
  <input type="submit" />
</form>
```

And the contents of the $_POST array will look like this:

```
Array (
  [p1] => Array (
    [a] => abc
    [b] => def
  )
  [p2] => 123
)
```

It is not necessary to have a HTML form to create a POST request. This can be done with an Asynchronous Javascript and XML request (AJAX). This is described in more detail in a later section of this chapter.

The same variable name can be used in the query string and the post body as shown in the next example:

```
<form method="POST" action="/?p2=value">
  <input name="p1[a]" type="text" />
  <input name="p1[b]" type="text" />
  <input name="p2" type="text" />
  <input type="submit" />
</form>
```

This will result in both the $_GET and $_POST arrays containing a value for p2.
The contents of $_GET will look like this:

```
Array (
  [p2] => value
)
```

And the $_POST array will still contain these values:

```
Array (
  [p1] => Array (
    [a] => abc
    [b] => def
  )
  [p2] => 123
)
```

Recipe 12-3. Cookies

Problem

Because of the nature of how web servers and browsers interact where every request is a new connection between the browser and the server, there is no easy way for the server to know that the request is coming from the same browser. The server could use the IP address of the request and/or the user agent string. But in an environment where multiple users can share the same public IP address (NAT) this does not guarantee that the requests are from the same user. Is it possible to identify the requests as coming from the same client?

Solution

One of the headers that can be exchanged between the client and server is the cookie header. This value originates on the server as part of a response. If the server sets a cookie, the browser will automatically include that cookie on subsequent requests to the same server. It can be set with the header() function but the format of the cookie is not trivial so PHP offers a SetCookie() function that takes a number of parameters that makes the setting and clearing of cookies relatively easy.

Browsers can store cookies in a couple of different places. A cookie can be stored on desk. This makes it possible to have cookies that will be persisted on the client for a long time, and they will be accessible even if the browser application is closed and restarted. All cookies must have an expiration time. When a non-zero value is set the cookie will automatically be written to disk and the browser will purge it after the expiration data/time.

Another option is to use an in-memory cookie, where the expiration time is set to 0. This will not be written to disk and it will be deleted when the browser is closed. In addition the SetCookie() function has a couple of options to set the cookie as secure, meaning it will only be used if the connection is over HTTPS and the cookie can be defined as HTTP only. This will prevent the client-side scripting code (javascript) from accessing the cookie.

The user of the browser can clear the cookies at any time, and as cookies are just files on a disk they can be faked. The code on the server side should take appropriate actions to handle cookies. In addition many countries require that the web site announce the use of cookies alongside with the purpose.

How it Works

This next example shows how a cookie can be used to track if a user has visited the web site before and print a special message accordingly.

```php
<?php
//12_3.php

if ($_COOKIE['visited']) {
  echo "Welcome Back!";
}
else {
  echo "Welcome to mydomain.com";
}
SetCookie('visited', time(), time() + 30 * 86400);
```

All parameters except the first (name) to the SetCookie() function are optional.

First we check the super global variable $_COOKIE for a key called visited. This is the way to check if a cookie is set. Based on that check the script will print one of two messages and then set the cookie with an expiration date 30 days in the future. The value of the cookie is set to the current time. This could used to show additional information about when the user was last visiting the site.

The first time a user requests the script they will get the generic welcome message and if the page is refreshed or the user returns within the 30 days they will get the welcome back message.

Cookies that are in-memory only are often used to store information about the user so the site can operate without the user has to log in again and again. This can be used as a timer that checks the time since the last request to the server and if too much time has gone by since the previous request, force the user to provide credentials again.

```php
<?php
//12_4.php

if (empty($_COOKIE['access']) || $_COOKIE['access'] < time() - 15 * 60) {
  SetCookie('access');
  Login();
}
else {
  SetCookie('access', time(), 0);
  // Perform action;
}
```

In this example we check for a cookie called access and if it's not defined or the value is older than 15 minutes the user is forced to perform the login, otherwise the value of the access cookie is set to the current time allowing the user another 15 minutes before the next action to stay locked in.

The SetCookie() function is also called with a single parameter, the name of the cookie. This will cause the cookie to be set but with an empty value. Deleting the cookie is done by setting the cookie with an expiration time in the past. Deleting a cookie will work for in-memory cookies as well as cookies written to disk.

In section 12-5 we will discuss the use of session data. When session data is used PHP will automatically generate a cookie called PHPSESSID. This is a memory-only cookie used to identify the data stored on the server side for the specific browser.

Recipe 12-4. Server Variables

Problem

We have seen how we can change the program flow based on the user's interaction with the web site, but what if we can't react to where the user is located in the world or whether they use the http or https version of the site?

Solution

There are a number of values stored in the $_SERVER super global that has to do with the request. These values can be used to provide specific content or to redirect the user to a different site. The request scheme can be checked with $_SERVER['REQUEST_SCHEME']. The values can be http or https.

You can also get the public IP address of the client machine with $_SERVER['REMOTE_ADDR']. This can be used to detect the country the user is originating from. This information is not always accurate as users can go though a number of proxies before accessing the Internet and thus it will be the IP address of the last proxy the request is coming from that will be populated in the $_SERVER variable.

If you decide to "trust" the IP address you can use services like GeoIP to translate the IP address to a location. This can be a country and perhaps a state/province and a city name depending on the type of subscription you are using with GeoIP.

How it Works

If you wanted to make sure a user is on the secure version of your site when they are accessing certain URL's you can add this to the script:

```php
<?php
// 12_5.php

if ($_SERVER['REQUEST_SCHEME'] == 'http') {
  $Location = $_SERVER['SERVER_NAME'] . $_SERVER['REQUEST_URI'];
  header("Location: **Error! Hyperlink reference not valid.**}");
  exit;
}
```

As an alternative you can use the browser's Geolocation API to get the user's location. This is available in most browsers that support the HTML 5 standard. Although the API is supported in most browsers it comes with the caveat that the user will have to approve the revealing of the information. Geolocation provides longitude and latitude data that can be used to locate the browser or to serve content that is relevant to the user's current location.

The Geolocation API is implemented in javascript and you will need a form or an AJAX request to submit the data to the server side. The next example shows a HTML 5 document that will detect if Geolocation is available, and if the user accepts the request it will get and print the latitude and longitude.

```
<!DOCTYPE html>
<!-Position.html->
<html>
<head>
<script>
function showPosition(position) {
    document.write("Latitude: " + position.coords.latitude +
```

```
      "<br>Longitude: " + position.coords.longitude);
}
if (navigator.geolocation) {
  navigator.geolocation.getCurrentPosition(showPosition);
}
else {
  document.write("Geolocation is not supported by this browser.");
}
</script>
</head>
<body>
</body>
</html>
```

If the device the browser is running on is equipped with a GPS receiver the position is more accurate than a laptop or desktop computer connected to the Internet.

Finally there are a number of third-party JavaScript libraries that can be used to collect useful information from the user. One I often use is the jstz library that makes it possible to get the user's time zone and use that as part of a request to sign up for an account on the web site. Knowing the user's time zone makes it possible to show date/time values according to the user's local time. The easy way is to provide a drop-down list with the valid time zones. This list is going to be quite long and it's nice to be able to have a value preselected for the user. The library can be found here: http://pellepim.bitbucket.org/jstz/. The library is very easy to use. After loading the library you can instantiate the time zone object with var timezone = jstz.determine(); and then access the name of the time zone with timezone.name();.

The full script for a user signup with automatic time zone selection could look like this.

```
<?php
// 12_6.php

if (empty($_POST)) {
  echo <<<HEREDOC
<!DOCTYPE html>
<html>
<head>
<script src="/js/jstz.js"></script>
</head>
<body>
<form method="POST" action="{$_SERVER['PHP_SELF']}">
  <div>
    <label for="user">User Name</label>
    <input name="user" type="text" required />
  </div>
  <div>
    <label for="timezone">Time Zone</label>
    <input id="tz" name="timezone" type="text" required />
  </div>
  <div>
    <input type="submit" />
  </div>
</form>
<script>
```

```
var timezone = jstz.determine();
var tz = document.getElementById('tz');
tz.value = timezone.name();
</script>
</body>
</html>
HEREDOC;
}
else {
  date_default_timezone_set($_POST['timezone']);
  $lt = date('M d Y H:i:s');
  echo <<<HEREDOC
<!DOCTYPE html>
<html>
<head>
<script src="/js/jstz.js"></script>
</head>
<body>
<div>Welcome: {$_POST['user']}</div>
<div>Local time is: {$lt}</div>
</body>
</html>
HEREDOC;
}
```

In this example we used a simple text input field and used JavaScript to fill in a value for the time zone. In my case that was America/Los_Angeles. The user can manually type another time zone (i.e., Europe/Paris) and when the form is submitted the script will show a welcome notice and the local time in the time zone entered.

This script does not validate any of the input and it would be a better user experience to present the user with a list of all the valid time zones. This will prevent mistyping and the user will not have to know the exact time zone names.

On the PHP side, when the form is submitted we use the function date_default_timezone_set() to set the current time zone before using any of the date functions. This function takes a mandatory parameter that is the string representing the time zone like "Europe/Paris."

Recipe 12-5. Session Data

Problem

As described in section 12-3 we can use cookies to store data in the client, but that is somewhat insecure, as the client will have access to manipulate the data between requests. It would be nice if there were a way to store the data on the server where only the server side scripts can access it.

Solution

Data can be stored on the server in a number of different ways. The server can write files, create records in a database, or other type of storage. Any of these are usually not linked to a specific session in a browser. By using the session data in PHP the system will generate a unique id that is used as a cookie. It's stored in the browser's memory and sent with all requests to the server. The session id is used to load or save a serialized array of data from disk (or other storage engine). This is all handled by the session_start() function. Calling this function before any output will look for the existence of a cookie called PHPSESSID. If it exists it will load all existing data matching the id and the same Id will be used for future references. If the cookie doesn't exist a new Id is generated and the cookie is set.

Any variable added to the $_SESSION variable will be stored when the script terminates or when the function session_close() is called and all the data written will automatically be populated in $_SESSION on the next request where session_start() is called.

Session data has a configurable expiration time. If no requests are made from the client to the server before the data expires, all the data will be removed from the session storage. The default value for the expiration is 1440 seconds or 24 minutes. This is configured in php.ini with the configuration value session.gc_maxlifetime = 1440. Each time the data is written the counter is reset.

There are a number of other configuration options that I recommend to use with the session configuration:

Session Id's can be initialized from many sources but by setting session.use_only_cookies = 1 in php.ini will restrict the source to cookies only. To ensure that the value of the cookie can't be accessed from scripting languages set the session.cookie_httponly = 1, and finally setting session.hash_function = 1 will make use of that SHA-1 function instead of the MD5 function to create the value for the cookie.

How it Works

In this example we use the session storage to store values that are linked to the browser through the cookie named PHPSESSID.

```php
<?php
// 12_7.php

date_default_timezone_set('UTC');
session_start();
if ($_SESSION['last_request']) {
  echo "Las access was " . date('M d Y H:i:s');
}
else {
  echo 'This is the first request to the site';
}
$_SESSION['last_request'] = time();
```

The first time a user requests the script they will get the message indicating that they have not been on the site before. As this is handled with a session cookie, they will get the same message if they close the browser and open it again or if they ways more than the configured lifetime for the garbage collector (24 min). In all other cases the script will show when they last accessed anything on the same server where the script started the session.

The $_SESSION array can contain values of any type of data. It can be used to store scalars as shown above, arrays, and even instantiated objects.

In example 12_3.php we used a cookie variable (visited) to store data about the time of access to the site. Using client-side storage makes it possible for the user to alter the data before sending subsequent requests making it an insecure form of storage. By moving the data to session data on the server we can link multiple values to a single session cookie and at the same time prevent the user from manipulating the data between requests.

The only security concern becomes the session cookie. If a user can take the value of the cookie and inject it in a different browser or other type of client they could potentially get access to data stored in the session data and thereby gain access to the site (of the session data contains information that identifies a user).

Recipe 12-6. Content Type and Disposition

Problem

Although PHP is designed to generate HTML documents it can also be used to generate other forms of content. The content can be used within the browser or saved to desk, but how can we tell the browser what type of content it is and how it's expected to use it?

Solution

There are some defaults that most browsers follow. If the content is identified with Content-Type defined as one of the headers and set to text/html or text/plain the browser will render the content as the document. The same way of the Content-Type is defined as application/octet-stream the browser will attempt to save the content to a file by opening the save as dialog to allow the user to select a folder and specify the filename.

In no Content-Type header is given from PHP the default value will be provided, and if the file is downloaded directly from the web server (image files, etc.) the web server will apply the appropriate header. If the wrong Content-Type is specified the browser might even look at the content and overwrite, rendering the content correct anyway. This is the case with images where it's possible to use image/jpeg for a GIF and it's possible to rename a .jpg file to .gif and the browser will still handle the image rendering correct.

The header Content-Type is intended to tell the browser what it is receiving in the body of the HTTP request. In the same way we can use the header Content-Disposition to tell the browser how to handle the response. The Content-Disposition can have two values. The value inline means the content should be rendered as part of the document if possible (text, html, image, etc.) and the value attachment indicates that the browser should save the file to disk. This is useful if you want the user to download a file that can be rendered in the browser. If you don't specify the Content-Disposition the browser will use its default behavior and the user will have to use the Save As function in the browser to save the content to desk.

Both of these headers can be set with the header() function. And both of them have additional options that can be provided. For the Content-Type we can add charset and specify if we are using utf-8 or iso-8889-1 or other character sets.

For the Content-Disposition we can add a filename option to suggest a file name that goes along with the content. If the filename is not provided the browser will default to the name of the file that is fetched from the server. That might be Ok if the file is served directly from the web server but if the file is generated with php the file name will be the name of the script.

How it Works

If you have an image file that you want to scale to a smaller size when the image is viewed in the browser but also allow the user to click a link and download the full-sized version of the image; you can use the code from example 8_3.php and add headers for downloading the image.

```php
<?php
// 12_8.php

$size = [160, 120];
$img_name = 'IMG_0099.JPG';
$orig = GetImageSize($img_name);

$a1 = $size[0] / $size[1];
$a2 = $orig[0] / $orig[1];
```

```php
if ($a1 > $a2) {
  $d = ceil($orig[0] / $size[0]);
}
else {
  $d = ceil($orig[1] / $size[1]);
}
$w = $orig[0] / $d;
$h = $orig[1] / $d;
header('Content-Type: ' . $orig['mime']);
if ($_REQUEST['Download']) {
  header('Content-Disposition: attachment; filename="' . $img_name . '"');
  readfile($img_name);
}
else {
  $img = ImageCreateFromJpeg('IMG_0099.JPG');
  $thumb = ImageScale($img, $w, $h);
  switch ($orig[2]) {
    case IMG_JPG :
    case IMG_JPEG :
      ImageJPEG($thumb);
      break;
    case IMG_PNG :
      ImagePNG($thumb);
      break;
    case IMG_GIF :
      ImageGIF($thumb);
      break;
  }
  ImageDestroy($thumb);
  ImageDestroy($img);
}
```

The HTML to show the image and provide a download link could look like this:

```html
<!DOCTYPE html>
<!- 12_8.html ->
<html>
<body>
<img src="12_8.php" />
<a href="12_8.php?Download=1">Download this image</a>
</body>
</html>
```

The image tag will render the thumbnail of the image and then a tag will provide a link to download the image in full size. Depending on the settings in the browser the user might or might not get a dialog box. In most browsers these days the default action is to save the file in a preconfigured download folder.

Recipe 12-7. Caching

Problem

Various types of content might end up changing at different frequencies. Static files like javascript and images might not change often and it would be a good idea to let the browser use the version already downloaded if it exists. This will save bandwidth and reduce the load on the server. This is usually handled with configurations of the web server. For content generated by PHP the default behavior is to generate and send the content to the client on every request, even if the client already has a copy of the content. That is using both bandwidth as well as CPU and memory resources on the server. In addition the script might use other resources to get the data. How can we dynamically handle the requests to determine if the client already has a copy of the content and whether it's Ok to use the copy already on the client?

Solution

The first step is to divide the content into various groups. Images, scripts, and other files that are served directly by the web server (without invoking PHP) should be handled by the web server configuration.

Content that is generally available to the public, no login or other user identification required could be served as a static file. Meaning when the content changes a process on the server will generate a new copy and all requests for the content will simply serve the pregenerated file. All this can be handled on the server without specific headers.

Content that changes more often could be given an expiration time. If that is done alone the browser will use the local copy until the time of expiration, but if we tell the browser that it must revalidate on every request the browser will add headers that can be tested and only of the content was changed on the server it will be regenerated; otherwise the server will simply tell the browser to use the copy it already has through a status code 304. This does require some communication between the browser and server but the server only spends time checking if the cache is still valid.

How it Works

The trick is to use a number of headers that identify that the browser can cache the content, how the cache should be handled, when the content was modified, and when it expires.

```php
<?php
// 12_9.php

function Cache($last_mod, $ttl = 86400) {
  $gmt_mod = gmdate('D, d M Y H:i:s', $last_mod) . ' GMT';
  $gmt_expires = gmdate('D, d M Y H:i:s', time() + $ttl) . ' GMT';

  header("Pragma: Cache");
  header("Cache-Control: max-age=0, must-revalidate");
  header("Last-Modified: " . $gmt_mod);
  header("Expires: " . $gmt_expired);

  if (!empty($_SERVER['HTTP_IF_MODIFIED_SINCE']) &&
      $_SERVER['HTTP_IF_MODIFIED_SINCE'] == $gmt_mod) {
    http_response_code(304);
    exit();
  }
}
```

```
// Lookup the timestamp when the data was changed
$LastMod = GetModified();
Cache($LastMod);

// Check for a cached version on the server
if (file_exists("cache_12_9.php")) {
  readfile("cache_12_9.php");
}
else {
  // Generate the content
}
```

In the example we use the Cache() function to check if the content was changed and to set the headers for the content. This function could be added to an include file so it can be used by multiple requests.

The format for the date/time values for the Last-Modified and Expires headers should be in the very specific format 'D, d M Y H:i:s' or by using one of the predefined constants DATE_RSS. The dates are also required to always be in GMT.

When the Cache-Control header is defined with must-revalidate the browser will always send a request to the server with the header HTTP_IF_MODIFIED_SINCE set to the modification last-modified date from the original response. That value will end up in the super global variable $_SERVER['HTTP_IF_MODIFIED_SINCE'] and can be compared directly to the modification date/time. If they are identical the script will send a status code 304 telling the browser to use the cached content and it exists so it does not have to spend resources on generating the content again.

For this to work the code that fetches the modification time must generate the same UNIX timestamp until the content actually changes.

The last section of the script checks for a cached version of the content on the server. If this file exists it will be sent to the client as is, otherwise the script will generate the content and perhaps save a cached version. The elements of code used to update the content could also generate the cached version when the new content is saved. This type of caching is relevant on sites that serve the exact same version of the content to many users in a high volume. For low-volume sites it might be fine to generate the content from scratch on every request.

Recipe 12-8. Remote Content

Problem

So far we have concentrated on the communication between the server and the browser, but what if the data needed is located on a different (web) server?

Solution

The fopen wrappers (as discussed in chapter 7) and stream functions in PHP can be used to communicate with other servers. The simplest for it is to use file_get_content() with a URL instead of a local file. This does not in itself provide a way to specify header values for the request or allow any access to the response headers. That's here the stream context comes in. It is possible to set the default stream context used with all functions (fopen(), file_get_contents() etc.) when used without a specified stream context. This is done with the stream_context_set_default() function. If a specific stream context is needed for individual function calls it can be created by calling the function stream_context_create(). The two functions both work on an array of options.

There is a long line of options available and the options are specific to the protocol used to communicate with the server. The supported protocols are HTTP, FTP, SSL, CURL, Phar, and MongoDB. These are available is the respective modules are installed. In this example we focus on the HTTP protocol, but the other protocols follow a similar pattern. More information can be found here: `http://php.net/manual/en/context.php`.

The important options available for the HTTP protocol are method, header, user_agent, and content. There are a number of other options to enable/disable redirects and other advanced features.

The method is either GET or POST and if it's not defined it defaults to GET. Headers can either be a string or an array of strings if more than one header should be sent. It follows the exact same pattern or syntax as is used with the header() function. The user_agent is a string that identifies the client. This can be anything and could be used to emulate various devices. If it's not defined the default value defined in php.ini will be used. If that is undefined the system will use PHP as the user agent. Finally the content should be the body of the POST request, following the standard formatting rules of a HTTP request.

How it Works

In the next example we look at how stream_context can be used to get content from a server acting as various different user agents. The first step is to identify the user agent strings to use. A few popular strings are the following:

Safari on an iPad:

```
Mozilla/5.0 (iPad; CPU OS 6_0 like Mac OS X) AppleWebKit/536.26 (KHTML, like Gecko)
Version/6.0 Mobile/10A5355d Safari/8536.25
```

Google Chrome on Windows:

```
Mozilla/5.0 (Windows NT 6.1) AppleWebKit/537.36 (KHTML, like Gecko) Chrome/41.0.2228.0
Safari/537.36
```

The web site `http://www.useragentstring.com/pages/useragentstring.php` keeps a list of the user agent strings used by many browsers and many different versions.

The next step is to create a stream context that sets the desired user agent and other parameters and finally we can make the request to the desired server.

```php
<?php
// 12_10.php

$options = array('http' => array(
  'user_agent' => 'Mozilla/5.0 (iPad; CPU OS 6_0 like Mac OS X) AppleWebKit/536.26 (KHTML,
like Gecko) Version/6.0 Mobile/10A5355d Safari/8536.25',
));

$context = stream_context_create($options);
$data = file_get_contents(
  'http://mydomain.com/myfile.php',
  false,
  $context
);
```

The second parameter indicates if the include path should be followed. It defaults to false but it is required to pass a value in order to specify the third parameter, the stream contact.

The only thing we changed here was the user agent string. If we wanted to use the POST method and add some actual content that would be included in the request we would still use the file_get_contents() function but the options to the stream context would look slightly different.

```php
<?php
// 12_11.php

function FormEncode($data) {
  $val = [];
  foreach($data as $key => $value) {
    $val[] = "$key=$value";
  }
  return implode("&", $val);
}

$content = [
  'a' => 1,
  'b' => 2,
];

$options = array('http' => array(
  'method' => 'POST',
  'content' = FormEncode($content)
));

$context = stream_context_create($options);
$data = file_get_contents(
  'http://mydomain.com/myfile.php',
  false,
  $context
);

var_dump($data);
var_dump($http_response_header);
```

The function FormEncode() is used to create the body of the POST request. When no special headers are used the form is expected to be a series of key value pairs separated by &.

The variable $data will contain the response form the request and the magic variable $http_response_header will be an array of all the response headers from the last stream operation. The dump of these will look something like this:

```
array(7) {
  [0] =>
  string(15) "HTTP/1.1 200 OK"
  [1] =>
  string(35) "Date: Sun, 28 Feb 2016 01:33:41 GMT"
  [2] =>
  string(62) "Server: Apache/2.4.18 (Unix) OpenSSL/1.0.1e-fips PHP/7.1.0-dev"
  [3] =>
  string(27) "X-Powered-By: PHP/7.1.0-dev"
```

```
[4] =>
string(18) "Content-Length: 47"
[5] =>
string(17) "Connection: close"
[6] =>
string(38) "Content-Type: text/html; charset=UTF-8"
}
```

Recipe 12-9. The HTTPS Protocol

Problem

The traditional protocol used to communicate between browser and web server is the HTTP protocol. This protocol sends all data in either direction in clear text. This allows proxy servers and other technologies to intercept and possibly change the content. How can this be avoided?

Solution

The HTTPS protocol uses encryption of the data in both directions. The encryption is based on a pair of encryption keys installed on the server. The web server handles all the encryption and decryption and for most PHP scripts there are no special things to take care of or do differently. The PHP script can use $_SERVER['REQUEST_SCHEME'] to determine the actual scheme used. This can be useful when creating rewrite responses or links to other parts of the site.

How it Works

HTTPS works like HTTP as far as creating a connection to the server. HTTP uses port 80 as the standard TCP port and HTTPS uses 443. It is possible to use any other port, but if nonstandard ports are used they must be specified explicitly as part of the URL.

When the socket connection is established the server will send the public key to the browser. The browser will use this key to encrypt the request and to decrypt the responses. By having the request and response encrypted it is no longer possible for proxies and others to know what's going on, with the exception of the fact there is a connection between the browser and server.

A redirect that matches the scheme used to formulate the request could look like this:

```
header("Location: " . $_SERVER['REQUEST_SCHEME'] .
    "://" . $_SERVER['SERVER_NAME'] . "/some/new/document");
```

Or if the request came in on HTTP and you wanted to force the request to use HTTPS:

```php
<?php
// 12_12.php
if ($_SERVER['REQUEST_SCHEME'] == 'http') {
  header("Location: https://{$_SERVER['SERVER_NAME']}" .
    $_SERVER['REQUEST_URI']);
  exit;
}
```

Recipe 12-10. AJAX Requests

Problem

PHP used to send complete HTML documents to the browser. The browser would then render the document and fetch additional resources like images and javascript from the same server or other servers. In order to minimize the amount of data and create sites that are more dynamic it us useful to send requests to the server to fetch just the latest information, get a status update, or get details about some content on the page.

Solution

From the PHP perspective there is no real difference between a request for a full HTML document, a request for an image, or some partial HTML or JSON document. It all follows the standard HTTP protocol and we have seen all the building blocks on how to create the response to any of those requests.

From the client side we have discussed GET requests as entered in the address bar or when a user clicks a link and we have seen how a HTML form can be used to generate a POST request. In this section we will work on generating a GET or POST request using JavaScript. It is possible to create these requests with pure Javascript or you can choose a library like jQuery that wraps some of the functionality into simple and easy-to-use functions.

How it Works

The basis of the functionality starts by the creation of a communication object. This is not done the same way in all browsers but when the object is created it does provide the same functionality.

```
if (window.XMLHttpRequest) {      // code for Mozilla, etc.
  xml xmlhttp = new XMLHttpRequest()
}
else if (window.ActiveXObject) {          // code for IE
  var xmlhttp = new ActiveXObject("Microsoft.XMLHTTP")
}
```

In this little example we test to see if the XMLHttpRequest object is defined on the window or if there is support for ActiveXObject in IE browsers.

The asynchronous nature of the XMLHttpResponse requires the definition of a function to process the response when it comes in. This can be done with a function like this:

```
ProcessStatus = function() {
  switch (xmlhttp.readyState) {
    case 4 :
      switch (xmlhttp.status) {
        case 0 :                        // Aborted
          break;
        case 200 :                      // if Ok
        case 304 :                      // if not modified
          resp = xmlhttp.responseText;
          break;
      }
  }
}
```

And the code to start the request would look something like this:

```
xmlhttp.onreadystatechange = ProcessStatus;
try {
  xmlhttp.open("GET", 'http://mydomain.com/12_12.php', true);
}
catch (e) {
  alert('Error');
}
```

On the PHP side the response should be formatted to how the JavaScript code expects the response. This can be a string or a Json encode string.

```
<?php
// 12_13.php
$resp = [
  'a' => 1,
  'b' => 2
];
header('Content-Type: application/json');
echo json_encode($resp);
```

The output will be a JSON encoded string of the response variable:

```
{"a":1,"b":2}
```

Recipe 12-11. Web Sockets

Problem

So far we have worked on problems that start by the client sending a request to the server and receiving a response. Nothing happens on the server unless there is a client sending requests. Is it possible to have a line of communication open as long as the browser stays of the page?

Solution

Web Sockets is a bidirectional (full duplex) communication pipe that allows browsers to connect to special purpose php scripts. The Web Sockets protocol does not use http or https as the basis for communication. Instead it uses ws or wss for SSL encrypted connections.

How it Works

Easy ways to get started with Web Sockets is to download, and extend an existing socket server. This could be https://github.com/ghedipunk/PHP-WebSockets. This is a stand-alone script that is executed from the command line. The scripts should not be placed in the web root and they can even be used on servers without a regular web server.

A simple server that receives a message and sends back a string with the characters in reversed order looks like this.

```php
#!/usr/bin/env php
<?php
// 12_14.php

require('./websockets.php');

class echoServer extends WebSocketServer {
  protected function process ($user, $message) {
    $this->send($user, str_reverse($message));
  }
  protected function connected ($user) {
  }

  protected function closed ($user) {
  }
}

$echo = new echoServer("0.0.0.0","9000");

try {
  $echo->run();
}
catch (Exception $e) {
  $echo->stdout($e->getMessage());
}
```

The WebSocketsServer class uses a couple of abstract methods that must be defined in the class even if they do nothing as in this example. These functions could be used to configure data and clean up on connect and disconnect from clients.

And an html document that can send and receive messages from the server could look like this:

```html
<!DOCTYPE html>
<!- 12_14.html ->
<html>
<head>
<script>
var socket;
function init() {
  var host = "ws://127.0.0.1:9000/echobot";
  try {
    socket = new WebSocket(host);
    socket.onmessage = function(msg) {
      var div = document.createElement("div");
      div.innerHTML = msg.data;
      document.getElementsByTagName('body')[0].appendChild(div);
    };
  }
```

```
  catch (e) {
    alert(e);
  }
}
function send(msg) {
  try {
    socket.send(msg);
  }
  catch (e) {
    alert(e);
  }
}
</script>
</head>
<body onload="init();">
<button onclick="send('This is a test');">Send</button>
</script>
</body>
</html>
```

CHAPTER 13

■ ■ ■

Creating and Using Forms

HTML Forms have many usages, ranging from a simple contact form to a way to collect and edit data in a web-based application. Forms can be created as a static section of HTML or it can be dynamically generated with PHP based on a set of data from a database or another source. No matter how the form is generated it's good practice to validate the input before the form is submitted. This will help prevent data errors and the user will be able to correct errors without having the data sent to the server for validations. It is also necessary to validate the contents of the POST request before data is inserted into the database or otherwise used on the server.

Recipe 13-1. Form Elements

Problem

There are a number of different types of input that can be used in an HTML form. How does these map to native PHP data types and even to column types in a database?

Solution

In general all input from a HTML form is treated as string values in PHP. This is because the type is not passed on from the client to the server. The POST request contains key/value pairs with no other information. The PHP script that receives the POST request has to perform the necessary type conversion.

There are a number of input types supported by HTML. The most generic type is a text field that can be used to enter any character the user can type on the keyboard. The basic HTML syntax for a text input looks like this:

```
<input type="text" name="text" />
```

The value of the name attribute will cause an index in the $_POST (or $_GET) array to be created with the same value and the value entered by the user can be accessed at that index.

A special type of text input is called password. This will replace the content of the input while the user is typing, preventing others from reading over the shoulder.

```
<input type="password" name="password" />
```

Each character is typically replaced with an asterisk *. Please note that the content on the form is still transferred in clear text, unless an encrypted connection is used between the client and the server. It is not necessary to encrypt the GET request that sends the empty form from the server to the client, but the POST that sends data back to the server should be encrypted to secure passwords.

Some types of input do not work well with free text input fields. If the form contains yes/no questions or other similar situations with a limited set of values where the user can select one of the options it's recommended to use radio button or drop-down lists. Drop-down lists are useful when there are many options, like a list of states as the total space needed for the form is reduced to a single line. The next few lines show an input structure for a variable called "agree." There are two options for the user to select. Only the selected value (if any) will be submitted as part of the form. Because the two inputs have the same name and the browser only allows the user to select one of the values the server only needs to check on variables.

```
<input type="radio" name="agree" value="0" />No
<input type="radio" name="agree" value="1" />Yes
```

Creating a drop-down lost is a bit more involved. Two html tags are needed. The other tag is called select and the inner tag is called option. The inner tag can be repeated as many times as needed.

```
<select name="state">
  <option value="AL">Alabama</option>
  <option value="AK">Alaska</option>
  <option value="AZ">Arizona</option>
  <option value="AR">Arkansas</option>
  <option value="CA">California</option>
...
  <option value="WY">Wyoming</option>
</state>
```

This element will create an index called state on the $_POST variable. It will contain only the selected value, in this case a two-letter code for the state.

Common for both radio buttons and drop-down lists are the fact that they can show a more readable version of the selection and simply send a short value back to the server.

If the user should have the option to select more than one value the form can contain check boxes or multiselect lists.

For check boxes to work it is necessary to name them with unique names for each option or use a name that will cause PHP to create an array of values. The yes/no example from above could be implemented with a single check box.

```
<input type="checkbox" name="agree" value="1" />I Agree
```

Submitting the form will only contain a value for the 'agree' variable if the value is checked. The PHP script will have to check if the index agree exists on $_POST. If it's undefined that means the value was not selected.

Creating a form that contains the selection of a user's programming skills could look like this:

```
<input type="checkbox" name="skill[]" value="1" />PHP
<input type="checkbox" name="skill[]" value="2" />JavaScript
<input type="checkbox" name="skill[]" value="4" />C/C++
<input type="checkbox" name="skill[]" value="8" />Java
```

If none of the values are selected when the form is submitted the $_POST array will not have an index called 'skill'. If one or more values are selected the variable will be an array of the selected values. Selecting PHP and JavaScript will create this content in $_POST.

```
Array (
    [skill] => Array
        (
            [0] => 1
            [1] => 2
        )
)
```

The possible values in the example are chosen to be the values of a single bit in an integer. That way the values can be ORed (bitwise disjunction) together to create an integer value that can be stored in a single column in a database.

The same example can be created with a multiselect list:

```
<select multiple name="skill[]">
  <option value="1">PHP</option>
  <option value="2">JavaScript</option>
  <option value="4">C/C++</option>
  <option value="8">Java</option>
</select>
```

This will produce the same content in the $_POST array as the check boxes. The user will have to hold down Ctrl (Windows) or Cmd (Mac) to select more than one value.

If the name is missing the square brackets [] at the end PHP will treat the values as one and it will only contain the value of the last selected option from the list.

In HTML 5 there were a couple of new input options introduced. The new types are listed here:

Type	Description
Color	Allows selecting of a color value from a color picker
Date	A date selector control for entering month, day, and year
datetime-local	A control for entering both date and time
Email	Control with simple e-mail validation
Month	Allows entering a month and a year
Number	Used for integer values
Range	An integer represented with a slider
Search	Defines a text field for entering a search
Tel	Allows input of a telephone number
Time	A control for entering time
url	A text field for entering a url
Week	A control to enter a week number and a year

It is up to each browser to define the look and feel of these new controls, and the browsers might not implement support for all of them.

There are plenty of resources online for HTML documentation. One of my favorites is W3Schools at http://www.w3schools.com. It's a reference for HTML, CSS, JavaScript, and Databases. It also contains some PHP documentation I prefer to use the PHP manual as it's more complete and it contains user-contributed code segments.

How it Works

The basic functionality of a form includes two steps. The first is to request a HTML document that contains the form definition. The second step is to submit the form with all the data to the server. This can be to the same server or a completely different one. A common implementation is to have a single PHP script that checks if a post was received. If no data was received it will show a form that will allow the user to enter data. If data was posted the data will be processed and the script will show some form of a thank you message.

The next example implements a simple Contact Us form with a number of input fields and the use of the jQuery library and Bootstrap framework.

```php
<?php
// 13_1.php

if (empty($_POST)) {
  // nothing posted show the form
  echo <<<HEREDOC
<!DOCTYPE html>
<html>
<head>
  <title>Contact Us</title>
  <!-- Latest compiled and minified CSS -->
  <link rel="stylesheet" href="https://maxcdn.bootstrapcdn.com/bootstrap/3.3.6/css/
  bootstrap.min.css" integrity="sha384-1q8mTJOASx8j1Au+a5WDVnPi2lkFfwwEAa8hDDdjZlpLegxhjVME1
  fgjWPGmkzs7" crossorigin="anonymous">
  <!-- Optional theme -->
  <link rel="stylesheet" href="https://maxcdn.bootstrapcdn.com/bootstrap/3.3.6/css/
  bootstrap-theme.min.css" integrity="sha384-fLW2N01lMqjakBkx3l/M9EahuwpSfeNvV63J5ezn3uZzap
  TOu7EYsXMjQV+0En5r" crossorigin="anonymous">
  <!-- jQuery (necessary for Bootstrap's JavaScript plugins) -->
  <script src="https://ajax.googleapis.com/ajax/libs/jquery/1.11.3/jquery.min.js"></script>
  <!-- Latest compiled and minified JavaScript -->
  <script src="https://maxcdn.bootstrapcdn.com/bootstrap/3.3.6/js/bootstrap.min.js"
  integrity="sha384-0mSbJDEHialfmuBBQP6A4Qrprq50VfW37PRR3j5ELqxss1yVqOtnepnHVP9aJ7xS"
  crossorigin="anonymous"></script>
</head>
<body>
<form name="contact" method="POST" action="{$_SERVER['PHP_SELF']}">
  <div>
    <label for="name">Name</label>
    <input class="form-control" name="name" type="text" />
  </div>
  <div>
    <label for="email">Email</label>
    <input class="form-control" name="email" type="text" />
  </div>
  <div>
    <label for="phone">Phone</label>
    <input class="form-control" name="phone" type="text" />
  </div>
  <div>
    <label>Best way to contact you</label>
    <div class="radio">
```

```php
      <label><input name="cnt" type="radio" value="0"/>Don't contact</label>
    </div>
    <div class="radio">
      <label><input name="cnt" type="radio" value="1"/>Email</label>
    </div>
    <div class="radio">
      <label><input name="cnt" type="radio" value="2"/>Phone</label>
    </div>
  </div>
  <button class="btn btn-default" onclick="document.contact.submit()">Submit</button>
</form>
</body>
</html>
HEREDOC;
}
else {
  switch ($_POST['cnt']) {
    case 0:
    default:
      $contact = "We will not contact you!";
      break;
    case 1:
      $contact = "We will contact you via email!";
      break;
    case 2:
      $contact = "We will contact you via phone!";
      break;
  }
  echo <<<HEREDOC
<!DOCTYPE html>
<html>
<head>
  <title>Thank You</title>
</head>
</body>
<div>Thank you for your input. We have received the following input from you:<div>
<div>Name: {$_POST['name']}</div>
<div>Email: {$_POST['email']}</div>
<div>Phone: {$_POST['phone']}</div>
<div>{$contact}</div>
</body>
</html>
HEREDOC;
  $mysqli = new mysqli("localhost", "user", "secret", "contact_db");
  $name = $mysqli->real_escape_string($_POST['name']);
  $email = $mysqli->real_escape_string($_POST['email']);
  $phone = $mysqli->real_escape_string($_POST['phone']);
  $cnt = (int)$_POST['cnt'];
  $SQL = "insert into contacts (contact_name, email, phone, cnt) values " .
         "('{$name}', '{$email}', '{$phone}', $cnt)";
  $mysqli->query($SQL);
}
```

It is not necessary to use the jQuery library or the Bootstrap framework but it makes the forms look a bit better than plain HTML forms.

The jQuery library is a de facto standard for interacting with the DOM from JavaScript. It allows easy access to elements by using a selector syntax that's close to that of CSS.

The Bootstrap framework is responsive and will cause the content to have a similar look and feel on mobile and laptop/desktop devices. As a growing portion of web requests is done from mobile devices it is highly recommended to create content that is responsive so it can adjust to the device. In fact many search engines will penalize content that is not mobile friendly in the search results.

After showing the collected data to the user the script will insert the values in a database using the mysqli extension. In this example the object- oriented style is used. The string values are escaped before they are used in the database query and the cnt value is cast to an integer to avoid errors if the value should be missing or contain a string value.

Recipe 13-2. Default Values

Problem

The forms used in the previous examples have all been empty when first loaded. There are a couple of use cases for adding default content to a form. One is to fill the form with common values or select the most common value of drop-down lists, etc. The other is to allow the user to edit a record that was previously submitted and saved on the server.

Solution

Setting the default value for an input tag depends on the type of input. For a text input the value is set with the value attribute.

```
<input type="text" name="name" value="Some default value" />
```

For check boxes and radio buttons the attribute checked it used to indicate if the value is checked. For radio button where only one value can be selected it's only the last element with the attribute checked that will be selected. Adding the attribute checked to the first value of the no/yes example from above will change the behavior of the form. In the original example none of the values were selected when the form was first loaded but by setting the checked on the No value this radio button will be selected when the form is loaded.

```
<input type="radio" name="agree" value="0" checked />No
<input type="radio" name="agree" value="1" />Yes
```

For check boxes where multiple values can be selected at once the same system can be used.

```
<input type="checkbox" name="skill[]" value="1" checked />PHP
<input type="checkbox" name="skill[]" value="2" checked />JavaScript
<input type="checkbox" name="skill[]" value="4" />C/C++
<input type="checkbox" name="skill[]" value="8" />Java
```

In this example the first two values will be preselected when the form is loaded.

Finally for the drop-down list the use of the attribute selected on the option that should be the default value will cause the drop-down to preselect that value. For a select with a single value it is possible to set the selected attribute on multiple values but only the last value with the attribute will be the selected option. If it's a multiselect list all options with the selected attribute will show as selected.

In the next example the state California will be the default value in the drop-down.

```
<select name="state">
  <option value="AL">Alabama</option>
  <option value="AK">Alaska</option>
  <option value="AZ">Arizona</option>
  <option value="AR">Arkansas</option>
  <option value="CA" selected>California</option>
...
  <option value="WY">Wyoming</option>
</state>
```

As with multiple checked check boxes we can use the selected attribute to select both PHP and JavaScript in the multiple select list.

```
<select multiple name="skill[]">
  <option value="1" selected>PHP</option>
  <option value="2" selected>JavaScript</option>
  <option value="4">C/C++</option>
  <option value="8">Java</option>
</select>
```

The attributes checked and selected are used without any values. It is allowed to add a value to these attributes. This could be checked="true" or selected="true", but be careful as checked="false" or selected="false" will still cause these to be set as the default values. It does not matter what the value is. If the attribute is present the element will be checked or selected.

How it Works

Extending Recipe 13-1, it's possible to do some checks on the server before inserting the data into the database. If the name or e-mail column is empty the form is regenerated with the values the user already submitted and a message is added to show the user that data is missing.

```
<?php
// 13_2.php

if (empty($_POST) ||
    empty($_POST['name']) ||
    empty($_POST['email'])) {
  $warning = empty($_POST) ? "" : "<div style=\"color:red;\">Please provide all required
fields</div>";
  // nothing posted or missing name or email show the form
  $checked0 = $_POST['cnt'] == 0 ? " checked" : "";
  $checked1 = $_POST['cnt'] == 1 ? " checked" : "";
  $checked2 = $_POST['cnt'] == 2 ? " checked" : "";
  echo <<<HEREDOC
<!DOCTYPE html>
<html>
```

```
<head>
  <title>Contact Us</title>
  <!-- Latest compiled and minified CSS -->
  <link rel="stylesheet" href="https://maxcdn.bootstrapcdn.com/bootstrap/3.3.6/css/
  bootstrap.min.css" integrity="sha384-1q8mTJOASx8j1Au+a5WDVnPi2lkFfwwEAa8hDDdjZlpLegxhjVME1
  fgjWPGmkzs7" crossorigin="anonymous">
  <!-- Optional theme -->
  <link rel="stylesheet" href="https://maxcdn.bootstrapcdn.com/bootstrap/3.3.6/css/
  bootstrap-theme.min.css" integrity="sha384-fLW2N01lMqjakBkx3l/M9EahuwpSfeNvV63J5ezn3uZzapT
  Ou7EYsXMjQV+OEn5r" crossorigin="anonymous">
  <!-- jQuery (necessary for Bootstrap's JavaScript plugins) -->
  <script src="https://ajax.googleapis.com/ajax/libs/jquery/1.11.3/jquery.min.js"></script>
  <!-- Latest compiled and minified JavaScript -->
  <script src="https://maxcdn.bootstrapcdn.com/bootstrap/3.3.6/js/bootstrap.min.js"
  integrity="sha384-0mSbJDEHialfmuBBQP6A4Qrprq5OVfW37PRR3j5ELqxss1yVqOtnepnHVP9aJ7xS"
  crossorigin="anonymous"></script>
</head>
<body>
{$warning}
<form name="contact" method="POST" action="{$_SERVER['PHP_SELF']}">
  <div>
    <label for="name">Name (required)</label>
    <input class="form-control" name="name" type="text" value="{$_POST['name']}" />
  </div>
  <div>
    <label for="email">Email (required)</label>
    <input class="form-control" name="email" type="text" value="{$_POST['email']}" />
  </div>
  <div>
    <label for="phone">Phone</label>
    <input class="form-control" name="phone" type="text" value="{$_POST['phone']}" />
  </div>
  <div>
    <label>Best way to contact you</label>
    <div class="radio">
      <label><input name="cnt" type="radio" value="0"{$checked0}/>Don't contact</label>
    </div>
    <div class="radio">
      <label><input name="cnt" type="radio" value="1"{$checked1}/>Email</label>
    </div>
    <div class="radio">
      <label><input name="cnt" type="radio" value="2"{$checked2}/>Phone</label>
    </div>
  </div>
  <button class="btn btn-default" onclick="document.contact.submit()">Submit</button>
</form>
</body>
</html>
HEREDOC;
}
```

```
else {
  switch ($_POST['cnt']) {
    case O:
    default:
      $contact = "We will not contact you!";
      break;
    case 1:
      $contact = "We will contact you via email!";
      break;
    case 2:
      $contact = "We will contact you via phone!";
      break;
  }
  echo <<<HEREDOC
<!DOCTYPE html>
<html>
<head>
  <title>Thank You</title>
</head>
</body>
<div>Thank you for your input. We have received the following input from you:<div>
<div>Name: {$_POST['name']}</div>
<div>Email: {$_POST['email']}</div>
<div>Phone: {$_POST['phone']}</div>
<div>{$contact}</div>
</body>
</html>
HEREDOC;
  $mysqli = new mysqli("localhost", "user", "secret", "contact_db");
  $name = $mysqli->real_escape_string($_POST['name']);
  $email = $mysqli->real_escape_string($_POST['email']);
  $phone = $mysqli->real_escape_string($_POST['phone']);
  $cnt = (int)$_POST['cnt'];
  $SQL = "insert into contacts (contact_name, email, phone, cnt) values " .
         "('{$name}', '{$email}', '{$phone}', $cnt)";
  $mysqli->query($SQL);
}
```

Now the form will be shown if the variable $_POST is empty (nothing posted) or if either $_POST['name'] or $_post['email'] are empty. In addition there is some added code to generate a warning message if needed and to set the checked attribute on the correct radio button. This allows the user to edit the values already entered and to fill in the missing data before submitting the form again.

The validation performed here is done on the server side only. This requires the entire form to be submitted and validated on the server and if there is an error sends back to the user for reentry.

Recipe 13-3. Form Validation

Problem

HTML 5 supports a new attribute on the input field called required. Setting this attribute will prevent the browser from submitting the form if the input field is blank/empty. This can be an easy way to add some validation but it might not be enough. A field marked required will still allow the form to be submitted if the field contains a space. How can form validation be added on the client side?

Solution

The solution is to use JavaScript to traverse through all the (or a few selected) input fields and validate that the content is as expected before the form is submitted. This will not eliminate the requirement to do server-side validation. The client submitting the form might not be a browser or it could have JavaScript disabled causing the validation to fail.

How it Works

In order to use jQuery it's necessary to have a way to identify the elements of the form. This can be done with the name of the form but it's a simpler syntax if an id attribute is added to the form.

```
<form id="cont" name="contact" method="POST" action="{$_SERVER['PHP_SELF']}">
</form>
```

To access this form via jQuery we use the selector '#cont', indicating that all elements with an id="cont" should be selected. If there are other elements with the same id adding the element type can reduce the number of elements selected. The selector 'form#cont' will select all elements of type form and with the id of cont.

The next step is to find all the inputs for the form. This is done by expanding the selector to 'form#cont :input'. This selector will select all inputs that are located inside of the form tag with the id of cont. Iterating over the elements and applying a validation rule to each of them could look like this:

```php
<?php
// 13_3.php

if (empty($_POST) ||
    empty($_POST['name']) ||
    empty($_POST['email'])) {
  $warning = empty($_POST) ? "" : "<div style=\"color:red;\">Please provide all required
  fields</div>";
  // nothing posted or missing name or email show the form
  $checked0 = $_POST['cnt'] == 0 ? " checked" : "";
  $checked1 = $_POST['cnt'] == 1 ? " checked" : "";
  $checked2 = $_POST['cnt'] == 2 ? " checked" : "";
  echo <<<HEREDOC
<!DOCTYPE html>
<html>
<head>
  <title>Contact Us</title>
  <!-- Latest compiled and minified CSS -->
```

```
    <link rel="stylesheet" href="https://maxcdn.bootstrapcdn.com/bootstrap/3.3.6/css/
    bootstrap.min.css" integrity="sha384-1q8mTJOASx8j1Au+a5WDVnPi2lkFfwwEAa8hDDdjZlpLegxhjVME1
    fgjWPGmkzs7" crossorigin="anonymous">
    <!-- Optional theme -->
    <link rel="stylesheet" href="https://maxcdn.bootstrapcdn.com/bootstrap/3.3.6/css/
    bootstrap-theme.min.css" integrity="sha384-fLW2N01lMqjakBkx3l/M9EahuwpSfeNvV63J5ezn3uZzap
    TOu7EYsXMjQV+0En5r" crossorigin="anonymous">
    <!-- jQuery (necessary for Bootstrap's JavaScript plugins) -->
    <script src="https://ajax.googleapis.com/ajax/libs/jquery/1.11.3/jquery.min.js"></script>
    <!-- Latest compiled and minified JavaScript -->
    <script src="https://maxcdn.bootstrapcdn.com/bootstrap/3.3.6/js/bootstrap.min.js"
    integrity="sha384-0mSbJDEHialfmuBBQP6A4Qrprq50VfW37PRR3j5ELqxss1yVqOtnepnHVP9aJ7xS"
    crossorigin="anonymous"></script>
</head>
<body>
{$warning}
<form name="contact" method="POST" action="{$_SERVER['PHP_SELF']}">
  <div>
    <label for="name">Name (required)</label>
    <input class="form-control" name="name" type="text" value="{$_POST['name']}" />
  </div>
  <div>
    <label for="email">Email (required)</label>
    <input class="form-control" name="email" type="text" value="{$_POST['email']}" />
  </div>
  <div>
    <label for="phone">Phone</label>
    <input class="form-control" name="phone" type="text" value="{$_POST['phone']}" />
  </div>
  <div>
    <label>Best way to contact you</label>
    <div class="radio">
      <label><input name="cnt" type="radio" value="0"{$checked0}/>Don't contact</label>
    </div>
    <div class="radio">
      <label><input name="cnt" type="radio" value="1"{$checked1}/>Email</label>
    </div>
    <div class="radio">
      <label><input name="cnt" type="radio" value="2"{$checked2}/>Phone</label>
    </div>
  </div>
  <button class="btn btn-default" onclick="$('form#cont').submit()">Submit</button>
</form>
<script>
$(document).ready(function() {
  $('form#cont').submit(function() {
    $('form#cont :input').each(function() {
        if (this.name == 'name' && $(this).val() == '') {
          alert('Name may not be empty');
              return false;
        }
```

```
            if (this.name == 'email' && $(this).val() == '') {
              alert('Email may not be empty');
                    return false;
            }
          });
    });
});
</script>
</body>
</html>
HEREDOC;
}
else {
  switch ($_POST['cnt']) {
    case 0:
    default:
      $contact = "We will not contact you!";
      break;
    case 1:
      $contact = "We will contact you via email!";
      break;
    case 2:
      $contact = "We will contact you via phone!";
      break;
  }
  echo <<<HEREDOC
<!DOCTYPE html>
<html>
<head>
  <title>Thank You</title>
</head>
</body>
<div>Thank you for your input. We have received the following input from you:<div>
<div>Name: {$_POST['name']}</div>
<div>Email: {$_POST['email']}</div>
<div>Phone: {$_POST['phone']}</div>
<div>{$contact}</div>
</body>
</html>
HEREDOC;
  $mysqli = new mysqli("localhost", "user", "secret", "contact_db");
  $name = $mysqli->real_escape_string($_POST['name']);
  $email = $mysqli->real_escape_string($_POST['email']);
  $phone = $mysqli->real_escape_string($_POST['phone']);
  $cnt = (int)$_POST['cnt'];
  $SQL = "insert into contacts (contact_name, email, phone, cnt) values " .
        "('{$name}', '{$email}', '{$phone}', $cnt)";
  $mysqli->query($SQL);
}
```

The addition of a small section of JavaScript code will iterate over all the elements of the form and validate if the name or e-mail fields are empty and show an error message if that is the case. Returning false in the case of a validation error will ensure the form is not submitted.

The validation can easily be extended to use regular expressions to check for leading/trailing spaces and even to validate that the e-mail address contains an e-mail address that could be used for sending e-mails.

When the same script is used to generate the form and process the post request, it's common practice to use $_SERVER['PHP_SELF'] at the action on the form tag. This will ensure the script is working even if it is renamed.

Recipe 13-4. Form Generation

Problem

Creating HTML forms using static HTML files or sections of HTML embedded in a php script can be tedious, especially when there are many types of data to edit in the application. How can form creation be made easier?

Solution

Most form elements that are used in multiple places follow the same pattern with each use. It's possible to create a generic function or class that can be used to generate HTML forms based on a simple form definition.

The first step is to define the types of inputs the form class should support, then the implementation can be stubbed out and finally the code created to handle the generation of the actual form tags.

As described earlier a form is defined with the form tag with one or more input elements inside. A basic form can have text, number, radio button, drop-down, check box, and multiselect options. Each of these options can have a predefined layout that can be reused as many times as needed.

The basic class to generate a HTML form can be created with a few methods.

```php
<?php

class HTMLForm {

    function __constructor($id, $action, $method = "POST") {
    }

    function AddInput($name, $type, $value = null) {
    }

    function __toString() {
    }
}
```

The first method is the constructor that is called when the object is instantiated. The constructor takes a few parameters that define some of the attributes on the form tag.

Next there is a function used to add inputs to the form. The parameters listed are a minimum set. As the class is developed there might be a need to add things like min and max values, options for a drop-down, and validations functions, but this is a good start. Finally the method __toString() is used to generate the output. When the object is used in a string context the __toString() function will be called and the returned value will be used as the value of the object.

How it Works

The purpose of the constructor is to initialize the object. In this case all it does is to store the parameters that are passed in. These values will be used later when the output is generated.

```php
<?php
// 13_4.php

class HTMLForm {
  private $id;
  private $action;
  private $method;
  private $inputs = [];

  function __constructor($id, $action, $method = "POST") {
    $this->id = $id;
    $this->action = $action;
    $this->method = $method;
  }

  function AddInput($type, $name, $label, $value = null) {
    $this->inputs[] = [
      $type,
      $name,
      $label,
      $value
    ];
  }

  function __toString() {
    $form = '<form id="%s" action="%s", method="%s>%s</form>';
    $inputs = [];
    foreach($this->inputs as $input) {
      switch($input[0]) {
        case "hidden" :
          $template = '<input type="hidden" name="%s" value="%s" />';
          $inputs[] = sprintf($template, $input[1], $input[3]);
          break;
        case "text" :
          $template = '<div><label for="%s">%s</label><input type="text" name="%s"
          value="%s" /></div>';
          $inputs[] = sprintf($template, $input[1], $input[2], $input[1], $input[3]);
          break;
        case "textarea" :
          $template = '<div><label for="%s">%s</label><textarea type="text" name="%s" />%s</
          textarea></div>';
          $inputs[] = sprintf($template, $input[1], $input[2], $input[1], $input[3]);
          break;
        case "number" :
          $template = '<div><label for="%s">%s</label><input type="number" name="%s"
          value="%s" /></div>';
```

```
      $inputs[] = sprintf($template, $input[1], $input[2], $input[1], $input[3]);
      break;
    case "select" :
      $template = '<div><label for="%s">%s</label><select name="%s" >%s</select></div>';
      $options = [];
      if (is_array($value)) {
        $option = '<option value="%s">%s</option>';
        foreach($value as $k => $v) {
          $options[] = sprintf($option, $k, $v);
        }
      }
      $inputs[] = sprintf($template, $input[1], $input[2], $input[1], implode("", $options));
      break;
    }
  }
  $form = sprintf($form, $this->id, $this->action, $this->method, implode("", $inputs));
  return $form;
  }
}
```

The AddInput() method is used to add new inputs to the form. The method has three mandatory and one optional argument and the main purpose is to create an array with the definition of all the input fields.

Finally the method __toString() is used to generate the actual form. This method uses a number of string templates for the HTML tags and the function sprint() to populate the placeholders (%s) with the actual values.

The HTMLForm class is defined in a file called 13_4.php. This file can be included and the object instantiated.

```php
<?php
// 13_5.php
require "./13_4.php";

$form = new HTMLForm('contact', $_SERVER['PHP_SELF']);
$form->AddInput('text', 'name', 'Name');
$form->AddInput('text', 'email', 'Email');
$form->AddInput('text', 'phone', 'Phone');
$form->AddInput('textarea', 'comment', 'Comment');

echo <<<HEREDOC
<!DOCTYPE html>
<html>
<body>
$form
</body>
</html>
HEREDOC;
```

This example does not add any specific styling so the browser will add the default styling for each element. It is relatively simple to add the Bootstrap css and it's straightforward to add more attributes to handle class, required, and other attributes on each element.

A couple of new input types were used in this example. The hidden type is a way to add additional information that is beyond the control of the user but the values are passed on to the server as part of the request. The text area type is a form of multiline input that will allow the user to enter longer text with line breaks.

The AddInput() method could be split into separate functions for each type of input where each method could have parameters that matches the specific type.

```php
<?php
// 13_6.php

class HTMLForm {
  private $id;
  private $action;
  private $method;
  private $inputs = [];

  function __constructor($id, $action, $method = "POST") {
    $this->id = $id;
    $this->action = $action;
    $this->method = $method;
  }

  function AddHidden($name, $value = null) {
    $this->inputs[] = <<<HEREDOC
<input type="hidden" name="{$name}" value="{$value}" />
HEREDOC;
  }

  function AddText($name, $label, $value = null, $required = false) {
        $attrib = $required ? " required" : "";
    $this->inputs[] = <<<HEREDOC
<div>
  <label for="{$name}">{$label}</label>
  <input type="text" name="{$name}" value="{$value}"{$attrib} />
</div>
HEREDOC;
  }

  function AddTextArea($name, $label, $value = null) {
    $this->inputs[] = <<<HEREDOC
<div>
  <label for="{$name}">{$label}</label>
  <textarea name="{$name}">{$value}</textarea>
</div>
HEREDOC;
  }
```

```php
  function AddNumber($name, $label, $value = null, $required = false, $min = null, $max = null) {
        $attrib = $required ? " required" : "";
        if (is_numeric($min)) {
          $attrib .= " min=\"{$min}\"";
        }
        if (is_numeric($max)) {
          $attrib .= " max=\"{$max}\"";
        }
    $this->inputs[] = <<<HEREDOC
<div>
  <label for="{$name}">{$label}</label>
  <input type="number" name="{$name}" value="{$value}"{$attrib} />
</div>
HEREDOC;
  }

  function AddSelect($name, $label, $values = [], $selected = null) {
        $options = [];
        if (is_array($values)) {
          $option = '<option value="%s"%s>%s</option>';
          foreach($values as $k => $v) {
                if ($k == $selected) {
          $options[] = sprintf($option, $k, " selected", $v);
                }
                else {
          $options[] = sprintf($option, $k, "", $v);
                }
          }
        }
        $options = implode("", $options);
    $this->inputs[] = <<<HEREDOC
<div>
  <label for="{$name}">{$label}</label>
  <select name="{$name}">$options</select>
</div>
HEREDOC;
  }

  function __toString() {
    $form = '<form id="%s" action="%s", method="%s>%s</form>';
    $inputs = [];
    $form = sprintf($form, $this->id, $this->action, $this->method, implode("", $this->inputs));
    return $form;
  }
}
```

In this case each of the Add..() methods is responsible for creating the HTML layout for the input. This makes the __toString() method simpler. Using this class is very similar to the previous example.

```php
<?php
// 13_7.php
require "./13_6.inc";

$form = new HTMLForm('contact', $_SERVER['PHP_SELF']);
$form->AddHidden('form', 'Contact');
$form->AddText('name', 'Name', null, true);
$form->AddText('email', 'Email', null, true);
$form->AddText('phone', 'Phone');
$form->AddSelect('ref', 'How did your find us?', ['Google', 'Bing', 'Ask', 'Yahoo', 'Other']);
$form->AddTextarea('comment', 'Comment');

echo <<<HEREDOC
<!DOCTYPE html>
<html>
<body>
$form
</body>
</html>
HEREDOC;
```

Recipe 13-5. File Upload

Problem

So far we have looked at HTML forms that are populated with input from the keyboard or mouse. This generates mostly textual input, but with the graphic nature of the web it is necessary to include files from the computer's hard drive.

Solution

Uploading files to a PHP script requires some settings to be enabled in php.ini. First of all there is file_uploads = On. If this is not set PHP will ignore all uploaded files. Secondly there is the limit on the upload size. This is used to prevent users from uploading very large files that eventually would fill up the disk drive. The setting to control this is called upload_max_filesize and it defaults to 2Mb. Finally there is the setting for maximum number of files per request, max_file_uploads and that has a default value of 20. In general there is also a setting for the maximum size of a post request. This value is defined by post_max_size and the default value is 8Mb. If you are going to allow large text inputs you will have to adjust this setting accordingly.

The special input type "file" allows the user to browse the local hard drive for a specific file. The selection of a file requires an action from the user. The browser can't be instructed with script code to select arbitrary files from the user's hard drive.

The file input will provide the user with a "browse" button. When the user clicks the browse button, the browser will open a file dialog. The browser, according to the guidelines from the platform, handles the look and feel of the browse button and the dialog. It is not possible to style these elements.

When the html form is created it is necessary to add the enctype attribute to the form in order for the form to handle file uploads. The value is defined as enctype="multipart/form-data" and the method must be set to POST. It's not possible to include file uploads as part of a GET request. Forgetting to set the enctype attribute will cause the name of the file to be stored in the $_POST array and the file is not available on the server.

On the server side the content of the upload is not available in the normal $_POST array but can be found in the $_FILES array. The upload of the file(s) take place before the PHP script starts executing. The file is given a temporary name and placed in the /tmp folder. The actual location is controlled with the upload_temp_dir setting in php.ini. It is also possible to restrict the max size of uploads and the entire POST with settings in php.ini. If you plan to allow your users to upload large files you will have to adjust these values accordingly.

The super global $_FILES will contain a number of values based on the name of the input, the name of the select file, and the size of the uploaded file.

How it Works

A file upload is handled with a form where the user selects the file and a PHP script that received the uploaded file. As before these can be in one php script. The next example shows a simple form with two inputs. The first is a text field and the second is a file.

```php
<?php
// 13_8.php

if (empty($_POST)) {
  // nothing posted show the form
  echo <<<HEREDOC
<!DOCTYPE html>
<html>
<head>
  <title>File Upload</title>
</head>
<body>
<form name="contact" method="POST" action="{$_SERVER['PHP_SELF']}" enctype="multipart/form-data" >
  <div>
    <label for="name">Name</label>
    <input name="name" type="text" />
  </div>
  <div>
    <label for="email">File</label>
    <input name="file" type="file" />
  </div>
  <button class="btn btn-default" onclick="document.contact.submit()">Submit</button>
</form>
</body>
</html>
HEREDOC;
}
else {
  print("<pre>");
  print_r($_POST);
  print_r($_FILES);
  print("</pre>");
}
```

The initial output of the script is the form and when the form is submitted it will show the contents of the two super globals $_POST and $_FILES.

```
Array (
    [name] => test
)
Array (
    [file] => Array
        (
            [name] => city.list.json
            [type] => application/json
            [tmp_name] => /tmp/phpOpdVpy
            [error] => 0
            [size] => 19208925
        )
)
```

The attribute of the $_FILES array is the name of the input. This is also an array that contains the name of the file, the mime type, the temporary name and path, an error code (0 means no errors), and the size in bytes of the uploaded file.

The temporary file is automatically deleted when the script terminates, unless there is a fatal error in the script. In order to keep the file on the server the script must move the file to a different location. Besides checking for error conditions with the upload there are a couple of functions that are useful to move files.

The function is_uploaded_file() will check if the file was actually uploaded via the HTTP POST. This function takes a single parameter, which usually is $_FILES['file']['tmp_name']. The other function move_uploaded_file() is used to move and rename the uploaded file into its permanent position. This function takes two parameters where the first is the temporary name and the second is the path and name of the new file/location. In the example above this would look something like this:

```php
<?php
// 13_9.php

if ($_FILES['file']['error'] == UPLOAD_ERR_OK &&
    is_uploaded_file($_FILES['file']['tmp_name'])) {
    move_uploaded_file($_FILES['file']['tmp_name'],
                    "/path/to/file/{$_FILES['file']['name']}");
}
```

Recipe 13-6. Form Data

Problem

In all the previous recipes we have used a HTML form to allow the user to enter data and a button to submit data to the server. Is it possible to submit forms without the submit button?

Solution

In most modern browsers (Firefox, Chrome, IE 10, and newer) there is an object called FormData. This object can be used to build and post forms with a dynamic number of fields.

How it Works

From the server side there is no difference in how the POST is received and managed but in the client the POST is created entirely with javascript and is submitted with a XMLHTTP request.

```
var content = new FormData();
content.append('name', 'Frank Kromann');
content.append('email', 'fmk@php.net');
xmlhttp = new XMLHttpRequest();
xmlhttp.open("POST", URL, true);
xmlhttp.send(content);
```

This can be used to validate a partial form without submitting the entire form. For example, you might want to check if a user name exists in the database before allowing the user to submit the form or if you want to use other server-side validation.

■ ■ ■

## CHAPTER 14

XML, RSS, WDDX, and SOAP

Web technology is more than HTML and JavaScript used by browsers and web servers. Other types of clients use other protocols and data formats to exchange and present data. This chapter contains recipes on how to create content in formats other than the usual HTML and JavaScript.

Recipe 14-1. Exchanging Data with XML

Problem

XML is a structured data format with tags and attributes like HTML. It is usually a bit stricter as tags without a corresponding closing tag will cause an error. In HTML it is allowed to have a <hr> or <br> tag without a corresponding </hr> or </br>. The XHTML standard enforces the XML convention and requires the tags to be written as <hr/> or <br/> which is valid XML.

XML is commonly used to exchange data, as it is a platform independent standard that is easy to read and parse. Just like PHP can be used to generate XML content the same way it generates HTML content but managing XML structures as strings is not always the most efficient, especially when it comes to parsing the values if the XML is used as an input to the PHP script. What tools does PHP provide to generate and consume XML content?

Solution

There are a number of different ways to generate XML with PHP. The simplest form is to create a string that contains the XML string and output that goes to the client with the correct headers. For small XML strings like a response to an insert or update command this can work well as the XML is relatively simple. The next example shows how PHP can be used to generate a simple response with an error or success XML structure.

```php
<?php
// 14_1.php
// Process request and make a response
header("Content-Type: text/xml");
if ($error) {
  $resp = <<<HEREDOC
<?xml version="1.0" encoding="UTF-8"?>
<error>
  <code>100</code>
  <message>The insert failed</message>
</error>
HEREDOC;
```

```
}
else {
  $resp = <<<HEREDOC
<?xml version="1.0" encoding="UTF-8"?>
<success>
  <message>The record was added</message>
</sucess>
HEREDOC;
}
```

When the XML structure becomes more complex or you want to convert from an XML structure to an object structure that can be used to iterate over values, there are a number of options in PHP. Most of them require the library called libxml to be installed on the system.

The DOM extension allows the manipulation of a XML document through the so-called DOM API. This is an object-oriented interface.

The libxml extension is the "wrapper" around the libxml library. It is mostly been used by many of the other XML extensions, but it does provide a few functions that can be called directly.

The SDO extension provides a way to work with data from different data sources using the same interface. The consumer of data does not have to know anything about the underlying data source and how to interact with it. The data sources can be XML files, Spreadsheets, and Database queries, etc.

The SimpleXML extension was introduced in PHP 5. This is a lightweight and simple-to-use extension for reading and writing XML content.

The WDDX extension makes it possible to do data exchanges between different programming languages over different protocols.

The XMLDiff extension can be used to compare two XML documents and to apply patches to XML documents in a similar way to how source control systems work.

The XML Parser extension is a set of functions that can be used to build XML parsers for specific document definitions. The parsers can work on small sections of a file so its not needed to load large XML documents into memory all at the same time.

The XML Reader extension acts as a cursor that reads the XML structure one node at the time.

The XML Writer extension can be used to create XML streams, where each node is processed and written without the need to load the entire data structure into memory to create the XML content.

Finally there is the XSLT extension that makes it possible to transform an XML structure. This extension requires the libxslt library.

How it Works

The SimpleXML extension is perhaps the easiest to use. Parsing and converting an XML document into a PHP object structure can be done in a few lines of code. In this example we are going to use an external source for the XML document. The example uses OpenWeatherMap.com and the source. This is a free source of weather data. It is only required that you sign up for an API key. The API key must be passed as a parameter to every request. In the example where <API KEY> is used you should replace it with your own key. You can get an API key here: http://openweathermap.org/appid.

To get the current weather in Los Angeles you can use this url with a few parameters:

```
http://api.openweathermap.org/data/2.5/weather
```

The API takes three parameters. The first is an indication of the location. This can be a city and a country code.

```
q=Los%20Angeles,us
```

The second is the mode. The API will default to a JSON response. To get an XML response, add this parameter:

```
mode=xml
```

And finally add a parameter with your api key:

```
appid=<API KEY>
```

When using the simplexml:load_file() function the filename provided as the first parameter can point to a file on the local file system or it can be a URL to read the XML content from a remote server:

```php
<?php
// 14_2.php
$xml = simplexml:load_file("http://api.openweathermap.org/data/2.5/weather?q=Los%20
Angeles,us&mode=xml&appid=<API KEY>");
print_r($xml);
```

In this simple example the XML structure is requested and passed in the same function call. The simplexml:load_file() function will return an instance of the class SimpleXMLElement as shown with the sample output.

```
SimpleXMLElement Object
(
    [city] => SimpleXMLElement Object
        (
            [@attributes] => Array
                (
                    [id] => 5368361
                    [name] => Los Angeles
                )

            [coord] => SimpleXMLElement Object
                (
                    [@attributes] => Array
                        (
                            [lon] => -118.24
                            [lat] => 34.05
                        )

                )

            [country] => US
            [sun] => SimpleXMLElement Object
                (
                    [@attributes] => Array
                        (
                            [rise] => 2016-04-10T13:26:29
                            [set] => 2016-04-11T02:21:43
                        )

                )

        )
```

```
[temperature] => SimpleXMLElement Object
    (
        [@attributes] => Array
            (
                [value] => 292.26
                [min] => 285.15
                [max] => 294.15
                [unit] => kelvin
            )

    )

[humidity] => SimpleXMLElement Object
    (
        [@attributes] => Array
            (
                [value] => 56
                [unit] => %
            )

    )

[pressure] => SimpleXMLElement Object
    (
        [@attributes] => Array
            (
                [value] => 1013
                [unit] => hPa
            )

    )

[wind] => SimpleXMLElement Object
    (
        [speed] => SimpleXMLElement Object
            (
                [@attributes] => Array
                    (
                        [value] => 6.2
                        [name] => Moderate breeze
                    )

            )

        [gusts] => SimpleXMLElement Object
            (
            )

        [direction] => SimpleXMLElement Object
            (
                [@attributes] => Array
```

```
                            (
                                [value] => 260
                                [code] => W
                                [name] => West
                            )

                    )
            )

    [clouds] => SimpleXMLElement Object
        (
            [@attributes] => Array
                (
                    [value] => 90
                    [name] => overcast clouds
                )

        )

    [visibility] => SimpleXMLElement Object
        (
        )

    [precipitation] => SimpleXMLElement Object
        (
            [@attributes] => Array
                (
                    [mode] => no
                )

        )

    [weather] => SimpleXMLElement Object
        (
            [@attributes] => Array
                (
                    [number] => 804
                    [value] => overcast clouds
                    [icon] => 04d
                )

        )

    [lastupdate] => SimpleXMLElement Object
        (
            [@attributes] => Array
                (
                    [value] => 2016-04-10T20:27:02
                )

        )

)
```

Using the var_dump() function is a quick way to get information about the XML object, but it's not very useful when it comes to generating content for a web site.

To make the example a bit more useful we can extract a few values from the XML and show them in a table. The values of interest are temperature, wind, and clouds. By passing the object to a foreach loop it's possible to list all the attributes that are available in the XML object.

```php
<?php
// 14_3.php

$xml = simplexml:load_file('http://api.openweathermap.org/data/2.5/weather?q=Los%20
Angeles,us&mode=xml&appid=<API KEY>');
foreach($xml as $attrib => $value) {
  echo $attrib . "\n";
}
```

This will generate the following output.

```
city
temperature
humidity
pressure
wind
clouds
visibility
precipitation
weather
lastupdate
```

Each of these attributes is also an object that is an instance of the SimpleXMLElement class. The temperature object has parameters for value, min, max, and unit. In this case the temperature unit is Kelvin so a bit of math is needed to show the current temperature in Celsius or Fahrenheit.

```php
<?php
// 14_4.php

$xml = simplexml:load_file('http://api.openweathermap.org/data/2.5/weather?q=Los%20
Angeles,us&mode=xml&appid=<API KEY>');

echo "City: {$xml->city['name']}\n";

if ($xml->temperature['unit'] == 'kelvin') {
    $k = $xml->temperature['value'];
    $c = $k - 273.15;
    $f = $c * 9 / 5 + 32;
}
printf("Temperature: %3.1f K / %3.1f C / %3.1f F\n", $k, $c, $f);
```

This will show the name of the city for the request as well as the temperature in Kelvin, Celsius, and Fahrenheit according to Open Weather Map on a 'cold' March evening.

```
City: Los Angeles
Temperature: 282.2 K / 8.9 C / 47.9 F
```

Note that the attributes on the top level (city, temperature, etc.) are accessed as member variables on the object and the members on the inner elements are accessed as array keys on the attribute. The difference can be seen in the raw dump of the $xml variable, where the @attributes element on each of the inner objects is marked as an array and not an instance of the SimpleXMLElement class. This can also be seen in the raw XML content where the name of the city and the temperature elements are attributes on the XML tags.

```
<current>
  <city id="5368361" name="Los Angeles">
    <coord lon="-118.24" lat="34.05"/>
    <country>US</country>
    <sun rise="2016-03-13T14:05:11" set="2016-03-14T01:59:41"/>
  </city>
  <temperature value="282.202" min="282.202" max="282.202" unit="kelvin"/>
  <humidity value="85" unit="%"/>
  <pressure value="966.32" unit="hPa"/>
  <wind>
    <speed value="0.84" name="Calm"/>
    <gusts/>
    <direction value="202.504" code="SSW" name="South-southwest"/>
  </wind>
  <clouds value="0" name="clear sky"/>
  <visibility/>
  <precipitation mode="no"/>
  <weather number="800" value="clear sky" icon="01n"/>
  <lastupdate value="2016-03-13T01:42:16"/>
</current>
```

To add the wind conditions (speed and direction) to the output a second level of indirection is needed. As the wind element contain three separate elements for speed, gust, and direction.

```php
<?php
// 14_5.php

$xml = simplexml:load_file('http://api.openweathermap.org/data/2.5/weather?q=Los%20
Angeles,us&mode=xml&appid=<API KEY>');

echo "City: {$xml->city['name']}\n";

if ($xml->temperature['unit'] == 'kelvin') {
    $k = $xml->temperature['value'];
    $c = $k - 273.15;
    $f = $c * 9 / 5 + 32;
}
```

```
printf("Temperature: %3.1f K / %3.1f C / %3.1f F\n", $k, $c, $f);

echo "Wind: {$xml->wind->speed['value']} mph, " .
     "direction: {$xml->wind->direction['name']}\n";
```

This will now produce the following output:

```
City: Los Angeles
Temperature: 282.2 K / 8.9 C / 47.9 F
Wind: 0.84 mph, direction: South-southwest
```

If you want to use these and other API's to fetch data for your web site it's recommended to build a caching system around each API call. This will prevent your site from calling the API each time a user accesses your site. First of all the data is only updated once an hour or even less often, and secondly it's always faster to fetch content from the local server than it is to run queries over the Internet to remote servers.

The SimpleXML parser used here could be replaced with the DOM parser, but that would require more code but at the same time also provide more features. The SimpleXML parser is just that: Simple.

Recipe 14-2. Generating XML Response

Problem

The previous recipe was focusing on parsing XML documents into a structure that can be used within PHP and where the elements can be accessed by a known path or by iterating over a SimpleXMLElement object. That is useful when the PHP script consumes data that's already in XML format. When the server is generating the XML response for other clients to consume we need a set of tools that can convert PHP arrays and other values to a XML document.

Solution

The SimpleXMLElement class can still be used, but instead of starting with a XML document we start with an empty instance of the SimpleXMLElement class. We can then use the methods addChild() and addAttribute() to build the XML object and finally we can use the method asXML() to convert the object to a XML string.

How it Works

This example starts with a list of planets. Each planet has a couple of parameters that describe the distance from the sun, the type of planet, number of moons, and the average surface temperature.

```php
<?php
// 14_6.php
$planets = [
  'mercury' => [
    'type' => 'rock',
    'dist' => 0.39,
    'moons' => 0,
```

```
      'temp' => 452
    ],
    'venus' => [
      'type' => 'rock',
      'dist' => 0.723,
      'moons' => 0,
      'temp' => 726
    ],
    'earth' => [
      'type' => 'rock',
      'dist' => 1,
      'moons' => 1,
      'temp' => 285
    ],
    'mars' => [
      'type' => 'rock',
      'dist' => 1.524,
      'moons' => 2,
      'temp' => 240
    ],
    'jupiter' => [
      'type' => 'gas',
      'dist' => 5.203,
      'moons' => 67,
      'temp' => 120
    ],
    'saturn' => [
      'type' => 'gas',
      'dist' => 9.539,
      'moons' => 62,
      'temp' => 88
    ],
    'uranus' => [
      'type' => 'gas',
      'dist' => 19.18,
      'moons' => 27,
      'temp' => 59
    ],
    'neptune' => [
      'type' => 'gas',
      'dist' => 30.06,
      'moons' => 13,
      'temp' => 48
    ],
    'plutu' => [
      'type' => 'rock',
      'dist' => 39,53,
      'moons' => 4,
      'temp' => 37
    ],
];
```

```php
$base = "<?xml version=\"1.0\" ?><planets></planets>";
$xml = new SimpleXMLElement($base);

foreach($planets as $name => $data) {
  $p = $xml->addChild('planet');
  $p->addAttribute('name', $name);
  $a = $p->addChild('dist');
  $a->addAttribute('value', $data['dist']);
  $a->addAttribute('unit', 'AU');
  $p->addChild('moons', $data['moons']);
  $a = $p->addChild('temp');
  $a->addAttribute('value', $data['temp']);
  $a->addAttribute('unit', 'kelvin');
}
header("Content-Type: text/xml");
echo $xml->asXML();
```

The method asXML takes an optional parameter for a filename. If a filename is passed in, the method will save the XML structure to the file. If no parameter is passed in, the method will simply return the XML structure as a string that can be sent to the client.

The raw output is one long string of data that can be hard to read for a human, but it's perfectly fine for a computer to parse.

```xml
<?xml version="1.0"?>
<planets><planet name="mercury"><dist value="0.39" unit="AU"/><moons>0</moons><temp
value="452" unit="kelvin"/></planet><planet name="venus"><dist value="0.723"
unit="AU"/><moons>0</moons><temp value="726" unit="kelvin"/></planet><planet
name="earth"><dist value="1" unit="AU"/><moons>1</moons><temp value="285"
unit="kelvin"/></planet><planet name="mars"><dist value="1.524" unit="AU"/><moons>2</
moons><temp value="240" unit="kelvin"/></planet><planet name="jupiter"><dist value="5.203"
unit="AU"/><moons>67</moons><temp value="120" unit="kelvin"/></planet><planet
name="saturn"><dist value="9.539" unit="AU"/><moons>62</moons><temp value="88"
unit="kelvin"/></planet><planet name="uranus"><dist value="19.18" unit="AU"/><moons>27</
moons><temp value="59" unit="kelvin"/></planet><planet name="neptune"><dist value="30.06"
unit="AU"/><moons>13</moons><temp value="48" unit="kelvin"/></planet><planet
name="plutu"><dist value="39.53" unit="AU"/><moons>4</moons><temp value="37"
unit="kelvin"/></planet></planets>
```

Adding a few line breaks and some indentation makes it easier to read.

```xml
<?xml version="1.0"?>
<planets>
  <planet name="mercury">
    <dist value="0.39" unit="AU"/>
    <moons>0</moons>
    <temp value="452" unit="kelvin"/>
  </planet>
  <planet name="venus">
    <dist value="0.723" unit="AU"/>
    <moons>0</moons>
```

```
      <temp value="726" unit="kelvin"/>
    </planet>
    <planet name="earth">
      <dist value="1" unit="AU"/>
      <moons>1</moons>
      <temp value="285" unit="kelvin"/>
    </planet>
    <planet name="mars">
      <dist value="1.524" unit="AU"/>
      <moons>2</moons>
      <temp value="240" unit="kelvin"/>
    </planet>
    <planet name="jupiter">
      <dist value="5.203" unit="AU"/>
      <moons>67</moons>
      <temp value="120" unit="kelvin"/>
    </planet>
    <planet name="saturn">
      <dist value="9.539" unit="AU"/>
      <moons>62</moons>
      <temp value="88" unit="kelvin"/>
    </planet>
    <planet name="uranus">
      <dist value="19.18" unit="AU"/>
      <moons>27</moons>
      <temp value="59" unit="kelvin"/>
    </planet>
    <planet name="neptune">
      <dist value="30.06" unit="AU"/>
      <moons>13</moons>
      <temp value="48" unit="kelvin"/>
    </planet>
    <planet name="plutu">
      <dist value="39.53" unit="AU"/>
      <moons>4</moons>
      <temp value="37" unit="kelvin"/>
    </planet>
  </planets>
```

Recipe 14-3. Sharing Data with RSS

Problem

The previous example used data that are reasonable static. It is not expected that new planets will be discovered in our solar system anytime soon and although the distance from the sun and the surface temperature is varying the values are not changing as often as the headlines on a news blog. In addition the example used valid XML for the list of planets and data, but without additional information about the content a consumer will not be able to use the data. How is it possible to share data that is easy to consume by multiple clients?

Solution

The use of XML is a good step in the right direction. Adding a predefined schema for the XML makes it possible for various clients to consume the data. There are many standards for how to use XML, either for specific purposes like a news summary or more generic uses. One of these is called Rich Site Summary or Really Simple Syndication: in short, RSS. There are a number of variants of the schemas used but the two most popular are called RSS 2.0 and Atom 1.0.

The two schemas provide almost the same values but use different tag names. Many browsers and e-mail clients have support for the RSS formats and there are a number of dedicated reader applications available too. Some of these have been discontinued due to the declining popularity of the RSS format.

How it Works

The top-level element of a RSS feed is called <rss></rss> and it is typically written with a version attribute <rss version="2.0"></rss>. Inside the top-level element is an element called <channel>. This is used to describe the content provider and includes fields for title, description, and link, etc. The channel element also contains one or more <item> elements. Each item describes an article or story.

Using the dom extension we can create a simple RSSWriter class that can be used to create RSS feeds for different types of data. The new class extends the class domDocument and in order to get the parent class initialized, there is a call to the parent::__constructor() method.

```php
<?php
//14_7.php

class RSSWriter extends domDocument {
  private $rss;
  private $channel;

  function __construct($xml = "1.0", $encoding = "UTF-8") {
    parent::__construct($xml, $encoding);
    $this->formatOutput = true;
    $this->rss = $this->CreateElement("rss");
    $this->rss->setAttribute("version", "2.0");
    $this->channel = $this->CreateElement("channel");
  }

  function SetChannel($title, $description, $link, $pubdate, $ttl=1800) {
    $element = $this->CreateElement('title');
    $element->appendChild($this->CreateTextNode($title));
    $this->channel->appendChild($element);

    $element = $this->CreateElement('description');
    $element->appendChild($this->CreateTextNode($description));
    $this->channel->appendChild($element);

    $element = $this->CreateElement('link');
    $element->appendChild($this->CreateTextNode($link));
    $this->channel->appendChild($element);
```

```php
    $element = $this->CreateElement('pubDate');
    $element->appendChild($this->CreateTextNode(gmdate("D, d M Y H:i:s", (int)$pubdate) . " GMT"));
    $this->channel->appendChild($element);

    $element = $this->CreateElement('ttl');
    $element->appendChild($this->CreateTextNode($ttl));
    $this->channel->appendChild($element);
}

function AddItem($title, $link, $description = null, $attribs = null) {
    $item = $this->CreateElement("item");

    if (!empty($title)) {
        $obj = $this->CreateElement("title");
        $obj->appendChild($this->CreateTextNode($title));
        $item->appendChild($obj);
    }

    if (!empty($link)) {
        $obj = $this->CreateElement("link");
        $obj->appendChild($this->CreateTextNode($link));
        $item->appendChild($obj);
    }

    if (!empty($attribs["description"])) {
        $obj = $this->CreateElement("description");
        $obj->appendChild($this->CreateTextNode($attribs["description"]));
        $item->appendChild($obj);
    }

    if (!empty($attribs["pubDate"])) {
        $obj = $this->CreateElement("pubDate");
        $obj->appendChild($this->CreateTextNode(gmdate("D, d M Y H:i:s",
        (int)$attribs["pubDate"]) . " GMT"));
        $item->appendChild($obj);
    }

    if (!empty($attribs["category"])) {
        $obj = $this->CreateElement("category");
        $obj->appendChild($this->CreateTextNode($attribs["category"]));
        $item->appendChild($obj);
    }

    if (!empty($attribs["author"])) {
        $obj = $this->CreateElement("author");
        $obj->appendChild($this->CreateTextNode($attribs["author"]));
        $item->appendChild($obj);
    }
```

```php
      if (!empty($attribs["guid"])) {
        $obj = $this->CreateElement("guid");
        $obj->appendChild($this->CreateTextNode($attribs["guid"]));
        $item->appendChild($obj);
      }

      if (!empty($attribs["comments"])) {
        $obj = $this->CreateElement("comments");
        $obj->appendChild($this->CreateTextNode($attribs["comments"]));
        $item->appendChild($obj);
      }

      $this->channel->appendChild($item);
    }

    function Output($file_name = "opensearch.xml") {
      $this->rss->appendChild($this->channel);
      $this->appendChild($this->rss);

      header("Content-Type: text/xml; name=\"{$file_name}\"");
      header("Content-Disposition: inline; filename=\"{$file_name}\"");
      echo $this->saveXML();
    }
}

$rss = new RSSWriter();
$rss->SetChannel("PHP & MySQL Recipes","A book about PHP and MySQL", "http://example.com", time());
$rss->AddItem("PHP 7", "http://php.net", "The new and faster version of php");
$rss->AddItem("MariaDB", "http://mariadb.org", "The open source database");
$rss->Output();
```

At the end of the script the $rss variable is assigned an instance of the RSSWriter() class, then the channel is defined and a couple of items are added.

To follow best practices the list of items should be limited to the latest 5 or 10 items of data. Each of the clients that subscribe to the feed can save copies of the elements for as long as the user wants. The client should not query the same feed again until the ttl value is exceeded. In this case it is set to 1800 seconds or a half hour. Requesting updates from the feed too often will create high load on the server.

Placing the RSSWriter() class in a separate file makes it possible to use the same class to generate multiple RSS feeds with different content.

Recipe 14-4. Consuming RSS Feeds

Problem

Depending on the definition used the last S in RSS stands for Syndication. Syndication is a way to share or distribute information. How can this be used to create a list of posts from a couple of space-related web sites?

Solution

We can use the SimpleXML extension to create a class that can read a feed, and perform extraction and formatting of the data.

How it Works

The constructor of the class takes a single parameter. This is the URL of the RSS feed. When the class is instantiated, it will read the content of the feed and store it in a private variable called $xml.

The method channel() also takes a single parameter. The parameter is used to identify and return the value. The can be used to fetch title and description value from the channel section of the feed.

Finally the method items() is used to extract some of the values for each of the items in the feed.

```php
<?php
// 14_8.php

date_default_timezone_set('America/Los_Angeles');

$feeds = [
  'https://www.nasa.gov/rss/dyn/breaking_news.rss',
  'http://www.nasaspaceflight.com/feed/'
];

class RSSReader {
  private $xml;

  function __construct($url) {
    $this->xml = simplexml:load_file($url);
  }

  function channel($name) {
      return $this->xml->channel->$name;
  }

  function items() {
      $i = [];
      foreach($this->xml->channel->item as $item) {
        $i[] = [
          (string)$item->title,
          (string)$item->description,
          (string)$item->link,
          strtotime((string)$item->pubDate)
        ];
      }
      return $i;
  }
}
```

```
foreach($feeds as $f) {
  $rss = new RSSReader($f);
  echo "<div>Channel: {$rss->channel('title')}</div>";
  echo "<div>{$rss->channel('description')}</div>";
  foreach($rss->items() as $item) {
        echo <<<HEREDOC
<div>
  <a href="{$item[2]}">{$item[0]}</a>
  <div>{$item[1]}</div>
</div>
HEREDOC;
  }
}
```

The example shows uses two feeds and it turns the content into a list of links that points to the full story on each site. Because the function strtodate() is used to convert the pubDate value into a Unix timestamp it is necessary to call the date_default_timezone_set() function or define the default time zone value in php.ini.

Best practice would be to save the values for each response in a database and only query for new data once an hour.

Recipe 14-5. Standard Data Exchange

Problem

Exchanging or syndicating data with RSS is simple and efficient, but it's also limited to the values that are defined in the definition. Adding new fields will most likely not work in all cases. Is there a way to exchange structured data (numbers, strings, and Booleans, etc.) in a format that can be described by the server allowing the client to consume the data?

Solution

In the early days of the web the Web Distributed Data eXchange (WDDX) platform was developed. It is built on XML where an element is defined with a couple of tags that defines the name of the value, the type, and the actual value. A simple example of the XML structure to exchange two values is shown below.

```
<wddxPacket version='1.0'>
  <data>
    <var name="language">
      <string>PHP</string>
    </var>
    <var name="version">
      <number>7</number>
    </var>
  </data>
</wddxPacket>
```

The WDDX format is very simple and easy to use but it has mostly been replaced by SOAP and XML-RPC, which offers more functionality.

How it Works

The WDDX extension is not enabled by default but it can be enabled if you have libxml and the expat library (bundled with Apache from version 1.3.7).

The extension provides a few functions to serialize and deserialize variables to and from the WDDX packet format.

To create a WDDX packet with a single value you can use the function wddx_serialize_value(). This function takes two parameters. The first is the value

```php
<?php
// 14_9.php

echo wddx_serialize_value("PHP & MySQL Recipes", "Packet");
```

This script will generate the following XML:

```
<wddxPacket version='1.0'>
<header><comment>Packet</comment></header>
<data><string>PHP &amp; MySQL Recipes</string></data>
</wddxPacket>
```

To convert a wddx packet back to PHP variables we can use the wddx_deserialize() function like this:

```php
<?php
// 14_10.php

$wddx = <<<HEREDOC
<wddxPacket version='1.0'>
<header><comment>Packet</comment></header>
<data><string>PHP &amp; MySQL Recipes</string></data>
</wddxPacket>
HEREDOC;

var_dump(wddx_deserialize($wddx));
```

This script will generate the following XML:

```
<wddxPacket version='1.0'>
<header><comment>Packet</comment></header>
<data><string>PHP &amp; MySQL Recipes</string></data>
</wddxPacket>
```

This can be used to exchange a single variable of any type, but with a bit more functions it's possible to exchange multiple variables.

```php
<?php
// 14_11.php

$int = 1234;
$str = "PHP & MySQL Recipes";
$arr = [
  12,
  "abc",
  [
    3.15,
    7.25
  ]
];
$packet_id = wddx_packet_start("Packet");
wddx_add_vars($packet_id, "int");
wddx_add_vars($packet_id, "str");
wddx_add_vars($packet_id, "arr");

echo wddx_packet_end($packet_id);
```

The output will look like this when formatted with line breaks and indentation:

```
<wddxPacket version='1.0'>
  <header>
    <comment>Packet</comment>
  </header>
  <data>
    <struct>
      <var name='int'>
        <number>1234</number>
      </var>
      <var name='str'>
        <string>PHP &amp; MySQL Recipes</string>
      </var>
      <var name='arr'>
        <array length='3'>
          <number>12</number>
          <string>abc</string>
          <array length='2'>
            <number>3.15</number>
            <number>7.25</number>
          </array>
        </array>
      </var>
    </struct>
  </data>
</wddxPacket>
```

Recipe 14-6. SOAP Server and Client

Problem

Although the WDDX extension from the previous section can be used to exchange data between different systems and different programming languages it only has support for limited data types and it works directly on variables in the programming language. Having a data exchange format that includes definitions of the data that is being exchanged and a description of how the data can be validated would greatly improve on the quality and flexibility of the exchange.

Solution

SOAP or as it was called in the beginning 'Simple Object Access Protocol' is the solution. As of version 1.2 of the standard, the acronym was dropped and it's now just called SOAP. SOAP is a XML-based format where the message definition is provided in a wdsl file (also XML format). With the use of the wdsl file it's possible for clients to consume SOAP API's in an automated fashion without prior knowledge of the API structure.

SOAP works over any type of transport protocol but is often used with HTTP/HTTPS.

PHP implements classes for creation of both SOAP Server and SOAP Client functionality. The basic functionality takes a PHP class and uses that to generate a SOAP Server. Each of the public methods in the class will be exposed as endpoints that can be accessed by the clients.

How it Works

The SOAP format supports passing parameters to the endpoints. These parameters can be used as input to the query as if the method was called locally.

In this first example we will create a SOAP server that can perform some simple math operations. The class called Math has three methods that can Add, Subtract, or Multiply two numbers.

```php
<?php
// 14_12.php

class Math {
  function Add($i, $j) {
    return $i + $j;
  }

  function Subtract($i, $j) {
    return $i - $j;
  }

  function Multiply($i, $j) {
    return $i * $j;
  }
}
```

To use this class in a SOAP server it is necessary to define an instance of the SoapServer class. The constructor of the SoapServer class takes two arguments. The first is a wsdl and the second is an array of options to use. The wsdl can be omitted by setting it to null and the minimum set of options in the second parameter is the URI of the API endpoint for the server. In this example the SOAP Server will be used on the localhost so the configuration of the server will look like this:

```php
<?php
// 14_13.php
include "./14_12.php";
$server = new SoapServer(null, ['uri' => 'http://localhost/14_13.php']);
$server->setClass('Math');
$server->handle();
```

The last two method calls are used to add the Math class to the server, exposing the public functions and to start the server.

The next step is to create a client that can consume the API's. Because there is no wsdl definition for the file the client must have prior knowledge about the available API's.

```php
<?php
// 14_14.php
$client = new SoapClient(null, array(
    'location' => "http://localhost/14_13.php",
    'uri'      => "http://localhost/14_13.php",
    'trace'    => 1
));

echo $return = $client->__soapCall("Add",array(5, 2)) . "\n";
echo $return = $client->__soapCall("Subtract",array(5, 2)) . "\n";
echo $return = $client->__soapCall("Multiply",array(5, 2)) . "\n";
```

The SoapCLient() class follows the same system as the SoapServer() and can be used with or without a WSDL file, but without a WSDL file it's necessary to pass in the location and url of the endpoints.

Creating a wsdl file can be a bit cumbersome but it's worth the work as the code for the client becomes simpler and more readable. As an example for the Math service above, we can create a wsdl file that defines the input and output of each procedure call and binds it all together in a service:

```xml
<?xml version="1.0" encoding="UTF-8" ?>
<definitions name="Math"
    targetNamespace="http://localhost/math.wsdl"
    xmlns:tns="http://localhost/math.wsdl"
    xmlns:soap="http://schemas.xmlsoap.org/wsdl/soap/"
    xmlns:xsd="http://www.w3.org/2001/XMLSchema"
    xmlns:soapenc="http://schemas.xmlsoap.org/soap/encoding/"
    xmlns:wsdl="http://schemas.xmlsoap.org/wsdl/"
    xmlns="http://schemas.xmlsoap.org/wsdl/">

    <message name="addRequest">
        <part name="i" type="xsd:int"/>
        <part name="j" type="xsd:int"/>
    </message>
    <message name="addResponse">
        <part name="Result" type="xsd:int"/>
    </message>
    <message name="subtractRequest">
        <part name="i" type="xsd:int"/>
        <part name="j" type="xsd:int"/>
    </message>
    <message name="subtractResponse">
```

```
        <part name="Result" type="xsd:int"/>
</message>
<message name="multiplyRequest">
        <part name="i" type="xsd:int"/>
        <part name="j" type="xsd:int"/>
</message>
<message name="multiplyResponse">
        <part name="Result" type="xsd:int"/>
</message>

<portType name="MathPortType">
        <operation name="Add">
            <input message="tns:addRequest"/>
            <output message="tns:addResponse"/>
        </operation>
        <operation name="Subtract">
            <input message="tns:subtractRequest"/>
            <output message="tns:subtractResponse"/>
        </operation>
        <operation name="Multiply">
            <input message="tns:multiplyRequest"/>
            <output message="tns:multiplyResponse"/>
        </operation>
</portType>
<binding name="MathBinding" type="tns:MathPortType">
        <soap:binding style="rpc"
         transport="http://schemas.xmlsoap.org/soap/http"/>
        <operation name="Add">
            <soap:operation soapAction="http://localhost/Add"/>
            <input>
                <soap:body use="encoded"
                 namespace=http://localhost/math.wsdl
                 encodingStyle="http://schemas.xmlsoap.org/soap/encoding/"/>
            </input>
            <output>
                <soap:body use="encoded"
                 namespace=http://localhost/math.wsdl
                 encodingStyle="http://schemas.xmlsoap.org/soap/encoding/"/>
            </output>
        </operation>
        <operation name="Subtract">
            <soap:operation soapAction="http://localhost/Subtract"/>
            <input>
                <soap:body use="encoded"
                 namespace=http://localhost/math.wsdl
                 encodingStyle="http://schemas.xmlsoap.org/soap/encoding/"/>
            </input>
            <output>
                <soap:body use="encoded"
                 namespace=http://localhost/math.wsdl
                 encodingStyle="http://schemas.xmlsoap.org/soap/encoding/"/>
```

```
            </output>
        </operation>
        <operation name="Multiply">
            <soap:operation soapAction="http://localhost/Multiply"/>
            <input>
                <soap:body use="encoded"
                 namespace=http://localhost/math.wsdl
                 encodingStyle="http://schemas.xmlsoap.org/soap/encoding/"/>
            </input>
            <output>
                <soap:body use="encoded"
                 namespace=http://localhost/math.wsdl
                 encodingStyle="http://schemas.xmlsoap.org/soap/encoding/"/>
            </output>
        </operation>
    </binding>

    <service name="MathService">
        <port name="MathPort" binding="MathBinding">
            <soap:address location="http://localhost/14_15.php"/>
        </port>
    </service>

</definitions>
```

With this new definition of the data structure the examples 14_13.php and 14_15.php can be simplified to the code shown in example 14_15.php and 14_16.php.

```php
<?php
// 14_15.php
include "./14_12.php";
$server = new SOAPServer('math.wsdl', ['encoding'=>'UTF-8']);
$server->setClass('Math');
$server->handle();
```

The code in 14_15.php is designed to work as the server side. In this case the math.wsdl file is located in the same folder as the PHP script and is loaded from the server.

```php
<?php
// 14_16.php
$client = new SoapClient('https://localhost/math.wsdl');

echo $return = $client->Add(5, 2) . "\n";
echo $return = $client->Subtract(5, 2) . "\n";
echo $return = $client->Multiply(5, 2) . "\n";
```

In the client example the wsdl file is loaded from the server. It could also be loaded locally to save a web request but the soap client supports caching of the wsdl file preventing it from being loaded on every request. The cache is usually stored in the /tmp directory and it must be cleared manually if the wsdl file is updated on the server.

With the use of a wsdl file the client becomes more like 'normal' PHP code. When the wsdl file is loaded the SoapClient will create magic functions for each of the methods defined and these can now be called directly.

If the server defines additional methods that are not included in the wsdl file it is still possible to call these, but only with the use of the __soapCall() method.

The soap functions can be used over HTTPS to make the requests more secure. It is also recommended that if sensitive data is being transferred the server the client should make use of additional parameters to pass credentials. This can be done in the same way as other parameters and the values can be exchanged by some other means before the client can make calls and the server will validate the credentials before returning any values to the client. This makes it possible to revoke the access to a client from the server side by invalidating the credentials.

■ ■ ■

## CHAPTER 15

Data Exchange with JSON

Chapter 14 covered the use of XML to exchange date between a client and a server. When the client is created with JavaScript in a browser it's much easier to exchange data with something called JSON. JSON is an acronym for JavaScript Object Notation. It is a sting-like notation that makes it easy to declare complex structures like arrays and object.

Recipe 15-1. Fetching Data with AJAX

Problem

Traditionally a browser is used to fetch HTML pages from a server. Navigation to a different page on the same or different server is done with links in the HTML document. When a user clicks on a link the browser will fetch and render the content of the new page.

As the web technology evolves and in order to reduce load time it's becoming more common to load part of a page and when the user clicks on a read more link or scrolls to the bottom of the page, the browser will fetch additional content and render it inline without reloading the existing document.

Solution

The technology to use is an AJAX request. This is a section of JavaScript code that will perform an HTTP request to a server (usually the same server where the page was loaded from) and the response will be used to insert additional content into the HTML document.

The simple approach is to have the server generate the HTML that needs to be added and simply append the returned value directly into the HTML document.

How it Works

Using the XMLHTTP object in the browsers is relatively simple but it can be made even simpler with the use of jQuery. jQuery is a JavaScript library that makes it very easy to manipulate the HTML document, add event listeners, and perform AJAX requests. All the recipes in this chapter will make use of the jQuery library.

The first example shows how to use jQuery and PHP scripts to load a simple document with a few rows of data and then make AJAX request to update the section of data without reloading the document.

```php
<?php
// 15_1.php
$languages = [
  'PHP', 'JavaScript',
  'C', 'C++', 'C#', 'Objective-C',
  'Python', 'Java', 'Ruby',
  'Visual Basic',
  'Scala'
];
shuffle($languages);
$data = array_slice($languages, 0, 3);

$html = "";
foreach($data as $lang) {
  $html .= "<li>$lang</li>";
}
if ($_REQUEST['data']) {
  echo $html;
}
else {
  echo <<<HEREDOC
<!DOCTYPE html>
<html>
<head>
<script src="https://code.jquery.com/jquery-1.12.2.min.js"
        integrity="sha256-lZFHibXzMHo3GGeehn1hudTAP3ScOuKXBXAzHX1sjtk="
        crossorigin="anonymous"></script>
</bead>
<body>
  <h1>Programming Languages</h1>
  <ul id="lang">
    $html
  </ul>
  <button onclick="Update()">Update</button>
<script>
function Update() {
  $.get("{$_SERVER['PHP_SELF']}?data=1", function(data) {
    $("#lang").html(data);
  });
}
</script>
</body>
</html>
HEREDOC;
}
```

The output of the initial load of this script will look like this:

Programming Languages

- Visual Basic
- C++
- JavaScript

[Update]

Every time the user clicks the Update button the same script is called with the parameter data=1 and it will return only the HTML for the 3 <li> elements. The returned string will be inserted into the <ul> element with the id="lang" attributes and replaces the content that was already there.

Recipe 15-2. Returning JSON

Problem

Returning the finished HTML string from the server makes it difficult for the client to manipulate the data, if needed. Is there was a way to get the data back in a structured form that would allow the client to manipulate the data and perhaps create the html needed to match the device it's rendering on?

Solution

PHP has functions to encode and decode variables to and from the JSON format. The function json_encode() will convert the variable into a stringified version and json_decode() will take a stringified JSON string and convert it back to a PHP variable. Encoding variables as JSON is often used to generate a response and decoding is used when PHP acts as a client to an API that returns a JSON response. In addition to the encode and decode function PHP also supports json_last_error(). This function does not take any parameters and can be called after encode or decode. It will return an integer value that represents the result of the last operation. The possible return values can be compared to one of the following constants:

Constant	Meaning	Available
JSON_ERROR_NONE	No errors detected	
JSON_ERROR_DEPTH	Maximum stack depth exceeded	
JSON_ERROR_STATE_MISMATCH	Invalid JSON	
JSON_ERROR_CTRL_CHAR	Invalid control character	
JSON_ERROR_SYNTAX	Syntax error	
JSON_ERROR_UTF8	Malformatted UTF-8 characters	5.3.3
JSON_ERROR_RECURSION	Recursive references	5.5.0
JSON_ERROR_INF_OR_NAN	NAN or INF values found	5.5.0
JSON_ERROR_UNSUPPORTED_TYPE	Unsupported type	5.5.0

When it's necessary to return more than one variable the easiest way is to add them into an array and return the JSON encoded version of the array.

How it Works

Changing the previous example to work with JSON instead of HTML strings only takes a few changes.

The first is to make sure the Content-Type is set correct. This simple example will work without it but it's always a good idea to set the correct Content-Type to tell the clients what to expect. The second step is to only generate the $html variable used on the full document load and to return the JSON encoded value of the $data variable. Finally there are some small changes to the JavaScript code. In this example the code will generate the final html segment to insert into the document. In this case the code looks at the data and if the language returned is PHP it will add a bold tag around it.

```php
<?php
// 15_2.php
$languages = [
    'PHP', 'JavaScript',
    'C', 'C++', 'C#', 'Objective-C',
    'Python', 'Java', 'Ruby',
    'Visual Basic',
    'Scala'
];
shuffle($languages);
$data = array_slice($languages, 0, 3);

if ($_REQUEST['data']) {
    header("Content-Type: application/json");
    echo json_encode($data);
}
else {
    $html = "";
    foreach($data as $lang) {
        $html .= "<li>$lang</li>";
    }
    echo <<<HEREDOC
<!DOCTYPE html>
<html>
<head>
<script src="https://code.jquery.com/jquery-1.12.2.min.js"
        integrity="sha256-lZFHibXzMHo3GGeehn1hudTAP3ScOuKXBXAzHX1sjtk="
        crossorigin="anonymous"></script>
</bead>
<body>
    <h1>Programming Languages</h1>
    <ul id="lang">
        $html
    </ul>
    <button onclick="Update()">Update</button>
<script>
```

```
function Update() {
  $.getJSON("{$_SERVER['PHP_SELF']}?data=1", function(data) {
    var html = '';
    $.each(data, function(key, value) {
      if (value == 'PHP') {
        html += '<li><b>PHP</b></li>';
      }
      else {
        html += '<li>' + value + '</li>';
      }
    });
    $('#lang').html(html);
  });
}
</script>
</body>
</html>
HEREDOC;
}
```

The jQuery function used in the first example was called $.get(). This is now replaced with a call to $.getJSON(). This function will automatically convert the JSON string into an array or object so the script can traverse through the values.

Recipe 15-3. Consuming a JSON API

Problem

When you are creating Web API's it's often a good idea to create a test client that can consume and validate the responses of API's.

Solution

PHP has built-in support for fetching remote content via the fopen wrappers that allow the user of URL's to fetch content from an HTTP based endpoint. We can use a combination of file_get_contents() and json_decode() to work with JSON-based API's.

How it Works

To create a simple command-line script that can call the API from example 15_2.php and show the output, it could look something like this:

```
<?php
// 15_3.php
$url = "http://localhost/15_2.php?data=1";
$response = file_get_contents($url);
$languages = json_decode($response);
var_dump($languages);
```

This script will produce output similar to this:

```
array(3) {
  [0] =>
  string(3) "PHP"
  [1] =>
  string(12) "Visual Basic"
  [2] =>
  string(1) "C"
}
```

Example 14_4.php was used to consume an XML-based API from openweathermap.com. That service actually works with JSON as the default format. It is relatively simple to convert the XML script to use JSON instead. The data structure is not exactly the same but it follows the same structure.

When I work with API's I like to create a simple script that fetches the data, convert it into a PHP variable, and dump the content to the console so it's clear what the response looks like. In the case of the weather API the data from the JSON response looks like this:

```
stdClass Object
(
    [coord] => stdClass Object
        (
            [lon] => -118.24
            [lat] => 34.05
        )

    [weather] => Array
        (
            [0] => stdClass Object
                (
                    [id] => 721
                    [main] => Haze
                    [description] => haze
                    [icon] => 50d
                )

        )

    [base] => stations
    [main] => stdClass Object
        (
            [temp] => 290.6
            [pressure] => 1018
            [humidity] => 72
            [temp_min] => 289.15
            [temp_max] => 292.15
        )

    [visibility] => 3219
    [wind] => stdClass Object
```

```
            (
                [speed] => 2.1
                [deg] => 260
            )

        [clouds] => stdClass Object
            (
                [all] => 40
            )

        [dt] => 1458413206
        [sys] => stdClass Object
            (
                [type] => 1
                [id] => 372
                [message] => 0.0446
                [country] => US
                [sunrise] => 1458395766
                [sunset] => 1458439495
            )

        [id] => 5368361
        [name] => Los Angeles
        [cod] => 200
)
```

The object stdClass is a built-in class definition that is used whenever an object is created without any class definitions. This happens because the JSON response returns an object and not an array.

In the JSON there is no unit on the temperature value. It is assumed that it always returns the temperature in Kelvin, so there is no need to have special check for that. The calculation of the temperature value in Celsius and Fahrenheit stays the same.

The elements for the name of the city and for the wind's speed, etc., are also structured slightly different but the concept is similar. The code to process the response looks like this:

```php
<?php
// 15_4.php

$json = file_get_contents('http://api.openweathermap.org/data/2.5/weather?q=Los%20
Angeles,usxxx&appid=<API KEY>');
$weather = json_decode($json);

echo "City: {$weather->name}\n";

$k = $weather->main->temp;
$c = $k - 273.15;
$f = $c * 9 / 5 + 32;

printf("Temperature: %3.1f K / %3.1f C / %3.1f F\n", $k, $c, $f);

echo "Wind: {$weather->wind->speed} mph, direction: {$weather->wind->deg}\n";
```

This script will generate output similar to the code in example 14_4.php.

```
City: Los Angeles
Temperature: 290.7 K / 17.6 C / 63.7 F
Wind: 1.31 mph, direction: 201.001
```

Recipe 15-4. JSON API

Problem

When a client consumes API's from multiple sources it's common that each source has its own definition for how the content is formatted and which elements are included in the response. This makes it more difficult to work with these API's.

Solution

In 2015 a new standard called JSON API reached version 1.0. This standard defines all the headers and other information about how API requests and responses should be formatted. The standard is documented at http://jsonapi.org. The goal is to improve caching and thereby reduce the amount of network traffic required to interact with the API's. Less network traffic makes it possible to serve a greater number of users on the same hardware.

The basic structure of all API's is a JSON structure with one or more of these three top-level objects; data, errors, and meta. In addition it is also allowed to include jsonapi, links, and includes as top-level objects.

The data object should contain the primary data for the response. This can be a single object or null for API's returning a single resource and an array of objects or an empty array for API's returning a list of resources.

A simple response of an API to get the number of visitors to a site could look like this:

```
{
  'data': {
    'type': 'statistics',
    'id': 'visitors',
    'attributes': {
      'value': 25
    }
  }
}
```

Each resource must include type and id and they must be strings. A link object can be added to the top level to show the link to the API.

```
{
  'data': {
    'type': 'statistics',
    'id': 'visitors',
    'attributes': {
      'value': 25
```

```
      }
    },
    'links': {
      'self': "http://localhost/statistics/visitors"
}
```

The link section can also be used to reference other data in the same dataset. If the API returns a single blog post and you want to link to the next, previous, first, and list posts in the same series the response could look like this:

```
{
   'data': {
      'type': 'articles',
      'id': '5',
      'attributes': {
          'title': 'PHP and MySQL Recipes'
      }
   },
   'links': {
      'self': "http://localhost/articles/5",
      'next': "http://localhost/articles/6",
      'prev': "http://localhost/articles/4",
      'first': "http://localhost/articles/1",
      'last': "http://localhost/articles/17"
   }
}
```

All requests and responses must use the Content-Type: application/vnd.api+json and the standard also describes how to handle related data like comments on a blog post, etc.

How it Works

One of the benefits of using a standard like JSON API is its ability to be handled with a common set of tools.

```php
<?php
// 15_5.php

class JsonResource {
  function __construct($type, $id) {
    $this->type = $type;
    $this->id = $id;
    $this->addLink('self', "$type/$id");
  }

  function addAttribute($name, $value) {
    if (!$this->attributes) {
      $this->attributes = new stdClass();
    }
    $this->attributes->$name = $value;
  }
```

```php
  function addLink($name, $value) {
    if (!$this->links) {
      $this->links = new stdClass();
    }
    $this->links->$name = "http://localhost/$value";
  }
}

class JsonApi {
  function addResource($data) {
    $this->data = $data;
  }

  function addLink($name, $value) {
    if (!$this->links) {
      $this->links = new stdClass();
    }
    $this->links->$name = "http://localhost/$value";
  }

  function __toString() {
    return json_encode($this, JSON_PRETTY_PRINT | JSON_UNESCAPED_SLASHES);
  }
}

$user = new JsonResource('user', 123);
$user->addAttribute('name', 'John Smith');
$user->addAttribute('age', 25);

$api = new JsonApi();
$api->addResource($user);
header("Content-Type: application/vnd.api+json");
echo $api;
```

This is a very basic example that only covers a few of the elements supported, but this simple structure can be used to generate valid API responses for any type of data. For this to be complete there would need to be a way to handle errors relations and other types of data. There are currently a number of different projects on GitHub that are more complete than this example shows.

The output from this script looks like this:

```json
{
    "data": {
        "type": "user",
        "id": 123,
        "links": {
            "self": "http://localhost/user/123"
        },
        "attributes": {
```

```
        "name": "John Smith",
        "age": 25
      }
    }
  }
}
```

More information about the standard and documentation can be found at http://jsonapi.org.

Recipe 15-5. Calling API's

Problem

API's often require parameters to be passed in order to return data about specific elements. Parameters can be passed as either GET parameters where they are simply added as key value pairs to the request URI or as POST parameters where they are key value pairs of the body of the request.

Some API's require a POST request simply to make it a bit more difficult for a user to request data (it's not possible to enter the request in the address bar of a browser to use wget to request the data), and some API's require special header values to be set. How can PHP and JavaScript be used to call such API's?

Solution

In PHP we can make use of the stream context to set the request method and add headers and body data and in JavaScript we can use the $.post() function that is part of the jQuery library. It is also possible to use the XMLHTTP object but it will take a few more lines of code. The browser will in most cases block XMLHTTP requests to any other domain than the one the html document came from. This is done for security reasons.

How it Works

The first example is a PHP script that builds a HTML form where a user can enter the endpoint URI and a couple of key value pairs. The form is submitted by PHP and is used to create an API request and show the result of the request. This can be used as a simple debugging tool when working with API's.

```php
<?php
// 15_6.php

$response = null;
if ($_POST) {
  $params = [];
  foreach($_POST['key'] as $i=>$key) {
    if (!empty($key) && array_key_exists($i, $_POST['value'])) {
        $params = "$key=" . urlencode($_POST['value'][$i]);
    }
  }
  $options = array('http' =>
    array(
      'method'  => $_POST['method'],
      'content' => implode("&", $params)
    )
  );
```

```php
    $context = stream_context_create($options);
    $response = file_get_contents($_POST['url'], false, $context);
    switch ($_POST['response']) {
      case 0 :
        $json = json_decode($response, true);
        $response_text = json_encode($json, JSON_PRETTY_PRINT);
        break;
      case 1:
        $dom = dom_import_simplexml($response)->ownerDocument;
        $dom->formatOutput = true;
        $response_text = $dom->saveXML();
        break;
    }
  }
}
echo <<<HEREDOC
<!DOCTYPE html>
<html>
<head>
<script src="https://code.jquery.com/jquery-1.12.2.min.js"
        integrity="sha256-lZFHibXzMHo3GGeehn1hudTAP3ScOuKXBXAzHX1sjtk="
        crossorigin="anonymous"></script>
<script src="https://maxcdn.bootstrapcdn.com/bootstrap/3.3.6/js/bootstrap.min.js"
        integrity="sha384-OmSbJDEHialfmuBBQP6A4Qrprq5OVfW37PRR3j5ELqxss1yVqOtnepnHVP9aJ7xS"
        crossorigin="anonymous"></script>
<link href="https://maxcdn.bootstrapcdn.com/bootstrap/3.3.6/css/bootstrap.min.css"
      rel="stylesheet"
      integrity="sha384-1q8mTJOASx8j1Au+a5WDVnPi2lkFfwwEAa8hDDdjZlpLegxhjVME1fgjWPGmkzs7"
      crossorigin="anonymous">
<script>
function AddParameter() {
  var \$params = $('#parameters');
  if (\$params) {
    var \$div = \$('<div>');
    \$div.html(\$params.html());
    \$div.insertAfter(\$params);
  }
}
echo <<<HEREDOC
<!DOCTYPE html>
<html>
<head>
<script src="https://code.jquery.com/jquery-1.12.2.min.js"
        integrity="sha256-lZFHibXzMHo3GGeehn1hudTAP3ScOuKXBXAzHX1sjtk="
        crossorigin="anonymous"></script>
<script src="https://maxcdn.bootstrapcdn.com/bootstrap/3.3.6/js/bootstrap.min.js"
        integrity="sha384-OmSbJDEHialfmuBBQP6A4Qrprq5OVfW37PRR3j5ELqxss1yVqOtnepnHVP9aJ7xS"
        crossorigin="anonymous"></script>
<link href="https://maxcdn.bootstrapcdn.com/bootstrap/3.3.6/css/bootstrap.min.css"
      rel="stylesheet"
      integrity="sha384-1q8mTJOASx8j1Au+a5WDVnPi2lkFfwwEAa8hDDdjZlpLegxhjVME1fgjWPGmkzs7"
      crossorigin="anonymous">
```

```
<script>
function AddParameter() {
  var \$params = \$('#parameters');
  if (\$params) {
    var \$div = \$('<div>');
    \$div.html(\$params.html());
    \$div.insertAfter(\$params);
  }
}
</script>
</head>
<body>
<form name="api" method="POST" action="{$_SERVER['PHP_SELF']}">
<div>
  <lable>API Endpoint</label>
  <input class="form-control" type="text" name="url" />
</div>
<div>
  <lable>Method</label>
  <select class="form-control" name="method">
    <option value="GET">GET</option>
    <option value="POST">POST</option>
  </select>
</div>
<div>
  <lable>Response</label>
  <select class="form-control" name="response">
    <option value="0">JSON</option>
    <option value="1">XML</option>
  </select>
</div>
<div id="parameters">
<div id="parameters">
  <lable>Parameters</label>
  <div style="width:30%; display: inline-block">
    <input class="form-control" type="text" name="key[]" />
  </div>
  <div style="width:50%; display: inline-block">
    <input class="form-control" type="text" name="value[]" />
  </div>
</div>
</form>
<button onclick="AddParameter()">Add Parameters</button>
<button onclick="document.api.submit()">Submit</button>
<pre id="response">
$response_text
</pre>
</body>
</html>
HEREDOC;
```

Note how the dollar signs in javascript section are escaped. The dollar sign is used as a shorthand for the jQuery() function as $() and also in some of the variable names, but as PHP performs variable replacement in the HEREDOC block these will be replaced by empty strings as these variables are not defined in the PHP scope.

The form has input fields for the URL, the method, how the response should be displayed, and a key/value for a single parameter. If more parameters are needed the user can click the Add Parameter button and the form will be expanded.

When the form is submitted the PHP side will create a HTTP request based on the data submitted and shows the response from the API call in the preformatted section of the HTML document.

Recipe 15-6. API Authentication

Problem

What is the best way to authenticate a user of an API?

Solution

First of all you should never send user names and passwords in clear text when you are calling an API, and you should never include any of the authentication parameters as part of the URI as that gets logged by the server. These should always be sent as headers or as part of the body.

Providers of API's will often issue an app key or other id that's unique for each user. This is typically some sort of hash value that can't be linked to a specific user account. Some sites also provide a secret code that should be used when generating a hash of the request, but the code should not be included with the request. The server will know the secret and it can generate the hash on the server side and compare it to the hash that was included with the request. If they match, the server can assume the requester is who they claim to be.

The hashing can be done with some of the request parameters but it can also include things like the public IP of the requester or the user agent string as long as both client and server use the same set of data to create the hash.

Some API's require the client to authenticate on every request, but the server can also include a session token with the response and any subsequent requests from the same client that include the session token will be considered valid. The server might use additional parameters from the request like the user agent string and IP address to validate the session token. If any of these are changed from one request to another the server will invalidate the session.

How it Works

There are many ways to generate app keys and secrets. The app key could be generated as a sha256 hash of some of the data associated with the account.

```php
<?php
$appkey = hash('sha256', $email . $first_name, $date);
```

In this example concatenating the e-mail address, first name, and some representation of a data creates a string that is then used to create a hash value from. The hash value is then stored with the account.

Hashing different account values that are unique to the user can generate a secret that will only be known by the server and the client and never included as part of the request.

```php
<?php
$secret = hash('sha1', $account_id . $email);
```

On the server side the app key and secret will be saved as additional account information. It is a god practice if the secret is generated on a web page to prevent showing of this element more than once, when it is generated. If the user forgets the secret a new one should be generated.

Between the client and the server there must be an agreement on how to generate the hash. This can be by taking all the parameters as a string, adding the secret and then create a hash of the string. The hash value is then added as an additional parameter to the request. On the server side all parameters except the hash will be combined to similar string and the app key is used to do a database lookup for the secret so a hash can be created to validate again the provided hash.

The next example shows who a client can use an include file with the $appkey and $secret variables. Make sure the include file is stored outside of the web root to prevent accessing it from a browser.

```php
<?php
// 15_7.php

require "api_credentials.inc";

$params = [
  "appkey=$appkey",
  "article=1"
];
$hash = hash('sha256', implode("", $params) . $secret);
$params['hash'] = $hash;

$options = array('http' =>
  array(
    'method'  => "POST",
    'content' => implode("&", $params)
  )
);
$context = stream_context_create($options);
$response = file_get_contents("http://example.com/articels", false, $context);
```

If the server side of the API call is process by a PHP script it would process the request like this:

```php
<?php
// 16_8.php

$params = [
  "appkey={$_POST['appkey']}",
  "article={$_POST['article']}"
];
$secret = GetSecret($_POST['appkey']);
$hash = hash('sha256', implode("", $params) . $secret);
if ($hash == $_POST['hash']) {
  // Request is allowed
}
else {
  // Error - the hash did not match
}
```

The GetSecret() function call should perform a database lookup to get the secret value based on the provided appkey.

■ ■ ■

## CHAPTER 16

Using MySQL Databases

Databases play an important role in web applications where content is constantly changing and being served according to users' preferences, location, or other parameters. Databases are also used to collect information from the users in the form of comments to a blog, personal information when accounts are created, etc.

PHP provides support for many different types of databases in the form of a set of functions to connect, perform queries, and get information about tables and columns in the database. Some of the database extensions are procedural and some offer an object-oriented interface. The open source database called MySQL is the most used database with PHP and both small and large companies like Facebook, Twitter, and Wikipedia use it. The extension is provided by default with most distributions.

The mysql extension is deprecated and replaced by the mysqli extension. The I stands for Improved. From PHP 7 the mysql extension is no longer provided.

The source code to the MySQL database is owned and maintained by Oracle today and there is a new open source version developed by the original MySQL team called MariaDB. This database is compatible with the MySQL API's and can be used as a drop in replacement for MySQL. The standard database provided by CentOS 7 today is MariaDB.

Another advantage is the small footprint that makes it possible to use MySQL on limited hardware or embedded systems.

In this chapter we are going to show how to perform common database tasks from PHP scripts using the mysqli extension.

Recipe 16-1. Connecting to MySQL

Problem

Although MySQL data in a database is stored in a file system it can't be accessed by opening and reading/writing a file using the `fopen()` or `file_get_contents()` functions. In order to issue commands and receive data it is necessary to have the database server running and use a TCP/IP connection between the client and the server. How can this be done from PHP?

Solution

The mysqli extension includes a function called `mysqli_connect()`. This function requires a host name, user id, password, name of the database, tcp port, and socket, as parameters and it will return a connection resource if the connection could be made and false if the connection failed.

It is also possible to connect to MySQL using the PHP Data Objects (PDO) extension.

© Frank M. Kromann 2016
F.M. Kromann, *PHP and MySQL Recipes*, DOI 10.1007/978-1-4842-0605-8_16

All the parameters can have default values provided as configuration options in php.ini. These are defined as the following:

```
mysqli.default_host = "127.0.0.1"
mysqli.default_user = "db_user"
mysqli.default_pw = "secret"
mysqli.default_port = 3306
mysqli.default_socket = ""
```

As a minimum it is required to provide values for host, user, and password. If the database is specified an attempt to connect to that database is made. The database can always be switched to a different database under the same host with the user of the mysqli_select_db() function.

If the database server and web server is running on the same box we can use localhost or the ip address 127.0.0.1 as the host name for the database server. If the two services are on different servers it's necessary to provide the remote host name or IP address. In a high-traffic environment it can provide better performance by using an IP address. In that case it's not necessary for the client to perform a DNS query to resolve a host name to an IP address on every connect request.

How it Works

In order to connect to a database we need one created on the server. Using the mysql command on the server can do this.

```
mysql -u root -p
```

This command will connect to the MySQL (or MariaDB) server on the local host using the root user. The connection will be interactive and can be used to create new databases, tables, and add/update or delete data.

In this example we will create a table called music to store albums, tracks, and artist information. The first step is to create the database:

```
create database music;
```

Use the command 'show databases;' to get a list of all databases available on the server.

```
MariaDB [mysql]> show databases;
+--------------------+
| Database           |
+--------------------+
| information_schema |
| book               |
| music              |
| mysql              |
| performance_schema |
+--------------------+
5 rows in set (0.00 sec)
```

It is also necessary to create a database user and grant that user access to the database. This is the user account that will be used when connecting to the database from PHP.

```
MariaDB [mysql]> CREATE USER 'php'@'localhost' IDENTIFIED BY 'secret';
Query OK, 0 rows affected (0.01 sec)
```

This will create a user account called php with the password secret. The final step is to grant the php user access to the music database.

```
MariaDB [mysql]> GRANT ALL PRIVILEGES ON music . * TO 'php'@'localhost';
Query OK, 0 rows affected (0.00 sec)
```

This statement will grant the user access to all tables in the music database.

Exit the mysql tool and enter it again with the new account:

```
mysql -u php -p
```

Enter the password (secret) and type the command to show the databases.

```
MariaDB [(none)]> show databases;
+--------------------+
| Database           |
+--------------------+
| information_schema |
| music              |
+--------------------+
2 rows in set (0.01 sec)
```

This will only list the databases the user has access to. The information_schema database is used by mysql to store data about tables, columns keys, and indexes, etc. It's a database all users can access (read-only).

In order to store data in a database we need to create one or more tables. Each table defines a number of columns of various data types (integer, char, datetime, etc.). Data is added to a table in the form of a row. Each row will contain a value for each column. The value of some columns can be empty if that is allowed by the schema definition but all rows will have the same number of columns.

```
MariaDB [music]> create table album (
    -> id int auto_increment,
    -> title varchar(250) not null,
    -> description varchar(2000),
    -> primary key(id)
    -> );
Query OK, 0 rows affected (0.02 sec)
```

The show tables; and describe album; commands can be used to show a list of available tables and the definition of the album table.

```
MariaDB [music]> show tables;
+-----------------+
| Tables_in_music |
+-----------------+
| album           |
+-----------------+
1 row in set (0.00 sec)

MariaDB [music]> describe album;
+-------------+---------------+------+-----+---------+----------------+
| Field       | Type          | Null | Key | Default | Extra          |
+-------------+---------------+------+-----+---------+----------------+
| id          | int(11)       | NO   | PRI | NULL    | auto_increment |
| title       | varchar(250)  | NO   |     | NULL    |                |
| description | varchar(2000) | YES  |     | NULL    |                |
+-------------+---------------+------+-----+---------+----------------+
3 rows in set (0.00 sec)
```

Columns included in the primary key can't have a null value so it's not necessary to specify a constraint disallowing null values on any column that is included in the primary key.

The auto_increment constraint is used to automatically assign a value to the column, if the insert statement does not provide a value.

We now have a database with a single table and a user that can be used to connect and interact with the database from a PHP script. In a procedural setting this could look like example 16_1.php.

```php
<?php
// 16_1.php
$con = mysqli_connect('127.0.0.1', 'php', 'secret', 'music');
if (mysqli_connect_error()) {
  die("Error connecting: " . mysqli_connect_errno() . ' '
      . mysqli_connect_error() . "\n");
}
else {
  echo "Connected to music\n";
}
```

As an alternative the same functionality can be obtained with an object-oriented approach.

```php
<?php
// 16_2.php
$mysqli = new mysqli('127.0.0.1', 'php', 'secret', 'music');
if ($mysqli->connect_error) {
  die("Error connecting: {$mysqli->connect_errno} {$mysqli->connect_error}\n");
}
else {
  echo "Connected to music\n";
}
```

If the script is called as a request from a web server it is not necessary to disconnect or release any resources. This is handled by PHP automatically when the script terminates. If the script is long running or no longer needs the connection to the database, it's a good idea to get rid of the connection. This can be done with the `mysqli_close()` function or the `mysqli::close()` method.

```php
<?php
// 16_3.php
$con = mysqli_connect('127.0.0.1', 'php', 'secret', 'music');
if (mysqli_connect_error()) {
  die("Error connecting: " . mysqli_connect_errno() . ' '
      . mysqli_connect_error() . "\n");
}
else {
  echo "Connected to music\n";
  mysqi_close($con);
}
```

Or in object-oriented code:

```php
<?php
// 16_4.php
$mysqli = new mysqli('127.0.0.1', 'php', 'secret', 'music');
if ($mysqli->connect_error) {
  die("Error connecting: {$mysqli->connect_errno} {$mysqli->connect_error}\n");
}
else {
  echo "Connected to music\n";
  $mysqli->close();
}
```

Recipe 16-2. Persistent Connections
Problem

Connecting to a database can be a process that takes some time, and if the same database is used by all, or most, requests to the web server, it can make sense to keep a pool of connections open and reuse them again and again.

Solution

Persistent connection in various database extensions has been available for a long time. Although persistent connections can save some time they can also cause problems. If a persistent connection is used to lock a table and the script is unable to release the lock the table might stay locked until the connection is killed manually (restart of the web server and possibly the database server) so be careful.

In the older database drivers it used to be a special connect function (`mysql_pconnect()` instead of `mysql_connect()`), but in the mysqli driver the persistent connection is created by adding the prefix 'p:' in front of the hostname.

The number of persistent connections allowed is configurable in php.ini and it should match the number of simultaneous requests to the web site. If the number is set too low some users might experience connectivity issues.

Persistent connections are closed when the web server is shut down or restarted. If the persistent connection is created from a script running under CLI the connection will be closed when the script terminates. In that case there will be no difference between persistent and non-persistent connections.

How it Works

The next example shows the use of the 'p:' prefix to the host name to create a persistent connection.

```php
<?php
// 16_5.php
$mysqli = new mysqli('p:127.0.0.1', 'php', 'secret', 'music');
if ($mysqli->connect_error) {
  die("Error connecting: {$mysqli->connect_errno} {$mysqli->connect_error}\n");
}
else {
  echo "Connected to music\n";
}
```

Don't use the close() function on a persistent link as that will remove it from memory.

The function phpinfo() can be used to display status about mysqli connections. Active Persistent Links is the number of links currently in use. Inactive Persistent Links is the number of available links not currently in use and Active Links is the number on non-persistent links currently in use.

mysqli

MysqlI Support	enabled
Client API library version	mysqlnd 5.0.12-dev - 20150407 - $Id: d8daadaf41e3cd81d7c6ae96c6091fd15b2c9382 $
Active Persistent Links	0
Inactive Persistent Links	0
Active Links	0

Recipe 16-3. Fetching Data
Problem

Databases use an internal format to store the data and are optimized to use indexes and memory to extract the data based on a query. If we use the mysql command-line tool the result of a query will be listed as text on the console. How can the data be extracted into PHP variables so it can be used in the script to perform action or generate output?

Solution

The net rectangular nature of SQL databases can easily be represented in PHP arrays. This will be an array of arrays. The outer array will correspond to the rows in the result and the inner array will represent the values of all columns in each row.

How it Works

In order to have some data in the table to fetch we need to insert some first. Use the mysql command-line tool to execute the following commands:

```
use music;
insert into album (title) values('Yellow Submarine');
insert into album (title) values('Sgt. Pepper''s Lonely Hearts Club Band');
insert into album (title) values('Help')
insert into album (title) values('Abbey Road');
```

And to verify the date select all columns from the table:

```
MariaDB [music]> select * from album;
+----+------------------------------------------+-------------+
| id | title                                    | description |
+----+------------------------------------------+-------------+
|  1 | Yellow Submarine                         | NULL        |
|  2 | Sgt. Pepper's Lonely Hearts Club Band    | NULL        |
|  3 | Help                                     | NULL        |
|  4 | Abbey Road                               | NULL        |
+----+------------------------------------------+-------------+
4 rows in set (0.00 sec)
```

Note how the insert statements for the second album have two quotes where the apostrophe is. This is necessary as the single quote is the string delimiter and in order to insert a single quote it must be escaped to tell the parser that it's not the end of the string.

The Id columns are added automatically as the insert statements did not provide them and the description field was left unspecified and shows the NULL value.

The next example shows how to create a class that extends the mysqli class.

```php
<?php
// 16_6.php

ini_set('display_errors', 1);

class music extends mysqli {
  function __construct() {
    parent::__construct('127.0.0.1', 'php', 'secret', 'music');
    if ($this->connect_error) {
      die("Unable to connect to music\n");
    }
  }
}
```

```
  function getAlbums() {
    $albums = [];
    $result = $this->Query("select * from album;");
    if ($result) {
      while($row = $result->fetch_assoc()) {
        $albums[] = $row;
      }
      $result->close();
    }
    return $albums;
  }
}

$music = new music();
print_r($music->getAlbums());
```

The constructor of the music class does not take any parameters, but it calls the parent class' constructor with some hard-coded parameters for host, user, password, and database. The getAlbums() method performs the query "select * from album;" and if the query was executed successfully it will loop over the result and insert each row into an array that is then returned. The result is closed before the function returns. This will free any memory used by the query.

The output of this script will look like this:

```
Array
(
    [0] => Array
        (
            [id] => 1
            [title] => Yellow Submarine
            [description] =>
        )

    [1] => Array
        (
            [id] => 2
            [title] => Sgt. Pepper's Lonely Hearts Club Band
            [description] =>
        )

    [2] => Array
        (
            [id] => 3
            [title] => Help
            [description] =>
        )

    [3] => Array
        (
            [id] => 4
            [title] => Abbey Road
            [description] =>
        )
)
```

There are a couple of different functions that can fetch data from a result set. The one used here is `fetch_assoc()`. It will return an associative array for each row. That's why each of the elements in the inner arrays have keys that match the column names for each of the columns selected. In this case the query uses "select * from album;" to select all columns but we could have written "select id, title from album;" to select only the first two columns.

Recipe 16-4. Inserting Data

Problem

The class in the previous example can be used to extract data from a specific table in a database, but how can new rows be added?

Solution

Before data could be extracted from the database they had to be added. This was done with the command-line tool with the use of the insert statement. The insert statement can work on a single table and it can be used to create new records with any number of columns. In the command-line example we only provided the title column. In this example that is a required column because it's defined with the constraint NOT NULL.

A simple function that can add rows to the database can be written like this:

```php
function addAlbum($title, $description = null) {
  $t = this->real_escape_string($title);
  if ($description) {
     $d = $this->real_escape_string($description);
     $sql = "insert into album (title, description) values ('$t', '$d')";
  }
  else {
     $sql = "insert into album (title) values ('$t')";
  }
  $this->Query($sql);
  return $this->insert_id;
}
```

This method uses the real_escape_string() function to make sure single quotes and other characters before they can be included in the query. The return value will be the id of the newly created row. This can be used later to link other data to the specific record.

How it Works

The full script to insert new albums and get the list of all albums is shown here:

```php
<?php
// 16_7.php

ini_set('display_errors', 1);

class music extends mysqli {
  function __construct() {
    parent::__construct('127.0.0.1', 'php', 'secret', 'music');
```

```
    if ($this->connect_error) {
      die("Unable to connect to music\n");
    }
  }

  function addAlbum($title, $description = null) {
    $t = $this->real_escape_string($title);
    if ($description) {
      $d = $this->real_escape_string($description);
      $sql = "insert into album (title, description) values ('$t', '$d')";
    }
    else {
      $sql = "insert into album (title) values ('$t')";
    }
    $this->Query($sql);
    return $this->insert_id;
  }

  function getAlbums() {
    $albums = [];
    $result = $this->Query("select * from album;");
    if ($result) {
      while($row = $result->fetch_assoc()) {
        $albums[] = $row;
      }
      $result->close();
    }
    return $albums;
  }
}

$music = new music();
$music->addAlbum("Let It Be");
$music->addAlbum("Twist and Shout");

print_r($music->getAlbums());
```

The table that contains albums is missing some information. So far only albums from a single band are added, but what if additional bands are to be added? The simple solution is to add an extra character column to the album table. This will allow insertion of a text value with each record. Using a text column makes it possible to use different values for each record, even if it's the same band. In this case we could use "The Beatles," "Beatles," "Beatles, The," and many other combinations. This could make it difficult to find all albums from a single band.

To solve this problem we can create a new tasble called artist and link the album table to this table. The SQL to perform these actions looks like this.

```
create table artist (
  id int auto_increment,
  artist_name varchar(250) not null,
  description varchar(2000),
  primary key(id)
);
```

And the SQL to update the album table with an extra column that will allow linking to the artist table:

```
Alter table album add artist_id int;
Alter table album add foreign key(artist_id) references artist(id);
```

The first statement changes the column definition for the album table and the second creates a foreign key relation between album and artist. This relation will prevent deletion of an artist of one or more albums that exist with a link to the artist.

So far only albums from The Beatles were created in the albums table. We can then create them as an artist and link the albums to the new artist.

```
insert into artist (artist_name) values ('The Beatles');
update album set artist_id=1;
```

In this case the first artist added will get the id=1 so the link will be made by setting artist_id=1 for all rows in the album table.

We can now expand the class to allow insertion of new artists and albums and to return artist_name as part of the query.

```php
<?php
// 16_8.php

ini_set('display_errors', 1);

class music extends mysqli {
  function __construct() {
    parent::__construct('127.0.0.1', 'php', 'secret', 'music');
    if ($this->connect_error) {
      die("Unable to connect to music\n");
    }
  }

  function addArtist($name, $description = null) {
    $n = $this->real_escape_string($name);
    if ($description) {
      $d = $this->real_escape_string($description);
      $sql = "insert into artist (artist_name, description) values ('$n', '$d')";
    }
    else {
      $sql = "insert into artist (artist_name) values ('$n')";
    }
    $this->Query($sql);
    return $this->insert_id;
  }

  function getArtists() {
    $artists = [];
    $sql = "select * from artist";
    $result = $this->Query($sql);
    if ($result) {
      while($row = $result->fetch_assoc()) {
```

```php
        $artists[] = $row;
      }
      $result->close();
    }
    return $artists;
  }

  function addAlbum($title, $artist_id = null, $description = null) {
    if (is_null($artist_is)) {
      $id = "NULL";
    }
    else {
      $id = (int)$artist_id;
    }
    $t = $this->real_escape_string($title);
    if ($description) {
      $d = $this->real_escape_string($description);
      $sql = "insert into album (title, artist_id, description) values ('$t', $id, '$d')";
    }
    else {
      $sql = "insert into album (title, artist_id) values ('$t', $id)";
    }
    $this->Query($sql);
    return $this->insert_id;
  }

  function getAlbums($artist_id = null) {
    $albums = [];
    if ($artist_id) {
      $sql = "select album.id, artist_id, artist_name, title from album, artist where album.
      artist_id=artist.id and artist_id=$artist_id";
    }
    else {
      $sql = "select album.id, artist_id, artist_name, title from album left outer join
      artist on (album.artist_id=artist.id)";
    }
    $result = $this->Query($sql);
    if ($result) {
      while($row = $result->fetch_assoc()) {
        $albums[] = $row;
      }
      $result->close();
    }
    return $albums;
  }
}

$music = new music();
$id = $music->addArtist("Pink Floyd");
$music->addAlbum("The Dark Side Of The Moon", $id);
$music->addAlbum("The Wall", $id);
$music->addAlbum("Widh You Were Here", $id);
```

344

```
print_r($music->getArtists());
print_r($music->getAlbums(1));
print_r($music->getAlbums(2));
print_r($music->getAlbums());
```

The script can now insert an artist and get a list of all artists and the function to insert an album has been modified to take an extra parameter for the artist id. If this is omitted the album will be created without a link to an artist.

The getAlbums() method was also modified to allow an optional artist id. If it's not included the query will perform a special join that will ensure all rows in the albums table are selected and linked to all the rows in the artist table. If there is no matching row in the artist table (artist_id is null) the row will still be selected but null will be returned for both artist_id and artist_name. This is called a 'left outer join."

If a value is provided for artist id the simple join is made, and only records that exist in both album and artist will be selected as seen in the output listed below where the four arrays represent all artists, all Beatles albums, all Pink Floyd albums, and finally all albums.

```
Array
(
    [0] => Array
        (
            [id] => 1
            [artist_name] => The Beatles
            [description] =>
        )

    [1] => Array
        (
            [id] => 2
            [artist_name] => Pink Floyd
            [description] =>
        )

)
Array
(
    [0] => Array
        (
            [id] => 1
            [artist_id] => 1
            [artist_name] => The Beatles
            [title] => Yellow Submarine
        )

    [1] => Array
        (
            [id] => 2
            [artist_id] => 1
            [artist_name] => The Beatles
            [title] => Sgt. Pepper's Lonely Hearts Club Band
        )
```

```
    [2] => Array
        (
            [id] => 3
            [artist_id] => 1
            [artist_name] => The Beatles
            [title] => Help
        )

    [3] => Array
        (
            [id] => 4
            [artist_id] => 1
            [artist_name] => The Beatles
            [title] => Abbey Road
        )

    [4] => Array
        (
            [id] => 5
            [artist_id] => 1
            [artist_name] => The Beatles
            [title] => Let It Be
        )

    [5] => Array
        (
            [id] => 6
            [artist_id] => 1
            [artist_name] => The Beatles
            [title] => Twist and Shout
        )

)
Array
(
    [0] => Array
        (
            [id] => 7
            [artist_id] => 2
            [artist_name] => Pink Floyd
            [title] => The Dark Side Of The Moon
        )

    [1] => Array
        (
            [id] => 8
            [artist_id] => 2
            [artist_name] => Pink Floyd
            [title] => The Wall
        )
```

```
    [2] => Array
        (
            [id] => 9
            [artist_id] => 2
            [artist_name] => Pink Floyd
            [title] => Widh You Were Here
        )

)
Array
(
    [0] => Array
        (
            [id] => 1
            [artist_id] => 1
            [artist_name] => The Beatles
            [title] => Yellow Submarine
        )

    [1] => Array
        (
            [id] => 2
            [artist_id] => 1
            [artist_name] => The Beatles
            [title] => Sgt. Pepper's Lonely Hearts Club Band
        )

    [2] => Array
        (
            [id] => 3
            [artist_id] => 1
            [artist_name] => The Beatles
            [title] => Help
        )

    [3] => Array
        (
            [id] => 4
            [artist_id] => 1
            [artist_name] => The Beatles
            [title] => Abbey Road
        )

    [4] => Array
        (
            [id] => 5
            [artist_id] => 1
            [artist_name] => The Beatles
            [title] => Let It Be
        )
```

```
    [5] => Array
        (
            [id] => 6
            [artist_id] => 1
            [artist_name] => The Beatles
            [title] => Twist and Shout
        )

    [6] => Array
        (
            [id] => 7
            [artist_id] => 2
            [artist_name] => Pink Floyd
            [title] => The Dark Side Of The Moon
        )

    [7] => Array
        (
            [id] => 8
            [artist_id] => 2
            [artist_name] => Pink Floyd
            [title] => The Wall
        )

    [8] => Array
        (
            [id] => 9
            [artist_id] => 2
            [artist_name] => Pink Floyd
            [title] => Widh You Were Here
        )

)
```

Recipe 16-5. Updating Data

Problem

Adding new records or rows to a table is not the only operation users might want to have. How can we create a method that can update one or more columns in a table?

Solution

In SQL the update statement can be used to update one or more columns of one or more rows in the table. Like insert statements update statements work on a single table. If it's necessary to update records in multiple tables, multiple updates statements are needed.

The structure of an update statement starts by identifying the table to update, followed by a comma separated list of column names and values and finally a where clause that identifies the rows to update. If the where clause is omitted the update statement will make the update to all rows in the table.

Identifying the primary key in the where clause is the easiest way to update a single record but it's possible to use other values to identify the row(s) to update.

How it Works

The following code section is an example of a method called updateAlbum() for the music class. This method takes two parameters. The first one is the id column that identifies the row to update and the second is an array of values, similar to the values returned from the getAlbum() method.

```
function updateAlbum($id, $data = []) {
  $schema = [
    "id" => "int",
    "title" => "char",
    "artist_id" => "int",
    "description" => "char",
  ];
  $columns = [];
  foreach($data as $k => $v) {
    if (array_key_exists($k, $schema)) {
      if (is_null($v)) {
        $column[] = "$k = NULL";
      }
      else {
        switch($schema[$k]) {
          "int" :
            $column[] = "$k = " . (int)$v;
            break;
          "char" :
            $column[] = "$k = '" . $this->real_escape_string($v) ."'";
            break;
        }
      }
    }
  }
  if (sizeof($columns)) {
    $sql = "update album set " . implode(", ", $columns) .
          " where id = $id;";
    $this->Query($sql);
  }
}
```

The function includes a schema definition. This is used to validate the content of the $data variable. Any value that is not found in the $schema definition will be ignored. This will eliminate SQL errors if the user were to update a nonexisting column. The schema also defines the types of the columns, allowing the code to perform the correct type casting.

The schema definition does not include column length or other restrictions that could be used for additional validation. This would be easy to add as additional parameters in the schema definition.

This function could be made a more generic by adding a private method that includes parameters for table name and the schema definition. This can then be used to add a method to update both the album and artist tables.

Both of these tables use the same type of primary key. In both cases it's an integer value that is incremented automatically. It is always a good idea to use a private key without any real information, especially if the primary key is used as a foreign key reference. Changing the value of such a key would require changing the value in all tables that references it. If the key is without any value there is never any reason to change it.

```php
  private function updateRow($table, $schema, $id, $data) {
    $columns = [];
    foreach($data as $k => $v) {
      if (array_key_exists($k, $schema)) {
        if (is_null($v)) {
          $column[] = "$k = NULL";
        }
        else {
          switch($schema[$k]) {
            "int" :
              $column[] = "$k = " . (int)$v;
              break;
            "char" :
              $column[] = "$k = '" . $this->real_escape_string($v) ."'";
              break;
          }
        }
      }
    }
    if (sizeof($columns)) {
      $sql = "update $table set " . implode(", ", $columns) .
             " where id = $id;";
      $this->Query($sql);
    }
  }

  function updateAlbum($id, $data = []) {
    $schema = [
      "id" => "int",
      "title" => "char",
      "artist_id" => "int",
      "description" => "char",
    ];
    $this->update("album", $schema, $id, $data);
  }

  function updateArtist($id, $data = []) {
    $schema = [
      "id" => "int",
      "artist_name" => "char",
      "description" => "char",
    ];
    $this->update("artist", $schema, $id, $data);
  }
```

Recipe 16-6. Deleting Data

Problem

The next problem is how do we get rid of data no longer needed in the table/database?

Solution

The solution is to use the delete SQL statement. This statement starts with delete from table and has an optional where clause to specify the exact rows to delete. Without the where clause all the rows in the specified table will be deleted.

If other tables have foreign key relations to any of the rows being deleted the query will fail because the foreign key relations will no longer point to a valid row. This can be handled by updating all the rows of the other tables that are related to the rows being deleted so they no longer points to them. That is if those rows should be kept in the database. If those rows should be deleted also it's possible to tell the database to delete the selecting rows and also all the rows in other tables that point to any of the rows being deleted. Adding the keyword 'cascade' to the end of the delete query does this.

The SQL statement to delete all rows in the album table looks like this:

```
delete from album;
```

The statement to delete all the rows that belongs to a specific artist looks like this:

```
delete from album where artist_id = 2;
```

If the Id of the artist is unknown this can be found by writing a sub query:

```
delete from album where artist_id in (select id from artist where artist_name='Pink Floyd');
```

The where clause uses the keyword in instead of =. This is helpful if the subquery results in multiple rows. This will ensure that all of the rows matching any of the id's returned from the subquery are deleted. If multiple rows are returned by the subquery and the main query use the = character the SQL query will fail with a cardinal exception. This indicates that artist_id can't be equal to more than one value but it can be in a list of multiple values.

How it Works

Inline with the update example from the previous recipe we can now write delete functions. The first one will be a private member that can delete data from any table, based on the table name and id provided. The other two functions will be public members to delete a specific id.

```
private function deleteRow($table, $id) {
  $sql = "delete from $table where id = " . (int)$id . ";";
  $this->Query($sql);
}

function deleteArtist($id) {
  $sql = "update album set artist_id=NULL where id = " . (int)$id . ";";
  $this->Query($sql);
  $this->deleteRow("artist", $id);
}
```

```php
  function deleteAlbum($id) {
    $this->deleteRow("album", $id);
  }
```

In the deleteArtist() function there is an extra statement to get rid of all constraints pointing to the row being deleted.

The entire class with insert, update, and delete functions can now be combined into one.

```php
<?php
// 16_9.php

class music extends mysqli {
  private $schema = [
    'artist' => [
      'id' => 'int',
      'artist_name' => 'char',
      'description' => 'char',
    ],
    'album' => [
      'id' => 'int',
      'title' => 'char',
      'artist_id' => 'int',
      'description' => 'char',
    ]
  ];

  function __construct() {
    parent::__construct('127.0.0.1', 'php', 'secret', 'music');
    if ($this->connect_error) {
      die("Unable to connect to music\n");
    }
  }

  function insertRow($table, $schema, $data = []) {
    $columns = [];
    $values = [];
    foreach($data as $k => $v) {
      if (array_key_exists($k, $schema)) {
        $columns[] = $k;
        if (is_null($v)) {
          $values[] = "NULL";
        }
        else {
          switch($schema[$k]) {
            case 'int' :
              $values[] = (int)$v;
              break;
            case 'char' :
              $values[] = "'" . $this->real_escape_string($v) . "'";
              break;
          }
```

```php
        }
      }
    }
    if (sizeof($columns)) {
      $sql = "insert into $table (" . implode(", ", $columns) . ") values (" .
            implode(", ", $values) . ");";
      $this->Query($sql);
      return $this->insert_id;
    }
    else {
      return false;
    }
  }

  function addArtist($name, $description = null) {
    return $this->insertRow(
      'artist', $this->schema['artist'], [
        'artist_name' => $name,
        'description' => $description
      ]
    );
  }

  function addAlbum($title, $artist_id, $description = null) {
    return $this->insertRow(
      'album', $this->schema['album'], [
        'title' => $title,
        'artist_id' => $artist_id,
        'description' => $description
      ]
    );
  }

  private function updateRow($table, $schema, $id, $data) {
    $columns = [];
    foreach($data as $k => $v) {
      if (array_key_exists($k, $schema)) {
        if (is_null($v)) {
          $column[] = "$k = NULL";
        }
        else {
          switch($schema[$k]) {
            case 'int' :
              $column[] = "$k = " . (int)$v;
              break;
            case 'char' :
              $column[] = "$k = '" . $this->real_escape_string($v) ."'";
              break;
          }
        }
      }
    }
```

```php
    if (sizeof($columns)) {
      $sql = "update $table set " . implode(", ", $columns) .
             " where id = $id;";
      $this->Query($sql);
    }
  }

  function updateArtist($id, $data = []) {
    $this->update("artist", $this->schema['artist'], $id, $data);
  }

  function updateAlbum($id, $data = []) {
    $this->update("album", $this->schema['album'], $id, $data);
  }

  private function deleteRow($table, $id) {
    $sql = "delete from $table where id = " . (int)$id . ";";
    $this->Query($sql);
  }

  function deleteArtist($id) {
    $sql = "update album set artist_id=NULL where id = " . (int)$id . ";";
    $this->Query($sql);
    $this->deleteRow("artist", $id);
  }

  function deleteAlbum($id) {
    $this->deleteRow("album", $id);
  }

  function getArtists() {
    $artists = [];
    $sql = "select * from artist";
    $result = $this->Query($sql);
    if ($result) {
      while($row = $result->fetch_assoc()) {
        $artists[] = $row;
      }
      $result->close();
    }
    return $artists;
  }

  function getAlbums($artist_id = null) {
    $albums = [];
    if ($artist_id) {
      $sql = "select album.id, artist_id, artist_name, title from album, artist where album.
      artist_id=artist.id and artist_id=$artist_id";
    }
    else {
```

```
    $sql = "select album.id, artist_id, artist_name, title from album left outer join
    artist on (album.artist_id=artist.id)";
  }
  $result = $this->Query($sql);
  if ($result) {
    while($row = $result->fetch_assoc()) {
      $albums[] = $row;
    }
    $result->close();
  }
  return $albums;
  }
}
```

The addArtist() and addAlbum() methods are also refactored to use the common schema definitions.

Recipe 16-7. Schema Information
Problem

In the previous example the schema definition for the two tables were hard coded and would need to be updated if there were any changes to the database. Would it be possible to extract the schema information from the database?

Solution

There is a special purpose database or schema in the MySQL database. This is called INFORMATION_SCHEMA and it contains information about all the tables and columns in any of the databases on the server. INFORMATION_SCHEMA is common among many SQL92 database engines.

The commands show databases; and show tables; that were used on the command line, and they can also be used from the Query() method of the mysqli class. These commands use the information in the INFORMATION_SCHEMA to extract data about the system.

The command show databases; is equivalent to this:

```
select schema_name `Database` from information_schema.schemata;
```

The ticks around the alias Database is there because database is a reserved word and it must be escaped to be used as a column name in the query.

In a similar way we can write a statement to get all the tables in the database called music. This will be equivalent to the following:

```
use music;
Show tables;
```

Using the information schema makes it possible to use this from any location. You don't have to select a specific database before querying this schema.

```
select table_name from information_schema.tables where table_schema='music';
```

And finally we can get the list of columns in each of the tables by using this SQL statement:

```
select column_name, column_type from information_schema.columns where table_name='album';
```

How it Works

With this information we can now change the constructor of the music class to query the database for the schema information.

```php
<?php
// 16_10.php

class music extends mysqli {
  private $schema = [];

  function __construct() {
    parent::__construct('127.0.0.1', 'php', 'secret', 'music');
    if ($this->connect_error) {
      die("Unable to connect to music\n");
    }
    $sql = "select table_name from information_schema.tables where table_schema='music';";
    $rs = $this->Query($sql);
    while ($table = $rs->fetch_assoc()) {
      $sql = "select column_name, column_type from information_schema.columns where table_
      name='{$table['table_name']}';";
      $rs1 = $this->query($sql);
      while($col = $rs1->fetch_assoc()) {
        $this->schema[$table['table_name']][$col['column_name']] = $col['column_type'];
      }
      $rs1->close();
    }
    $rs->close();
    print_r($this->schema);
  }
}

$music = new music();
```

Index

A

addArtist() and addAlbum() methods, 355
AddInput() method, 285–286
Anonymous functions, 243
Apache Lounge, 14
array_merge() function, 237
Array of arrays, 86–88
Arrays
    addition, elements, 79–81
    array_merge() function, 82–86
    creation, 77, 79
    debugging, variables, 105–107
    definition, 107
    each() and reset() functions, 88
    json_decode(), 107
    json_encode(), 107
    print_r() function, 108
    range() function, 81
    removal, elements, 81
    serialize(), 107
    slicing and splicing arrays, 102, 104–105
    sorting, 79
        arsort(), 90, 93
        asort(), 90, 93
        insensitive string sorting, 91–92
        krsort(), 90
        ksort(), 90, 93
        rsort(), 90, 93
        sort() function, 93–96
        SORT_LOCALE_STRING, 96
        SORT_NATURAL, 92, 97
        SORT_NUMERIC, 96
        SORT_STRING, 96
        usort() function, 97–100
    stacks, 100–101
    traverse process, 88–90
    unserialize(), 107
array_slice() function, 102–103
array_splice() function, 103–104

B

Binary safe string, 125

C

Cache() function, 262
Calculated function names, 242
__constructor() method, 304
Coordinated Universal Time (UTC), 109
CSV files, 156–158

D

date_default_timezone_set() function, 308
Date functions
    date() function, 112–113
    gmmktime(), 112
    RFC 2822-formatted string, 116
    storage, 122–123
    week numbers, 117
DateTime Class, 118–122
define() function, 219
DeleteRows() function, 238
Dynamic imaging
    adding text, 191
    caching, 193
    changing colors, 180
    creation, 169
    crop, 173
    drawing function, 182
    flip, 177
    ImageArc() function, 188
    ImageEllipse() function, 187
    ImageFilledArc(), 189
    ImageFilledPolygon(), 189
    ImageFilledRectangle() function, 185
    ImageFillToBorder() function, 186
    ImagePolygon() function, 185, 188
    ImageRectabgle() function, 185

F.M. Kromann, *PHP and MySQL Recipes*, DOI 10.1007/978-1-4842-0605-8

Dynamic imaging (*cont.*)
   resize, 171
   rotate, 176
   transparency, 190
   watermark, 178

■ E

error_log option, 20
Escaping strings, 130–132
ExecCGI, 17

■ F

FastCGI interface, 17
File permissions, 152–153
File properties, 150–152
Files and Directories
   copy() function, 149
   downloading, 164
   fopen(), fclose(), and
      fwrite(), 147–148
   include and require, 143, 145
   iterators, 162–163
   mkdir() function, 155
   readfile() and fpassthru(), 145–147
   rename(), 149
   rmdir() function, 155
   single class definition, 143
   Stream Context, 160–161
   streams, 159–160
   Test(), 145
   unlink() function, 149
   uploading, 165
$_FILES array, 290
FormEncode(), 264
Forms
   data, 290
   default values, 276
   elements
      $_POST (or $_GET) array, 271
      Bootstrap framework, 274, 276
      check boxes/multiselect lists, 272
      html tags, 272
      implementation, 274
      jQuery library, 274, 276
      multiselect list, 273
      PHP script, 272
      text input, 271
      types, 273
      user's programming skills, 272
   file upload, 288
   generation, 283
   validation, 280
function_exists(), 241

Functions
   anonymous functions, 243
   calculated function names, 242
   calling functions, 231
   function_exists(), 241
   get_defined_functions(), 241
   is_callable(), 241
   optional parameters, 236
   passing parameters, 234
   return values, 239
   type declarations, 238
   variable parameter list, 246
   variable scope, 232

■ G

getAlbums() method, 345
get_defined_functions(), 241
GetSecret() function, 331

■ H

header() function, 263
HTMLForm class, 285

■ I

ImageChar(), 192
ImageCopyResampled() function, 175–176
ImageCreateFrom*() functions, 169
ImageFilledRectangle() function, 185
ImageFillToBorder() function, 186
ImageFlip() function, 177–178
ImageLoadFont(), 191
ImagePolygon() function, 185
ImageRectabgle() function, 185
ImageRotate() function, 176
ImageScale() function, 173
ImageString() function, 191
ImageTTFText() function, 191
Internet Information Services (IIS version 7), 9
is_callable(), 241
is_finite(), 216
is_infinite(), 216
ISO formats, 116–117
isset() function, 226
is_uploaded_file(), 290

■ J, K

jQuery() function, 321, 330
JSON
   API authentication, 324, 330
   consume and validation, 321
   Content-Type, 320

debugging tool, 327
fetching data, AJAX, 317
HTML strings, 320
jQuery() function, 330
json_last_error(), 319
return values, 319
stringified version and json_decode(), 319
$.post() function, 327
json_last_error(), 319

■ L

Linux, 6
list() construct, 227

■ M, N

Math functions
  base values, numbers, 62–64
  binary representation, 65–66
  binary shift, 67, 69
  binary values, integers, 64
  built-in functions, 61
  complex numbers, 74–75
  data types, 61
  exponential expression, 61
  exponential functions, 71–72
  floating point numbers, 69
  hexadecimal numbers, 66
  logarithmic functions, 71
  randomization functions, 70
  trigonometry, distance and direction, 73–74
Memory allocation, PHP, 21
method __toString(), 285
Microsoft Visual Studio, 12
MySQL database installation, 26–27
MySQL databases
  auto_increment constraint, 336
  deleting data, 351
  fetching data, 338
  file_get_contents() functions, 333
  fopen(), 333
  INFORMATION_SCHEMA, 355
  inserting data
    array, 345
    code implementation, 343
    column definition, 343
    command-line tool, 341
    getAlbums() method, 345
    left outer join, 345
    list, 341
    real_escape_string() function, 341
    simple function, 341
  MariaDB, 333
  mysql command, 334

mysql extension, 333
mysqli::close() method, 337
mysqli_select_db() function, 334
object-oriented approach, 336
PDO, 333
persistent connections, 337
php user access, 335
root user, 334
show databases, 334
updating data, 348
mysqli_select_db() function, 334

■ O

Object-oriented programming, PHP
  abstract classes, 31–32
  access method, 38
  applications, 29
  autoloading classes, 59
  base class, 30
  class hierarchy, 39
  class properties and methods, 36–37
  collisions of names, 57–58
  directory iteration, 52–53
  initialization, classes, 39–40
  interface classes, 33–34
  magic function __clone(), 46–47
  magic method __invoke(), 47
  magic method __toString(), 41
  member variables/methods, 38
  method __debugInfo(), 49–50
  method getType(), 37
  MethodOverload, 48–49
  object context, 35–36
  object context __call(), 48
  Reusable Code, 53–56
  __set_state(), 49
  simple class definition, 29
  static and object context, 37–38
  static context, 35–36
  types, classes, 30
  variable overloading functions, 42–44
object stdClass, 323

■ P, Q

PHP
  administrative tools, 10
  Apache installation, 12
  Apache module, 15
  compiling, 21–24
  configuration, 2
  default-installed modules, 7–8
  display_errors and error_reporting, 20
  E_NOTICE option, 20

PHP (*cont.*)
    extensions, 21
    FastCGI version, 16
    httpd, 2
    IIS configuration, 10
    IIS Web server, 13
    installation, 3, 6–7
    open source scripting language, 1
    package manager yum, 2
    php.ini-development, 17–18
    php.ini-production, 18
    redistribution libraries, 13
    standard Apache 2.4 configuration, 3
PHP Data Objects (PDO), 333
phpinfo() function, 338
POSIX system, 152
$.post() function, 327
preg_match() function, 201, 203–204
preg_match_all() function, 206
preg_replace(), 205

■ R

real_escape_string() function, 341
Really SimpleSyndication. *See* Rich site
        summary (RSS)
Reformatting Strings, 132–133
Regular expressions
    character class, 198
    ereg(), 197
    eregi_replace(), 197
    ereg_replace(), 197
    erigi(), 197
    format validation, 200
    metacharacter, 197
    meta characters, 198
    metacharacters, 198
    modifiers, 199
    special characters, 199
    string replacement, 205
    str_pos() and substr() functions, 197
    str_replace() function, 197
    subexpressions/sub patterns, 198
    sub patterns, 203
Rich site summary (RSS)
    date_default_timezone_set() function, 308
    definition, 304
    method channel(), 307
    method items(), 307
    sharing data
        channel element, 304
        __constructor() method, 304
        RSS 2.0 and Atom 1.0, 304
        RSSWriter() class, 306
    strtodate(), 308
rmdir() function, 149

■ S

Serializing PHP variables, 44–45
session_start() function, 257
SetCookie() function, 253
Simple Object Access Protocol (SOAP)
    API structure, 311
    code implementation, 312
    Math class, 311–312
    math.wsdl file, 314
    parameters, 311
    PHP implements classes, 311
    quality and flexibility, 311
    Server and Client functionality, 311
    __soapCall() method, 315
    SoapCLient() class, 312
    transport protocol, 311
    wsdl file, 312, 314
simplexml:load_file() function, 295
__soapCall() method, 315
SoapCLient() class, 312
stdClass, 51
stream_context_create(), 262
Strings
    array of characters, 126–127
    character replacement, 127–128
    creation, 125–126
    Hash values, files, 139–140
    HTML Entities, 137–138
    Long Strings, Heredoc and Newdoc, 128–130
    passwords storage, 141–142
    storage, 125
    Substrings, 135–137
    Trimming Whitespace, 133
Strings in Strings, 133–135
strpos() functions, 134
Symbolic links, 153–155

■ T, U

Time functions
    date function, 110
    elapsed time calculation, 123–124
    PHP 5.1, 111
    strftime() function, 113–116
    strtotime() function, 111
    UNIX timestamp, 113
Timestamps, 110–111, 113, 116
Time Zones, 109–110
__toString() method, 283, 288

■ V

Variable parameter list, 246
Variables
    accessing global variables, 233
    allocating memory, 210

comparing variables, 221
constants, 219
construct include(), 229
converting variable type, 209
definition, 232
each() construct, 229
foreach() construct, 229
global variable problems, 214
handling floating point
        numbers, 224
include_once(), 229
language constructs, 225
memory use, 212
output generation, 229
reducing memory use, 216
require_once(), 229
reset() function, 229
scope, 213
type, 215
variable variables, 220
with strings, 223
$_GLOBALS array, 233
Virtual Machines, 27–28
Visual Studio 2015 (VC14), 12

■ W

wddx_deserialize() function, 309
wddx_serialize_value(), 309
Web Distributed Data eXchange
        (WDDX) platform, 308
Web fundamentals
    $_GET and $_POST, 250
    AJAX requests, 266
    caching, 261
    content type and disposition, 259

cookies, 253
headers, 249
HTTPS protocol, 265
remote content, 262
server variables, 255
session data, 257
web sockets, 267
WebSocketsServer class, 268
World Wide Web Services, 9

■ X, Y

XML
    exchanging data
        api key, 295
        API key, 294
        DOM extension, 294
        indication, 294
        libxml extension, 294
        mode, 295
        SDO extension, 294
        SimpleXMLElement class, 298–299
        SimpleXML extension, 294
        simplexml:load_file() function, 295
        structure, 293
        var_dump() function, 298
        WDDX extension, 294
        XMLDiff extension, 294
        XML Parser extension, 294
        XML Reader extension, 294
        XML Writer extension, 294
    generating XML response, 300

■ Z

Zipped Files, 166–167

Get the eBook for only $5!

Why limit yourself?

Now you can take the weightless companion with you wherever you go and access your content on your PC, phone, tablet, or reader.

Since you've purchased this print book, we're happy to offer you the eBook in all 3 formats for just $5.

Convenient and fully searchable, the PDF version enables you to easily find and copy code—or perform examples by quickly toggling between instructions and applications. The MOBI format is ideal for your Kindle, while the ePUB can be utilized on a variety of mobile devices.

To learn more, go to www.apress.com/companion or contact support@apress.com.

CPSIA information can be obtained
at www.ICGtesting.com
Printed in the USA
FSOW04n0710160616
21627FS

9 781484 206065